THE RESILIENCE OF CONSERVATIVE RELIGION

The resurgence and persistent appeal of conservative religion – not just in the United States, but around the world in the past few decades – present a great challenge to sociologists and to modernization theory. The recent growth and popularity of conservative churches contradict the idea that late-modern societies – with their emphases on the individual, the separation of church and state, and the cultural fragmentation and secularization that they foster – have outgrown the need for such relics of the past as traditionalist religions. In this book, Joseph Tamney offers an explanation for this apparent incongruity by looking at the case of growing, popular, conservative Protestant congregations in the United States.

From about 1972 through the late 1980s, more Americans switched from mainline Protestant churches to conservative Protestant churches than the reverse, and the trend continues. Tamney uses four cases studies of successful Protestant congregations in middle America to examine why people join conservative churches and what people like about them. He uses these cases – three that represent diverse strands of conservative Protestantism and one that represents a mainline church – to test the relevance of Dean Kelley's "strong church" theory, which posits that strictness accounts for the appeal and resilience of conservative religion. Tamney finds that while strictness holds some appeal, the most successful churches are not really traditionalist at all, but what he calls "modernized traditionalist." These conservative congregations survive and continue to attract members because they both accommodate secular changes and compensate for the failures of late-modern society. They are able to maintain the appealing stance of being "against the world," without in fact being isolationist.

This book is filled with enlightening interviews with church members and data gleaned from participant observation; it offers both ethnographic and theoretical contributions. Tamney's findings represent a synthesis of ideas from supporters of secularization theory and from those who stress the competitive market of churches in America as a factor in church growth. Tamney's conclusion, that the most popular conservative churches in practice accommodate modern society, is more consistent with modernization theory than Kelley's explanation, which emphasizes the appeal of the conservative church as a strictly traditional, unchanging, self-sufficient, and absolutist social unit. Tamney offers a new, alternative way to look at the phenomenon of conservative churches in the modern age – one that may be applied more broadly to explain the appeal and survival of conservative religion and congregations in other parts of the world.

JOSEPH B. TAMNEY is Professor of Sociology at Ball State University in Muncie, Indiana. His previous books include *The Resilience of Christianity in the Modern World* (1992), *American Society in the Buddhist Mirror* (1992), and *The Struggle over Singapore's Soul* (1996). Professor Tamney was the editor of *Sociology of Religion* from 1995–2000. He has published articles in the *Journal for the Scientific Study of Religion*, *Sociology of Religion*, *Review of Religious Research*, *Journal of Church and State*, *British Journal of Sociology*, and *Sociological Forum*.

THE RESILIENCE OF
CONSERVATIVE RELIGION

THE CASE OF POPULAR, CONSERVATIVE

PROTESTANT CONGREGATIONS

JOSEPH B. TAMNEY

Ball State University

CAMBRIDGE
UNIVERSITY PRESS

PUBLISHED BY THE PRESS SYNDICATE OF THE UNIVERSITY OF CAMBRIDGE
The Pitt Building, Trumpington Street, Cambridge, United Kingdom

CAMBRIDGE UNIVERSITY PRESS
The Edinburgh Building, Cambridge CB2 2RU, UK
40 West 20th Street, New York, NY 10011-4211, USA
477 Williamstown Road, Port Melourne, VIC 3207, Australia
Ruiz de Alarcón 13, 28014 Madrid, Spain
Dock House, The Waterfront, Cape Town 8001, South Africa

http://www.cambridge.org

First published 2002

Printed in the United Kingdom at the University Press, Cambridge

Typeface Goudy 10.5/13 pt.   System LaTeX 2ε [TB]

A catalog record for this book is available from the British Library.

Library of Congress Cataloging in Publication Data
Tamney, Joseph B.
The resilience of conservative religion : the case of popular, conservative Protestant
congregations / Joseph B. Tamney.
   p. cm.
Includes bibliographical references and index.
ISBN 0-521-80396-9 – ISBN 0-521-00867-0 (pbk.)
1. Sociology, Christian. 2. Protestant churches – United States – Case studies. I. Title.
BT738 .T253 2001 2002
280'.4'0973 – dc21   2001025763

ISBN 0 521 80396 9 hardback
ISBN 0 521 00867 0 paperback

CONTENTS

v

LIST OF TABLES

Acknowledgments

The material in this book is based on personal interviews by Peggy J. Shaffer, Susan P. Ryan, and myself. The work done by Peggy and Susan was invaluable, and I thank them for it. Their assistance was possible because of a grant from the Lilly Endowment. Garnell Jones transcribed many of the taped interviews; she worked without material compensation. Because of her help, I am able to provide the actual comments of the people with whom we talked. Garnell also transcribed two taped sermons, parts of which appear in Chapters 3 and 4.

Ball State University gave me a Summer Research Grant, which allowed me to oversee the project and do some of the interviews. For the preparation of the manuscript, I am indebted to Kara Keaffaber, Jill Lochtefeld, Matt Morris, Justin Rummel, and Vanessa Schooley – all Ball State students – who were trained and supervised by Nancy Annis. Nancy also did most of the initial copyediting of the manuscript.

Two friends served as consultants: George Jones (retired Ball State professor and former director of religious programs at the university) and George Saunders (pastor of the First Baptist Church, Muncie, Indiana). These gentlemen read several drafts of all the manuscript chapters. While the final words are mine, the two Georges did their best to help me avoid misunderstanding the congregations I studied. They polished my writing, forced me to clarify my ideas, and contributed their own insights. They are a part of this book. I am eternally grateful for their time and support.

Finally, Peggy, Susan, and I want to thank the pastors and people in the congregations we studied. Their willingness to talk with us made this book possible.

INTRODUCTION

It is commonplace today to divide American Protestantism into dying and thriving groups. The old mainline Protestant churches, especially the United Methodist Church and the Presbyterian Church (USA), are shrinking. In contrast, conservative Protestant churches are holding on to their share of the expanding American population. This book is about the survival of the latter type of religious groups. Members of such churches may consider it arrogant to question why conservative churches are doing relatively well. Yet it seems true that objectively the strength of conservatism should be a puzzle. After all, we live in a time of rapid change. It is not obvious why at such a moment leaders who advocate conserving old ways are relatively popular.

Several reasons for the continuing strength of conservative Protestantism are straightforward. Compared to the mainline groups, conservative Protestants have more children. Moreover, their leaders discourage conditions associated with being unchurched: childlessness and divorce. People stay in or join churches because they want their children to have a religious education. Divorced people stay away from churches, in part, because so many congregations are family-oriented.

Conservative Protestants also devote more time and energy to evangelism. A congregation's outreach program is important. Sponsoring revivals and advertising programs at a church may aid growth. Of more importance, however, is whether a congregation is encouraged to reach out to others. Even near-strangers can be influential, especially if the strangers tell a conversion story that makes clear a need shared with the potential newcomers to a congregation. Almost all of the people discussed in this book first became interested in their new congregations because of some comments made by a member of the congregation who

1

was also a newcomer's family member, friend, neighbor, or coworker. Conservative Protestant churches survive, in part, because they try harder to do so.

Such churches also retain more of the people who grow up in the churches. Any significant changes in lifestyle or religious affiliation are often influenced by exposure to new options but deterred by social pressure from others favoring the status quo. Urban living and education are likely indicators of exposure to new ideas; conservative Protestants are more likely to live in rural areas and less likely to be highly educated. The degree of social pressure to remain the same is related to the frequency of interaction with similar people. White conservative Protestants have the highest marriage rates and, among those living in multi-adult households, conservative Protestants are more likely than members of other religious groups to live in religiously homogeneous households. Moreover, conservative Protestants tend to live together in the same parts of the United States. Because they live in households and regions where people share similar religious beliefs, conservative Protestants experience greater social pressure not to switch religions.[1]

But it is also true that many people switch from having no religious preference or from being a member of a mainline religion to being a member of a conservative Protestant church because they find such churches to be appealing. During the period 1972–87, about one out of five people raised in mainline Protestantism left that religious family to join a conservative Protestant church. Within conservative Protestantism, one out of seven switched to mainline churches. Why the difference?[2] The purpose of this book is to further our understanding of what people like about conservative Protestant congregations. As Coalter, Mulder, and

1. The data confirming my description of conservative Protestants can be found in Kosmin and Lachman (1993:71–2, 258, 240, 107).
2. Such differences cannot be interpreted as moving from a liberal to a conservative congregation. For instance, in Middletown (Delaware Country, Indiana), almost all white conservative congregations have theologically conservative pastors, but the white mainline congregations are led by pastors who are roughly equally divided among three theological categories: conservative, moderate, and liberal (Johnson and Tamney 1986:52). Thus, an unknown number of people switching to conservative denominations in Middletown would have been members of mainline congregations with conservative pastors or of congregations that had had such pastors. The data about the 1972–87 period is in Greeley (1989:34–6).

Weeks (1996:33) emphasized, "People join or leave congregations, not denominations." To understand national changes, it is necessary to study specific congregations.

In 1996 my assistants (Peggy Shaffer and Susan M. Ryan) and I began a study meant to find out why people joined successful conservative churches and what currently appeals to them about the churches they joined. The interviewees were residents of "Middletown," who recently joined Protestant churches. "Middletown" refers to the county containing the city of Muncie, Indiana. Robert and Helen Lynd (1929) wrote the classic study of this community, giving the town its sociological label. They believed that Middletown was reasonably representative of white, Anglo-Saxon culture. What is important about Middletown for our purposes is that it contains a variety of Protestant churches.

The issue is not why people are religious but why they have joined a specific congregation. These are distinct matters. For example, a person might be religious because she wants to believe in a life after death and attends a specific church because her friends are members. In another type of case, the two matters may be closely connected. For instance, a person might be religious because he wants to feel loved by Jesus, and the person may belong to a specific church because the congregation's liturgy makes him feel close to Jesus. Our objective was to discover why the person was attracted by a specific congregation.

Whether or not a particular congregation is popular certainly depends, in part, on the resources available to it. Congregations with money, paid staff, and abundant volunteers are more likely to offer attractive programs and thus to be popular, all else aside. Similarly, groups with skilled workers such as eloquent preachers and talented musicians are better candidates for success, at least within Protestantism. In the text, I will note from time to time the presence of such resources, but they are not my primary concern. What I wanted to know was what it is about conservative Protestant theology and rituals that people find appealing.

Chapters 3 through 6 concern the four congregations in the 1996 study. In them I describe what people found attractive in each of the congregations. In writing Chapter 2, I used other sources of information. In order to understand the appeal of conservative Protestantism in the early-modern United States (i.e., prior to World War II), I used historical research and some classical sociological studies, including the work of the Lynds in the 1920s and 1930s. Knowing what made conservative congregations appealing during early-modernity helps give us a better perspective on more recent developments.

In Chapter 1, I develop the framework used throughout the book by discussing both the nature of conservative religion and theories about what makes the content of a religion appealing to contemporary Americans.

EXPLANATIONS FOR THE
SUCCESS OF CONSERVATIVE
RELIGIONS

Diverse forms of religion exist in every society. The different responses to the publication of Salman Rushdie's novel *The Satanic Verses* illustrate these different forms. The appearance of this novel aroused such strong feelings that Islamic fundamentalists placed a bounty on the author's head, prompting the British government to protect Rushdie by moving him from one "safe house" to another. I use the reaction of Islamic fundamentalists to Rushdie and of Westerners to the Muslim responses, as well as the defense put forth by Rushdie and those sympathetic to him, to develop the concepts of traditionalist, modern, and late-modern religions. In the latter part of this chapter, I present alternative explanations for the appeal of traditionalist religion. The term "conservative religion" is used to refer to religions that are either clear-cut cases of the traditionalist type or approximations of it.

THE EPISODE

On 26 September 1989, Salman Rushdie's novel *The Satanic Verses* was published in Great Britain. Beginning with India in October of that year, the book was banned not only in Muslim societies but also in Kenya, Singapore, South Africa, Tanzania, Thailand, and Venezuela. All these societies, except the last, have significant Muslim minorities. In February 1989, a radio announcer read a statement on Tehran radio from Ayatollah Khomeini, who was the spiritual leader of Iran's Muslims at the time. The statement included the following remarks:

> I inform all the intrepid Muslims in the world that the author of
> the book entitled *The Satanic Verses*, which has been compiled,

printed, and published in opposition to Islam, the Prophet, and the Koran [Quran], as well as those publishers who were aware of its contents, have been sentenced to death.

I call on all zealous Muslims to execute them quickly... (*Observer*, 19 February 1989).

Prior to this *fatwa* (i.e., an Islamic legal opinion), eight thousand Muslims took part in a protest march in London, and six people died in Pakistan participating in a riot linked to the publication of *The Satanic Verses* in the West. The Ayatollah's death sentence captured the world's attention and further inflamed the situation. Demonstrations occurred in various parts of the world, including London and New York City, in which people chanted "Death to Rushdie" (*New Straits Times* [Malaysia], 27 February 1989).

A small part of the novel, but the part from which the book's title most immediately derives, concerns an incident in the life of Muhammad that was recorded by two early Arab historians, but which Quranic commentators later discredited because it implied that one cannot take for granted that the Quran is literally and totally the work of God (Mojtabai 1989:3). According to these "Satanic Verses," Muhammad briefly allowed Muslims to use female intercessors with Allah, naming three goddesses who were worshipped in Mecca at the time when Muhammad was trying to convert the Meccans. Rushdie "used the incident as an extended metaphor for both the ambiguity of revelation and the ostensible willingness of the Prophet to compromise in unfavorable circumstances" (Piscatori 1990:772).

In another incident, the scribe, Salman, alters the verses dictated by Mahound (the name of the character who bears some resemblance to Muhammad) and supposedly revealed to him by God's messenger, Gabriel. In the novel, when the text is read back to him, Mahound does not at first notice the changes. When Mahound becomes suspicious, Salman leaves for another city, fearful for his life. "There could hardly be a more direct attack on a fundamentalist construal of the holy word" (Steiner 1995:105). In another episode, a poet, Baal, hides in a brothel and conceives a plan to name the whores after Muhammad's wives. It is easy to understand why the novel would offend Muslims.

Translators and publishers of Rushdie's books have been personally assaulted or killed (*New York Times* 1991; Weisman 1991). In 1997, the Iranian foundation that originally promised $2 million to Rushdie's killer raised the bounty by $500,000. The following year, the Iranian government disassociated itself from the death sentence given Rushdie, but bounty hunters may not be swayed by this action (Goshko 1998). Subsequent to the government's action, the reward for Rushdie's death was increased to $2.8 million (*Wall Street Journal*, 13 October 1998).

The Satanic Verses won Britain's Whitbread Prize as best novel of the year. The editors of the *New York Times Review of Books* chose it as one of the best books of 1989 (there were thirteen in all).

Khomeini's judgment was based on the Quranic verse, "Those who molest God's messenger, for them awaits a painful punishment" (9:61). According to Islamic law, such a sentence must be passed by an Islamic court, which would have jurisdiction only in countries under Islamic law (Ahsan and Kidwai 1991:54–5). Thus the validity of Khomeini's *fatwa* is debatable. The nature of the punishment Khomeini decreed was based on a precedent set by Muhammad: "Shortly after he had captured Mecca in January 630, he had Kaab ibn al Ashraf, a poet, decapitated for mocking the Quran" (Hiro 1989:298). Khomeini's condemnation, although not always his death sentence, was popular among both the elite and the common people in the Muslim world (Hiro 1989:299).

Rushdie's Islamic critics were especially upset because the author was raised in a nominally Muslim home, first in India and later in Pakistan. Because Rushdie was born a Muslim, even though he never considered himself religiously Islamic and now claims only a cultural Muslim identity (Rushdie 1991b), he was charged with apostasy. While Islam emphasizes the importance of personal commitment for salvation, the traditional belief lingers that an individual is born into a religion. Individuals are not free to renounce their religious heritage; at the extreme, apostates are to be killed. This attitude exemplifies a crucial aspect of traditionalist religion, namely the subordination of the value of the individual to the preservation of the group.

That Rushdie should die has been accepted by many Muslims. *International Guerillas* is a Pakistani film that was popular with local audiences. The film presents Rushdie as a Rambo-like figure pursued by four Pakistani guerillas. God kills him using bolts of lightning, a scene that evoked shouts of approval from audiences (*The Australian*, 16 May 1990). Rushdie has not been the only target. When the Japanese translator was stabbed to death in 1991, a spokesperson for the Pakistan Association in Japan said, "the murder was completely 100 percent connected with the book.... Today we have been congratulating each other. Everyone was really happy" (quoted in Bedford 1993:163; see also Dempsey 1997). Traditionalist religion may be linked to violence because the group and not the individual is significant. The group symbolizes the sacred, thus any insult to its culture is blasphemy.

Most Islamic political leaders rejected the death sentence against Rushdie. The foreign ministers at a meeting of the forty-six-member Organization of Islam Conference condemned Rushdie's book but also rejected the death sentence. The Conference urged member-states to ban *The Satanic Verses* (Associated Press 1989) and asked all countries to pass laws protecting religious beliefs against insult and abuse (Appignanesi and Maitland 1989:145). Measures less extreme than murder, such as censorship, may be used to "protect" traditionalist religions. Killing and censorship are ways to preserve the group.

Rushdie's novel created such a sensation because of political processes occurring among Muslims at the time of its publication. In Great Britain, South Asian imams (Muslim religious leaders) were trying to establish themselves as political spokespersons for their discriminated-against constituency. Simultaneously Khomeini was struggling with pragmatists for control of the Iranian revolution (Keppel 1994:33–9; Milani 1994). The imams and Khomeini tried to use *The Satanic Verses* episode to rally people to their political programs. The episode occurred because the Islamic world is far from united. Thus it must be kept in mind that what I am describing as Islamic fundamentalism represents only one faction in the Islamic world.[1]

TRADITIONALIST RELIGION

The fundamentalist response illustrates what I mean by "traditionalist religion." *Traditionalism* means "a deliberate effort to regenerate tradition and make it socially significant again.... [It] is a form of engagement with the modern world" (Lechner 1993:23). In the process, traditionalists may support important social changes. What traditionalists seek to preserve, above all, is valuing the group more than the individual, even to the point of being willing to kill someone who symbolizes a threat to the group or to that for which the group stands. People such as Rushdie

---

1. Of course, there were quite varied responses to Rushdie's book among Muslims. Muslim writers especially have called for the end of state censorship (Naïm 1994; see also Evans 1996). In this book, the term "Islamic fundamentalist" refers to Khomeini and those expressing sympathy for his attitude toward Rushdie.

must be killed because their example is a threat to the cohesion of the group:

"We believe in collective justice," a right-wing Jewish leader explained. By that he meant that any individual who was part of a group deemed to be the enemy might justifiably become the object of a violent assault, even if he or she were an innocent bystander (Juergensmeyer 1993:165).

Extremists in various traditions think in collective or group terms that implicitly devalue individual life. Because the focus is on the group, some Pakistanis in Japan could feel "really happy" about the death of the Japanese translator of Rushdie's book.

Such tragedies have occurred in the United States. After studying violence at abortion clinics, Dallas A. Blanchard and Terry J. Prewitt (1993:225–6) included "a justification for violence" among a list of six commonalities shared by Protestant, Catholic, and Mormon fundamentalisms. They found violence to be a result both of the substitutionary theory of the atonement, which assumes that a sacrificial offering must precede divine forgiveness for sin, and of a stress on "a literal, fiery hell of eternal punishment," which reinforces "the notion of a God who is vindictive and unremittingly violent, a God of self-congratulating cruelty" (p. 262). However, my suggestion is that the acceptability of violence is not dependent on specific beliefs about atonement and hell. Rather, violence is acceptable because traditionalists devalue the individual compared to the group.[2]

Traditionalism means not only the superiority of the religious group over the individual but also the dominance of the religious group over all the other institutions of society. Khomeini spoke as both a religious and a political ruler in Iran. Similarly, traditionalism means the cultural triumph of the group's ideology. Artists such as Rushdie have no literary license. Iranian fundamentalists in state institutions have tried to eliminate the influence of Western and pre-Islamic Persian cultures (Milani 1994; Riesèbrodt 1993:128). In the traditionalist worldview, there is no

2. The Fundamentalism Project, organized by Martin E. Marty and R. Scott Appleby, has documented the willingness of traditionalists in various religious traditions to use violence – among Jews (Aran 1991), among Muslims (Voll 1991), among Sri Lankan Buddhists (Manor 1994), and among Hindus (Embree 1994).

separation of church and state, and traditionalist religious values are hegemonic.

The justification of labeling such a religious culture "traditionalist" requires an understanding of the modernization process.

TRADITIONALISM AND MODERNIZATION

Modernization theory assumes that we are part of a historical process dating back to premodern times. There is no definitive list of characteristics of this process, nor do all sociologists agree on the usefulness of this theory (for a general discussion of this topic, see Sztompka 1993). However, modernization theory remains an important part of sociology, and I have found it useful for studying change in Western and Eastern societies (Tamney 1992a, 1996).

Modernization can be viewed using long or short timeframes. For the moment, I limit the discussion to the long term. As such, modernization means the process of change from small, traditional societies up to the contemporary world. It is assumed that when the most technologically advanced societies existing at various points in time are compared, they will reveal directions of social change. That is, it is assumed that increasing technological sophistication produces social changes in a predictable manner.

The modernization process, as I conceive it, has five basic components: technological development, societal expansion, structural differentiation, the fragmentation of a society's culture, and the growing importance of the individual at the expense of groups. In this book, I will not dwell on the first two factors but shall simply assume that over time societies have become more technically sophisticated and have integrated larger numbers of people. As I shall argue, a traditionalist religion seeks to eliminate the last three components of the modernization process.

A traditional society is essentially a large family with a unique culture. Thus modernization means development from a society "in which all the major roles are allocated on an ascriptive basis, and in which the division of labor is based primarily on family and kinship units" (Eisenstadt 1964:376). Political, religious, and educational tasks, for instance, are assigned to people with certain family statuses, such as the oldest heads of families. Each group (i.e., an extended family or a tribe) has its own culture, which is permeated by religious beliefs and values. However, religion per se does not exist. For instance, "In the traditional cultures of western Africa, 'religion' did not exist as an indigenous category, but was introduced by missionaries..." (Peel 1993:89). Ethnic or communal identity is foremost, and specific religious beliefs are just part of the group's identity. "In Africa, people only recognize themselves as having 'a religion' when they adopt Islam or Christianity, religions which not only define themselves as such, but construct 'paganism' as their opposition" (Peel 1993:89).

"Primitive" religion assumes the complete identification of an individual with a collectivity, usually a real or fictitious extended family. This "identification is typically apprehended as being congenital and thus inevitable for the individual" (Berger 1967:60). Individual death and suffering are transcended through the immortality of the collectivity. Rituals affirming the continuity of generations are emphasized. "The individual finds his ancestors continuing mysteriously within himself, and in the same way he projects his own being into his children and later descendants" (p. 62).

With technological development and societal expansion, societies cease to be families writ large. Over time, new institutions such as armies and religious organizations appear. Recently in the West, new professions have formed committed to the spirit of capitalism (entrepreneurs), reason (lawyers, accountants), humanism (teachers, caring professionals such as social workers or therapists), or aesthetics (artists). The proliferation of institutions has lessened the social influence of religious organizations. Each profession exists independent of any religious organization. Moreover, its values or goals may or may not be affected by religious notions. For example, artists may infuse their works with religious meaning, but they may not, preferring perhaps the philosophy of art for art's sake. Rushdie's opponents, however, refused to allow such choice to artists.

Such structural differentiation has been accompanied by cultural fragmentation. Prior to modernization, social control processes are used to protect religious beliefs and values and to ensure their influence on every aspect of life, whether familial, economic, or whatever. Over time, social observers have found it necessary to talk about subcultures based on ethnicity and social class within societies. Illustrative of cultural fragmentation in the West, while the Bible remains a best seller, popular culture is more related to "the secular scripture" (Frye 1976), epitomized by love stories, and elite culture to "a secular canon" (Bloom 1995), exemplified for English-speaking people by Shakespeare.

Moreover, as societies have become larger – a process whose facets have been described as urbanization, nation-building, and more recently globalization – they have also become more religiously pluralistic. In response, the state separates from any one religious group and sponsors the development of a national culture. It has been argued that, in the English-speaking world, English literature became an important school subject in the late nineteenth century as a consequence of "the failure of religion" to unify the nation (Eagleton 1983:22). Thus states develop their own civic codes that are at least somewhat independent of religion. In contrast, the Iranian constitution, written under the influence of Ayatollah Khomeini, makes the Quran the foundation of the state.

A result of structural differentiation and cultural fragmentation is individuation: a sense of self not completely defined by social roles and group memberships (Coser 1991). As the social structure becomes differentiated, the various roles one plays involve the individual with diverse role partners who may not all have the same expectations, thus forcing individuals to make personal choices consciously. Cultural fragmentation has a similar consequence. Thus people are more and more self-conscious about a personal identity that is increasingly unique.

Modernization, then, is a process in which structural differentiation, cultural fragmentation, and individuation become more characteristic of a society. By "traditionalist religion" I mean a religious group that resists this process. Traditionalist religion is an attempt to approximate the situation of traditional religion: The individual is absorbed into a clearly defined group (in effect, birth determines a person's religion), culture is governed by the group's religion, and no institutions are free from religious control. However, traditionalist religion is not the same as traditional religion.

The Satanic Verses episode cannot be understood without considering the international context at the time. Among the Western critics of Khomeini, a recurring motif was that the death sentence against Rushdie must be condemned by "the civilized world, " implying that at least parts of the Orient are barbaric (Appignanesi and Maitland 1989:130, 162, 164). In Great Britain, after some British Muslims publicly burned a copy of *The Satanic Verses*, "Muslims were called 'barbarians,' 'uncivilized,' 'fanatics,' and compared to the Nazis" (Parekh 1990:76). It was the well-known writer Anthony Burgess who compared Muslims to Nazis. Another novelist, Fay Weldon, commented, "The Koran is food for nothought." In East London, and perhaps elsewhere, white youths taunted their Muslim counterparts by calling them "Rushdie." A British Muslim claimed that the media portrayed the event as a cultural war "between a 'backward and uncultured' Muslim community and an 'enlightened' world community" (Parekh 1990:195).

The first deaths related to the publication of *The Satanic Verses* were simultaneously related to anti-Westernism. The occasion for the protest in Islamabad was the forthcoming publication of the book in the United States (Ruthven 1990:108). At least five people were killed by police fire on anti-Rushdie protesters who attacked the U.S. Information Center in the Pakistani capital (Appignanesi and Maitland 1989:81). Later, police in Bombay killed protesters who were threatening the British Council (Ruthven 1990:114). In India, a condemner of *The Satanic Verses* labeled it an example of "literary colonialism" (Shahabuddin 1989:49). The Islamic fundamentalist reaction to Rushdie's book was, in part, an expression of outrage on the part of Muslims who believed they were portrayed as barbarians by those who influenced their economic destiny and who dominated the world's mass media.

Unlike premodernists, then, traditionalists feel alienated from a hostile world. In traditional society, there is one important group whose religion is an undifferentiated part of its culture. In modern society, traditionalists fight against a dominant group that defines the traditionalists as inferior. The latter either tries to separate from this hostile environment or seeks to gain control of it. The goal is to approximate the premodern situation: Individuals are to identify with their religious group; this group is to control the state, and through it all other institutions; the group's values and beliefs are to infuse and dominate all of culture. If successful, traditionalists would create a society unified by their religious culture and organization, and in which each individual's identity would be unified by religious values and rules. Traditionalists would create Christian societies, Muslim societies, and so on.

THE MODERN RESPONSE

At the time of the incident, Rushdie was a British citizen. The British government was forced to react because the *fatwa* violated the principle of state sovereignty. As the foreign secretary said, "Nobody has the right to incite people to violence on British soil or against British citizens" (Appignanesi and Maitland 1989:109). In the modern context, only a state may legitimately kill someone residing in its territory. Khomeini's *fatwa* undermined the principle of state sovereignty. Moreover, the *fatwa* violated the moral foundation of British society, although this would not have been the case a relatively short time ago.

Long into the process of Western modernization, verbal offenses against sacred matters – that is, blasphemy – were considered criminal offenses (Levy 1993). In the seventeenth century a British lord chief justice explained the social significance of blasphemy: "to say religion is a cheat is to dissolve all those obligations whereby civil societies are preserved..." (quoted in Lee 1990:77). However, in 1949 a British lord described the law as obsolete. He commented, "The reason for this law was because it was thought that a denial of Christianity was liable to shake the fabric of society, which was itself founded upon Christian religion. There is no such danger to society now and the offense of blasphemy is a dead letter" (quoted in Webster 1990:24). Today the law is rarely enforced.

In reaction to *The Satanic Verses* episode, Home Office Minister of State John Patten circulated a news release "On Being British" (Asad 1993). Britishness was equated with valuing freedom, showing tolerance, and respecting the rights of others (p. 244). This civic code, the minister was implying, was now what held together the fabric of British society. Thus, Great Britain officially condemned the *fatwa* because it violated the foundations of the state: sovereignty and a modern civic code.

Artists were also quite vocal in defending Rushdie. The *New York Times* (12 March 1989) asked writers to speak to Rushdie "from their common land – the country of literature." Indeed, they spoke as representatives of the writing profession. The common theme was that a novel's content is irrelevant, because the issue is the freedom to create. To be a writer requires a feeling of freedom. To be a creative writer, said Robertson Davies, means to say "what entrenched opinion considers unspeakable" (*New York Times*, 12 March 1989).

Another defense of Rushdie emphasized the independent importance of aesthetic pleasure. Wendy Steiner criticized those who would deny us of pleasure such as "the Islamic fundamentalists who could not tolerate Rushdie's wicked fun..." (1995:207). As Steiner wrote, "art is virtual. We will not be led into fascism or rape or child abuse or racial oppression through aesthetic experience" (1995:211). We should be able to experience aesthetic bliss, "secure in the belief that whatever similarities art may have to reality will not determine either us or that reality, and whatever pleasures it provides will hurt no one" (p. 211).

But these positions did not go unchallenged in the wake of the publication of Rushdie's novel. Great Britain continues to have a law against insulting Christianity. (Thus Rushdie did not break the law, since he insulted Islam.) Valuing individual rights does not necessarily mean rejecting the protection of religion. So, Western (modern) reactions to *The Satanic Verses* episode were mixed.

IN CRITICISM OF RUSHDIE

In 1976 the *Gay News* had published a poem expressing an erotic fantasy about a Roman centurion who makes love to Christ after piercing His side. The British law on blasphemy was used in 1977 to prosecute the publisher. The presiding judge made clear that the issue was not simply content but the manner of expression:

Blasphemous libel is committed if there is published any writing concerning God or Christ, the Christian religion, the Bible, or some sacred object, using words that are scurrilous, abusive, or offensive and which tend to vilify the Christian religion (and therefore have a tendency to lead to a breach of the peace) (quoted in Ruthven 1990:49).

The principle is that in a pluralistic society, since religion is so emotionally important to people, not only must religious differences be tolerated but also religious beliefs and practices must be protected against ridicule and contempt (Webster 1990:64–5).[3]

A commentator, critical of Rushdie's judgment, noted that to label a character Mahound, a medieval corruption of Muhammad that connoted a devil, "is to play a very dangerous game indeed: about as dangerous as writing 'FUCK THE POPE' on the walls of the Catholic Falls Road in Belfast" (Ruthven 1990:162). The commentator rejected the freedom to insult (see also Lee 1990 and Webster 1990).

According to a Gallup poll in 1990, a majority of the British believed Rushdie should apologize to Muslims for what he wrote in *The Satanic Verses* (Bedford 1993:153). Indeed, the conservative British historian, Hugh Trevor-Roper, commented in a British paper that Rushdie's

offense is one of manners, not a crime, and the law cannot notice it. That being so, I would not shed a tear if some British Muslims, deploring his manners, should waylay him in a dark street and seek

---

3. Internationally, absolute freedom of speech is not accepted. Article 19 of the International Covenant on Civil and Political Rights defends the right to freedom of expression. However, this right may be restricted (1) to protect the rights or reputations of others, or (2) to ensure national security, public order, public health, or public morals (Appignanesi and Maitland 1989:211–2). Some democratic countries banned Rushdie's book because laws required them to prohibit the public expression of hostile religious attitudes.

to improve them. If that should cause him thereafter to control his pen, society would benefit and literature would not suffer (quoted in Barnes 1994:102).

Religious leaders of various faiths, while condemning Rushdie's death sentence, expressed sympathy for Muslims and were critical of *The Satanic Verses*. The archbishop of Canterbury and the chief rabbi of Great Britain advocated the prohibition of publishing obscenely defamatory material likely to inflame a section of society by showing contempt for that section's religious beliefs (Appignanesi and Maitland 1989:70, 124, 143, 181, 216; Webster 1990:67). George Carey, who followed Runcie as the archbishop of Canterbury, said, "Muslims shocked by Mr. Rushdie's book felt the same pain as Christians outraged at [the movie version of] *The Last Temptation of Christ*" (Gledhill 1991:5). He called for greater tolerance of the Muslim feelings about *The Satanic Verses*. An article in the Vatican newspaper called *The Satanic Verses* blasphemous and implied that blasphemers had no right to free speech (Ahsan and Kidwai 1991:127). Some Catholic intellectuals in the United States supported the banning of *The Satanic Verses*; civility, they argued, includes respect for religions (Allitt 1994).

The Islamic Society of North America (1989) expressed support for restricting religious insults. The society's statement affirmed commitment to human rights such as freedom of expression, but added that "it is the spirit of harmony, goodwill, and mutual respect among the members of society that ensures the full and balanced enjoyment and responsible exercise of these rights by all." The statement condemned the threat of violence against Rushdie. It also said that *The Satanic Verses* is a slanderous stab at Islam "from beneath the cloak of literature." Thus, the Islamic Society tried to achieve a voluntary ban on the book in the name of harmony and mutual respect among the members of a pluralistic society.

MODERN SOCIETY

To understand the nature of modern religion, we must return to the modernization process. A crucial period in the history of humanity was the Axial Age (c. 600 B.C.E. [Before the Common Era; same as B.C.] to c. 600 C.E.), so called because during this period civilizations around the world experienced profound events that are still relevant, notably the

Greek philosophers, the Jewish prophets, Christianity, the Roman state, Buddhism, Confucianism, and Islam.[4] It is customary for textbooks on Western Civilization to begin with ancient Israel, classical Greece, and the Roman Empire.

During the Axial Age, world religions appeared that broke the tie between a religion and a group (Mensching 1973). New religions, such as Buddhism and Christianity, focused on the salvation of individuals. The fundamental change was the new importance of the person. This change was most fully accepted in the West and over time increasingly became a fundamental part of all social institutions. Individuation, I assume, had been becoming a more common experience for a long time. What was new was a cultural change: Religions ascribed ultimate importance to each and every individual. "Individualism" was born.[5]

Individualism – the cultural acceptance of the ultimate significance of the individual – has implications for all aspects of society.

[It] means that the value of the person exceeds that of any group as such. Take the case of a family. According to individualism, the well-being of each member of the family is equally important, and the happiness of the members is more important than the status of the family as such; thus divorce can be justified in terms of improving the aggregate well-being of the individuals composing the family. Individualism is not egoism. The latter means being selfish, making one's self more important than anyone else. Individualism is not a glorification of the self. Rather, it is expressed in a respect for each person including the self (Tamney 1996:11).

The British civic code previously referred to spells out some of the implications of individualism: Freedom is to be protected, individual differences are to be tolerated, and each person must respect the human rights of everyone else. Many of the specific cultural differences across the globe that are related to politics, family, and religion are really differences about individualism.

---

4. For a discussion of the idea of the Axial Age, which was originally proposed by Karl Jaspers, see Eisenstadt 1986.
5. My analysis here is, of course, based on the work of Émile Durkheim (1973a; see also Tamney 1996:22).

MODERN RELIGION

A modern society, then, accepts the notion of state sovereignty, with the state promulgating a civic code that is an expression of individualism. A modern society is also characterized by structural differentiation and cultural fragmentation. For example, writers are not dependent on "church" or state for survival and they defend the values of the artistic institution: being creative, airing the "unspeakable, " producing beauty.

Modern religion accepts such a society – up to a point. Religious leaders did not criticize John Patten's notion of British culture (freedom, tolerance), nor did they challenge the right of artists to be independent of church and state. Moreover, Christian leaders implied their acceptance of a pluralist society with their sympathetic comments about Islam. Finally, the modernist's commitment to individualism is at least to some extent applied within the religious group – religious leaders did not demand acceptance of their judgments, but simply presented arguments for them.

In contrast, traditionalists do not accept a state based on a secular civic morality. In 1993, the host of a San Francisco television show asked a Baptist minister if he agreed with a statement in the Book of Leviticus to the effect that men who have sex with other men should be stoned to death. The minister replied, "That's what it says. . . . That's what God says. . . . That's what the Bible says." In reaction, the mayor of San Francisco said in a statement, "It is intolerable, indefensible, and inexcusable for anyone in San Francisco . . . to be associated with statements, be they biblical or otherwise, which justify violence" (Associated Press 1993:3). Christian traditionalists not only give ultimate allegiance to the Bible as they understand it, they also want biblical injunctions to be enforced by the state, regardless of their consequences for such things as human rights.

As I said previously, modern religious leaders accept the modern context up to a point. They continue to expect public respect and state protection. During the 1980s, when a special commission held hearings on Britain's blasphemy law, most religious groups favored retention of the law in some form (Levy 1993:555). Thus they are not willing to give writers such as Rushdie "free reign." Indeed, *The Satanic Verses* episode evoked a resentment about the importance of the state. An Anglican bishop analyzed the modern condition thusly: The "supreme reality on which we rely for welfare is the nation-state. To betray the interests of the nation is therefore the supreme crime, but blasphemy is a joke" (quoted in Ahsan and Kidwai 1991:86).

British popular opinion also did not support Rushdie's action. What R. Stephen Warner said of the United States applies to any modern people: While a religion is not "a property of the whole society," it is "a fundamental category of identity and association" (Warner 1993:1046, 1059). Because specific religions remain important to them, modernists espouse the notion of respectful tolerance of established creeds, or at least for all religions that accept the prevailing civic culture (Tamney 1994:203–4). Religious insults are informally or formally punished, although not by death.

An article about Taslima Nasrin, "the Salman Rushdie of Bangladesh" who is also hiding from some Islamic fundamentalists who want her dead, recorded Nasrin as saying, "Religion is the great oppressor, and should be abolished." The article's author commented, "Even by Western standards, her views are radical..." (Weaver 1994:49). Indeed, sympathetic Westerners have been "outraged" by Nasrin's criticism of the Quran and other religious texts as "out of place and out of time" because such observers believed her statements were unnecessarily provocative (Weaver 1994:56).

Wendy Kaminer (1996:25) recently wrote that an op-ed piece on spirituality which she wrote for the New York Times "was carefully cleansed by my editors of any irreverence toward established religion." As she said,

If I were to mock a religious belief as childish, if I were to suggest that worshipping a supernatural deity, convinced that it cares about your welfare, is like worrying about monsters in the closet who find you tasty enough to eat..., I'd violate the norms of civility and religious correctness (1996:24).

Kaminer described the modern world.

As these examples imply, modernity involves inconsistency because people value both free speech and the social protection of religion:

Many self-proclaimed defenders of free speech are tying themselves in strange knots. People tell me privately they believe in free speech and then say Rushdie should not have given offense.... None of these positions makes clear how a writer is "to respect" other people's views without putting on the iron mask of self-censorship (Ignatieff 1989:250).

Moreover, avowedly modern people do not apply the norm of toler-ance consistently. A British commission set up to examine the country's blasphemy law criticized some religious beliefs, such as the injunction that adulterers should be stoned to death, and some religious groups, such as the one involved in mass suicide/murder at Jonestown (Levy 1993:554). In fact, absolute tolerance does not exist in modern societies. In the aftermath of *The Satanic Verses* episode, some people publicly doubted that tolerance should mean "respecting religious expressions such as Islamic fundamentalism" (Parekh 1990:79; see also Asad 1993).

A modern religion, then, accepts being part of a modern society, but not completely. In fact, it expects to have a special, protected sta-tus. Moreover, commitment among religious people to a code founded on tolerance coexists with an unwillingness of those ostensibly com-mitted to the code to tolerate all religions. The inconsistencies within modern religion suggest further change will occur. Indeed, the kind of religion represented by Rushdie would seem more consistent with moder-nity. The question addressed in this book is why traditionalist religion, which is Rushdie's target in *The Satanic Verses*, remains resilient in a time that included the great success of this novel – a book that sym-bolizes the latest form of religion to appear during the modernization process.

THE LATE-MODERN RESPONSE

I follow Anthony Giddens in labeling the present period of Western history "late-modern," because Westerners are now experiencing the consequences of modernity in their most radical form (1990:3). I shall elaborate on the meaning of late-modernity by describing Rushdie's response to his critics.

Rushdie wrote that while "reality and morality are not givens but imperfect human constructs, " the challenge for writers is to "find a way of fulfilling our unaltered spiritual requirements" (Rushdie 1990b:105). In the words of another writer, the question is, "Can the religious mentality thrive outside of religious dogma and hierarchy?" (Fuentes 1989:248). Spiritual needs will not disappear. We want to understand our place in the universe, and we need rules for living. Late-modernity is not the end of religion.

In a late-modern culture, artists are the equal of any in having the authority to explore spiritual issues. "Joyce's wanderers, Beckett's tramps, Gogol's tricksters, Bulgakov's devils, Bellow's high-energy meditations on the stifling of the soul by the triumphs of materialism; these, and many more, are what we have instead of prophets and suffering saints" (Rushdie 1990b:106). It is not that late-modern people will cease to read the writings of prophets and saints, but that spiritual issues are increasingly explored outside any established religious context. Late-modern religious seekers may read the pope *or* Rushdie. Rushdie intended "to affirm that, like fiction, religion is a product of the creative imagination" (Piscatori 1990:772). Cultural categories such as art and religion remain, but late-modernists are blurring the distinctiveness of the categories.

The key point, however, is not the elevation of artists to new heights of social status. In his novel, Rushdie raised the issue, who has control over "the grand narrative, the Story of Islam." He wants everyone to have such power "because those who do not have power over the story that dominates their lives, power to retell it, rethink it, deconstruct it, joke about it, and change it as times change, truly are powerless, because they cannot think new thoughts" (Rushdie 1991b:A16). The crucial matter is to democratize control of all grand narratives.

Beyond such matters, Rushdie and his supporters affirmed the desirability of doubt and the need to attack religious institutions.

DOUBT

The Satanic Verses opens with a quotation from Defoe's *The History of the Devil*; Satan is described as a vagabond, a person without any fixed place. The story itself begins with the explosion of an airborne plane carrying the two main characters, both of whom are actors. The debris falling from the plane includes "stereophonic headsets, drinks trolleys," as well as "broken memories, sloughed-off souls, [and] severed mother-tongues" (Rushdie 1989:4). According to the author, *The Satanic Verses* "is written from the very experience of uprooting, disjuncture and metamorphosis . . . that is the migrant condition . . . from which, I believe, can be derived a metaphor for all humanity" (Rushdie 1990a:52). "Satanic" culture, then, is built on the acceptance of doubt, which Rushdie believes is "the central condition of a human being in the 20th century . . . " (quoted in Appignanesi and Maitland 1989:30).

Nothing is sacred. Ideas, texts, and people can be made sacred, but "the act of making sacred is in truth an event in history," and such events must be subject to questioning, "even to declarations of their obsolescence" (Rushdie 1990b:99).

The Satanic Verses does not exemplify social realism. Rushdie "deliberately prevents his readers from being caught up in a story with its own 'organic' life, that progresses uninterrupted, and that creates a completely imagined world" (Brennan 1989:85). Rushdie's book is an example of the magical realism associated with South American writers such as Gabriel García Márquez. A work seems realistic, yet objects or people have magical (unusual) properties that undermine the realism, thus both distancing the audience from the artistic work and calling reality into question (Sadri 1994). One critic described Rushdie's style as a mix of myth and realism, a style meant to destroy the status quo: "The point of view that emerges is not anti-Islam but anticlosure, opposed, in principle, to any dualistic, fixed way of looking at things" (Afzal-Khan 1993:168–9). The method for dealing with perennial spiritual issues should approximate more magical realism than dogmatic theology: Answers should be understood as real yet always provisional.

RELIGIOUS ATTACK

The Satanic Verses is an attack on religion. But, it is an attack that takes religion seriously. One of Rushdie's characters describes a movie he is about to make in India. The movie is of the "theological type" so popular in that country, but of a new kind. Although about the temptation of a prophet, it would not be seen as blasphemous.

> Our purpose is not to make some farrago like that movie *The Message* in which, whenever Prophet Muhammad (on whose name be peace!) was heard to speak, you saw only the head of his camel, moving its mouth. *That* – excuse me for pointing out – had no class. We are making a high-taste, quality picture. A moral tale: like – what do you call them? – fables (Rushdie 1989:272).

In dissenting from "imposed orthodoxies, " Rushdie produced his own moral lessons.

Rushdie writes as he does because he does have values. In the disputed section of the novel concerning Mahound, a theme is the religious leader's prejudice against women. For example, the "Satanic Verses" concern the status of three goddesses. As Rushdie wrote, "I thought it was at least worth pointing out that one of the reasons for rejecting the goddesses was that *they were female*. The rejection has implications that are worth thinking about. I suggest that such highlighting is a proper function of literature" (1991a:399–400). Given the pain caused by aspects of Islam, such as its use in the defense of patriarchy (Ruthven 1990:5), Rushdie felt justified in assaulting Islam.[6]

LATE-MODERN RELIGION

Rushdie does not repudiate modernity. He accepts the aforementioned modern civic code as the basis for the state. For example, Rushdie showed his commitment to tolerance when he supported a law against inciting racial and religious hatred (Johnson 1990). (He does not believe he would have been found guilty of violating such a law. Simon Lee [1990:87] reaches the same conclusion in his examination of the Rushdie case.) Artistically, modernism has been identified with the motto "art for art's sake," implying that only aesthetic values should be used in judging art. Using this definition, Rushdie rejects modernism because social issues and spiritual values shape his artistic works. Rushdie continues what Jürgen Habermas called the "project of the enlightenment": the arts and sciences being used to promote moral progress and personal happiness (Habermas 1981). Rushdie is political, spiritual, and artistic – thus he refers to himself as "postmodern." In my framework, postmodern artists are a characteristic of late-modern society.

Rushdie is *late*-modern, then, because while he defends the institutional separation of the arts from religion and the state, he does not judge artistic worth using only aesthetic criteria.[7] The British politician and literary critic Michael Foot defended Rushdie, arguing that if fanatics are to be stopped, "they must be mocked in the name of a common human decency with a claim to take precedence over any religion"

6. Readers perceived the feminist theme in *The Satanic Verses*. Some Asian women staged a counterdemonstration against an anti-Rushdie rally in the name of Women Against Fundamentalism (Ruthven 1990:5).
7. Although Rushdie uses "postmodern" to describe his philosophy (e.g., Rushdie 1990b:107), I find this label misleading, since Rushdie does not repudiate modernity as I have described it. Marshall Berman called Rushdie a modern, not postmodern, author, because while postmoderns "repudiate any sort of universal quest . . . ," Rushdie struggles "to break through to visions of truth and freedom that all men and women can embrace" (Berman 1992:54; see also Edmundson 1989:68).

(Foot 1989:244). In effect, all religions are judged by a morality based on individualism. Authoritarian and dogmatic religion is condemned in the name of such things as upholding women's rights, democratizing control of religious grand narratives, and respecting each person's decision about a proper spiritual path.

Rushdie is also late-modern because he accepts doubt as a permanent condition. Rushdie told an interviewer that people ask him "are you Indian? Pakistani? English?" He went on to say that people must accept those like himself with plural identities: "We are increasingly becoming a world of migrants, made up of bits and fragments from here, there. We are here. And we have never really left anywhere we have been" (quoted in Marzorati 1989:100). Appropriately, spiritual life would include fragments from various traditions and doubts about all of them. The symbolic importance of the migrant emphasizes that the late-modern religious person both incorporates doubt into a philosophy and borrows across cultures in arriving at a tentative credo.

In sum, a traditionalist religion seeks to approximate the premodern religious condition while maintaining a hostile attitude toward those not of like mind. A modern religion accepts being part of a modern society but expects to have a protected status, is ambivalent about the importance of the state and its civic code, and is inconsistent in expressing tolerance. More than the other religious types, late-modern religion expresses respect for each and every person. As a consequence, late-modernists give no religion a protected status, and tolerance depends on conformity with a modern civil code. Moreover, late-modern religion evidences the consequences of cultural fragmentation and the resulting exposure of people to diverse religions. Late-modernists, therefore, value borrowing from different religious traditions and accept religious uncertainty as permanent. The three religious forms – traditionalist, modern, and late-modern – represent an increasing accommodation of modernity. What distinguishes contemporary society is the simultaneous existence of all three forms of religion.[8]

8. An alternative typology has been developed by Ernst Troeltsch (1931). He used "church," "sect," and "mysticism" to understand the history of Christianity (Steeman 1975). However, Troeltsch used his concepts to describe both how a religion responds to modernization and the struggle between idealists and compromisers that occurs in all utopian movements (O'Dea 1966:67). My suggestion is that the categories developed in this book be used to analyze the

Explaining the Appeal of Traditionalist Religion

There are two broadly different ways to explain the popularity of a particular form of religion (or, for that matter, of a particular religion). First, popularity can be explained in terms of a timeless theory – that is, a theory supposedly applicable any time and any place. Second, popularity can be accounted for using historical theory – that is, a theory that sees the cause of popularity in the fit between a religion and the particular needs of a people in a certain time and place. I shall illustrate both approaches in trying to explain the appeal of traditionalist religion in a late-modern society.

COSTLY RELIGIONS SUCCEED

In the 1970s, Dean Kelley (1977) wrote a book that remains influential: *Why Conservative Churches Are Growing.* He had noticed that while mainline Protestant churches such as the Presbyterian and Methodist denominations were in decline, more conservative denominations such as the Southern Baptist Convention and the Assemblies of God were growing. Kelley tried to explain this difference using a theory not limited to contemporary society. He wanted to show that religion "has its own elemental drives, dynamics, and necessities that are not to be explained in terms of 'extraneous' factors such as economics, geography, demographics, or climate" (Kelley 1977:VII).

He imagined what "an ideal type of religion might be," and concluded that such a religion would attend to its essential business: "explaining the meaning of life in ultimate terms" (Kelley 1977:37,56). But while many organizations, religious and otherwise, offer interpretations of life, all are not equally successful. The appeal of a doctrine, Kelley argued, is not a function of its content but the apparent seriousness of its adherents: "More significant than the content of the faith for its success are the demands made upon the would-be members and the commitment with which they respond" (p. 53). Seriousness is signaled by costliness;

relationship between modernization and religion, and that "church" and "sect" be used to analyze the inevitable cyclical processes affecting all religious (indeed, all utopian) traditions. A "church" would be a religious group that compromises itself religiously out of neglect, avarice, self-defense, and such; a "sect" would be a religious group that tries to remain saintly by allowing for no compromises with its religious purpose.

the group's demands are costly in themselves, and the members' commitment indicates a willingness to accept future costs, such as sacrificing time, money, or one's life.

Costliness in Kelley's work takes two broad forms: control over members' lifestyles (strictness) and a certain kind of congregation (a strong church). Kelley emphasized that if a church has many strict rules and enforces them, it will appear to others to be a serious religion. For instance, a church that requires members not to gamble, drink alcohol, or attend dances and movies is taken as more serious than one that does not have these or similar rules.

But Kelley went beyond – far beyond – idealizing lifestyle demands being placed on church members. As Kenneth W. Inskeep (1993:136) put it, "If a group was to grow, the community must be everything and the individual nothing." He then quoted Kelley:

The appreciation of individual worth and freedom is one of the highest achievements of modern man, but it does not do much for social strength. If each member is unwilling to give *unquestioning* obedience (or even much questioning obedience) to a leader or group, it makes for an atomistic aggregation of individuals rather than a cohesive deployable organization (Kelley 1977:85).

In a strong church, each person is wholeheartedly committed to the group – "each individual's goals being highly or wholly identified with – or derived from – those of the group . . ." (p. 57).

Kelley's strong church requires (a) absolutism, i.e., uncritical members accept an ideology that explains everything, and, correspondingly, members obey the leader's commands without question; (b) homogeneity, i.e., deviants are not tolerated but are corrected by group confessions or are excommunicated; (c) fanaticism, i.e., members do not want to hear ideas different from their own and may isolate themselves or engage only in one-way communications meant to spread their message; and (d) totalitarianism, i.e., the church controls all aspects of a member's life, including work, family, recreation, dress, and demeanor (Kelley 1977:58–9, 79–81, 101).[9]

---

9. Kelley's strong church resembles the Cosers' (1979) "greedy institution," Kanter's (1972) "successful commune," and Goffman's (1961) "total institution." In all, the group consumes the lives of the members and discredits the individual self. Cohesion is of utmost importance because the preservation of the group is the ultimate goal.

My colleague Stephen Johnson and I were interested in how many people thought that churches should be "strong." In 1994, we asked a sample of residents in Middletown the following question: "If you had to select a new church to attend, how important would each of the following eight things be?" The offered responses were "very important," "somewhat important," and "not important at all." If the person answered, "I don't know," this response was recorded.[10] The eight characteristics were:

- The church is led by a pastor who is certain that what he or she teaches is the truth (TRUTH).
- The church has strict rules about things such as how to dress in church and how much money to give the church (STRICT).
- The church makes people who do not follow the rules leave the church (KICKOUT).
- The church service makes you feel joyous (JOYOUS).
- The people at the church go out of their way to be your friends (BEFRIEND).
- The pastor encourages meeting people from other denominations and religions (OTHERDEN).
- The pastor encourages members not to associate with nonreligious people during their free time (AVOID).
- The church places a major emphasis on programs to help the poor and needy (HELPPOOR).

Half of these traits are represented in Kelley's model: TRUTH, STRICT, KICKOUT, and AVOID. The last three were, by far, the least chosen characteristics for an ideal church; about 10 percent of the respondents said it would be very important for a church to have strict rules, to kick out deviants, or to encourage avoiding nonreligious people. In contrast, about two-thirds of the respondents said it would be very important in choosing a new church for it to emphasize helping the poor, to have a joyous church service, and to have a preacher certain about the content of her or his sermon; only the last of these popular traits (TRUTH) is part of Kelley's model.

A year later we asked a sample of people in Middletown similar questions about the actual churches they attended. We asked each

10. The sample consisted of 576 people who resided in the county that contains the Lynds' (1929) "Middletown" (Muncie, Indiana). For details of the study, see Tamney and Johnson (1998).

respondent who gave a religious preference the extent to which the following statements described the church that the respondent attended.

- My church has strict rules about things such as how to dress in church and how much money to give the church.
- My church pressures people who do not follow the rules to leave the church.
- My pastor encourages members not to associate with nonreligious people during their free time.

The possible responses were "generally describes person's church," "somewhat describes the church," and "does not describe the church."[11] Out of the 421 people we interviewed, fifteen people (about 4 percent) said having strict rules about dress and tithing generally describes their churches, eight people gave this response to the question about pressuring deviants to leave, and four people said that generally their pastors encourage members not to spend their free time with nonreligious people.

The two Middletown projects suggest that "strong" religious institutions are neither popular nor prevalent. Kelley's theory would explain the appeal of traditionalist religion, since his ideal church resembles this type of religion inasmuch as the individual is totally subordinated to the group. However, the decided lack of appeal in Middletown of Kelley's strong church suggests that his theory does not explain the success of churches in the United States.

However, aspects of Kelley's theory may be useful. The importance of lifestyle strictness in explaining religious popularity remains unclear.[12] Perhaps our question about dress codes and tithing focused on the wrong rules. Undoubtedly, the churches that have grown in the United States

---

11. The sample consisted of 421 residents of "Middletown" who stated that they were going to vote in the 1996 presidential election.
12. Kelley is not logically consistent about strictness. At times, he argues that excessive strictness has limited appeal, citing examples of excessiveness that are quite unusual, such as the Inquisition (1977:95–6, 124). At times, Kelley seems to be saying that people who will join a high-demand movement are not numerous (1977:101,112). Yet the message that Kelley intended, and the one received by his readers, is that strictness results in growth. While all of Kelley's book is about "conservative" groups, he allows that "radical" groups could also be demanding by requiring poverty or pacifism and thus be strong groups (p. 177). But he does not explain the lack of success of such groups as Dorothy Day's Catholic Worker movement.

are the ones with more rules against drinking, dancing, and so forth. It is possible that some form of lifestyle strictness connotes religious serious-ness to people and validates the doctrines promulgated by traditionalist groups. In addition, we did find that people in Middletown liked au-thoritative pastors, and this might explain the appeal of traditionalist religion.[13]

Moreover, it cannot be ignored that people studying church suc-cess continue to use Kelley's argument. His ideas are the theoretical basis for one of the most influential sociological studies of American church history, Roger Finke and Rodney Stark's (1992) *The Church-ing of America 1776–1900*. Studies of church growth and decline rou-tinely refer to Kelley's argument (cf., Hoge, Johnson, and Luidens 1994; Perrin, Kennedy, and Miller 1997), as does Laurence Iannaccone's (1994) frequently referenced essay "Why Strict Churches Are Strong," which analyzes the success of denominations in attracting committed participants.[14] Appropriately, an excerpt from one of Kelley's essays in which he explains his strictness thesis is included in a new anthology de-voted to "religion in modern times" (Woodhead and Heelas 2000). Thus church traits emphasized by Kelley – lifestyle strictness and authoritative pastors – will be discussed throughout this book.

Previously I described the crucial aspect of traditionalist religion to be the subordination of the individual to the group; the belief that one is born into such a religion symbolizes the ideally unbreak-able bond between the individual and the group. This trait can now be restated thusly: A traditionalist religion seeks to embody Kelley's notion of a strong church. The lack of broad appeal of such churches implies that traditionalist religion in its pure form cannot be success-ful in late-modern societies. Because popularity may accrue only to approximations of traditionalist religion, I shall use the broader category

---

13. Interestingly, authoritative pastors were more important to Protestants of all kinds than to Catholics (Tamney and Johnson 1998). This result probably reflects the relative importance of sermons to Protestants. It also makes the point that the specific determinants of popularity vary by religious tradition.

14. Laurence R. Iannaccone recasts Kelley's argument using the idea of free riders. Specifically, Iannaccone (1994) argues as follows: Strictness means that mem-bership is costly, thereby eliminating free riders; as a result, average levels of commitment are high, which increases the congregation's capacity to produce collective rewards, a source of success. I doubt the usefulness of this argument (Tamney and Johnson 1997; see also Ammerman 1997:302).

"conservative religion" to refer to religious groups that appear to be variants of traditionalist religion.

RELIGIONS ACCOMMODATING MODERNIZATION SUCCEED

Modernization theory assumes that the popularity of a religion depends on how well it fits each historical situation. The implication is that secular change precedes religious change. However, modernization theory does not portray religious institutions as continually only reacting to secular changes. Rather, the theoretical assumptions are that the most significant causes of change are secular, and that the consequences of such change are affected by the religious response to them.

In addition, as previously noted, modernization theory assumes there is a direction of social change, and it argues that successful groups or movements will be those that accommodate the pattern of change. Thus, based on what I have written so far, the theory predicts that religions are more likely to succeed to the extent that they adjust to increasing individuation, structural differentiation, and cultural fragmentation. The lack of popular appeal of Kelley's strong church is consistent with this prediction.

To develop the theoretical framework further, I shall consider modernization as it has occurred in the West. David Gress (1998) distinguished the "old West" and the "new West." The former is a "synthesis of classical, Christian, and Germanic culture that took shape from the fifth to the eight centuries A.D." (p. 1). The "new West" is the more recent "synthesis of reason, liberty, and progress" (p. 10). Many writers (e.g., Giddens 1991) restrict the notion of the modern West to Gress's "new West." Such an approach overlooks the obvious continuity between classical culture and both modern philosophy (especially the faith in reason) and a democratic ideology, between Christianity and individualism, and between Germanic culture and Anglo-Saxon notions about freedom (Cantor 1994; Gress 1998). However, it is also true that much of what Gress calls the "old West" is not considered part of modernity, such as the Christian emphasis on sinful human nature or the Germanic idealization of the warrior. While all that Gress discussed is part of Western Civilization, only a part of what he described should be understood as reflecting modernization as I use that term.

Gress's "synthesis of reason, liberty, and progress" would certainly be considered part of modernization. Liberty is one of the consequences of individualism. Perhaps less obviously, the emphasis on reason is

another such consequence. The Enlightenment is a European philosophical movement of the eighteenth century based on the belief in
the superiority of reason as the means of discovering truth, deciding on
what is beautiful, and determining what is moral. This faith in reason
was fueled by what has come to be called the Scientific Revolution of the
preceding century, but it also found a receptive audience in the growing
intellectual class, among whom reasoning became the means used to
critique established authorities. In practice, the Enlightenment meant
that beliefs and values could no longer be established by reference to
either tradition or classical sources (i.e., the Bible or secular writers such
as Plato). A new faith in reason spread among the educated people because it gave them a new freedom to think for themselves (Anderson
1990:33). Such a faith can be traced back to classical Greece but became
a dominant part of culture only in the "new West."

   This faith was affirmed by new technological developments. The process of developing our knowledge of how things work and of inventing
substitutes for natural products and processes became institutionalized.
As Alfred North Whitehead (1925: 98) wrote, "The greatest invention
of the nineteenth century was the invention of the method of invention." The development of scientific procedures and the social commitment to research and development are profoundly important. One
consequence, at least until now, has been an optimism about the future,
a sense that humanity can and will create a better world – thus Gress
includes a belief in progress in his depiction of the new West.

   Since World War II, however, several crises have developed that,
although not inconsistent with modernization, imply that Western culture is changing in important ways. First, the implications of individualism for private life are becoming obvious, creating in part a crisis of
the family. Second, the faith in reason seems to be declining. Third,
Westerners are experiencing greater anxiety about the consequences of
new technological developments. Conceivably each of these crises is
resulting in the greater appeal of conservative religion. In other words,
I shall argue that some recent developments in the West may favor
the kind of religion supposedly incompatible with the modernization
process.

SELF-REALIZATION AND FAMILY

   After World War II, widespread affluence allowed Americans to think
beyond survival needs (Inglehart 1990), and the expansion of higher
education exposed more people to new ideas, among them the varied

expressions of psychoanalysis. Previously when Americans talked about the individual, they would glorify liberty and independence. Freedom from the control of others was the ideal. In contrast, the Freudian legacy referred to the need to free ourselves from the tyranny of our personal pasts. People were said to be controlled by repressed wishes or fears resulting from earlier emotional experiences. Therapy was a way to face this repressed material so that people could start living in the present and cease reenacting past events or reliving their consequences. In the late-modern context, this psychoanalytic legacy became widely known through the reinterpretations of Freud by Karen Horney, Erich Fromm, and Abraham Maslow. Maslow called their ideas "Third Force Psychology."[15]

Horney (1950), whose ideas were influenced by Fromm and who in turn influenced Maslow (Paris 1994), assumed that human nature is basically constructive, moving us toward the realization of our potentialities. Her morality was built on this supposed natural tendency: We should seek self-understanding, be honest with ourselves, and take responsibility for self-development.

Illness means being alienated from the real self (Horney 1950). Horney believed that the past enslaves us through an idealized self that when compared to the actual self makes us dislike, possibly despise, our actual selves. This idealized self is made up of beliefs about how we should feel, think, or act. The "tyranny of the should" may result in our completely losing touch with how we do feel, think, and want to act: "We consciously believe or feel then as we should believe or feel" (p. 82). The first step to health is to reconnect with how *we* believe and feel. The need is to listen to the authentic voices from within rather than to a superego within or an authority figure without.

Maslow (1968, 1971) praised the actualized person – one whose inner nature is freely expressed, one in whom all potentialities are fully developed. But self-realization requires a nurturing environment that allows a person to get to know herself and to be herself. The significant others must allow the individual to feel secure and must convey that they value the individual. These relationships must tolerate reasonably free self-expression. Given the importance of the family in shaping our personalities, Third Force recommendations were considered especially applicable to the family: The family should be a

15. The school is called *Third* Force because it followed Freudianism and Behaviorism.

nurturing environment that allows each person to develop her or his potentialities.

Until recently, a quite different kind of family life, identified with patriarchy, was supported by conservative religion. Patriarchy has been an unquestioned aspect of all societies until recently, so inevitably traditionalist forms of religion legitimate male dominance.[16] The Islamic defense of patriarchy is one of the reasons Rushdie wrote *The Satanic Verses*. During the 1920s, the women's emancipation movement was portrayed as a sign of the approaching end times within American Protestantism. Women were idealized as preservers of morality and were shielded from the world by their male protectors. Institutionally, churches segregated women in women's groups associated with "female" tasks such as nurturing the sick. These developments occurred in all branches of Christianity, but within Protestantism the segregation of women was strongest and longer lasting in the conservative branch (Kosmin and Lachman 1993). Thus, it would seem that modernization would undermine both patriarchy and conservative Protestantism.

During late-modernity, however, some conservative churches have moved away from the attitudes so strongly defended in the 1920s. While supporting the authority of the father, such churches are encouraging men to become involved in the home. Mary Jo Neitz summarized the findings from her own and others' research about a "neotraditional" family model. Some conservative husbands have changed, as has their image of God, who has been transformed "from an authoritarian patriarch to the 'Daddy-God'.... He is still the Father, but what he offers is unconditional love to His children ... " (Neitz 1993:172).

Arguably such neotraditional norms may be appealing. Family life is changing. New expectations drawn from the democratic tradition and the recent literature about maximizing one's potential are transforming home life. Yet traditions die slowly. Some women have settled for something short of a revolution in order to gain a more caring or helpful husband: "They traded formal authority for their husbands' emotional expressiveness and involvement in family life" (p. 172). A shared acceptance of the chain of command – God, husband, wife – has

---

16. Riesèbrodt (1993:178–184) specified six "basic patterns of fundamentalist ideology," one of which is patriarchal moralism, that is, a morality valuing asceticism and patriarchy. I am not sure that asceticism characterizes all non-Abrahamic religions; however, I agree that the defense of patriarchy could be added to my traditionalist ideal type.

allowed women to remain married to potentially dominating husbands (Ammerman 1987). While the women are subordinate to their spouses, both partners are subordinate to God; conceivably the women could use God (i.e., biblical passages) to influence men. Converts to conservative Protestant churches have claimed that the religion saved their marriages. Said one woman, "I learned to be submissive to Burt, but he learned to treat me with respect and give me space" (quoted in Warner 1990:133).

Some Americans, then, seem to be seeking a third way between patriarchy and spousal equality. My argument is that such people are drawn to conservative churches preaching neotraditional ideas about what it means to be a husband or a wife. Thus conservative churches that try to maintain tradition *and to* accommodate new ideas about the family would appeal to contemporary people – women who want less authoritarian and more caring husbands, and men who either want to be nurturing or simply are willing to compromise to gain peace at home.

REASON AND LEGITIMACY

Giddens (1991) has emphasized the importance of reflexivity in the modernization process. The authority of tradition is disappearing. Modern individuals have been freed from life-long group bonds. They may choose memberships in groups, even changing citizenship and gender. The need to make important personal choices (e.g., what job to take, whom to marry, whether to change a job or spouse) pressures individuals to think about who they are and what they want out of life at periodic intervals, if not continually. Moreover, taught to be self-conscious, as we learn more about ourselves, we alter our self-image and our aspirations. Modernization has pushed people to search for the unique person beyond group memberships and social roles.

Modern people ask questions: What do I want? What is the best way to get it? Reasoning calls attention to what the individual wants and favors comparing alternative means – that is, having choices. Reasoning encourages people to review habits (or traditions) and make their own individual choices. So, individuals develop styles of living that are unique. Food preferences, dress, favorite leisure activities, job choice, mate selection, and churchgoing become choices that are more or less integrated into a lifestyle. Over time, individuals become conscious of their personal styles, and being true to one's self (having integrity, being authentic) becomes important in itself.

Thus, as Gress (1998) emphasized, the use of reason to establish culture and to determine one's personal life is a distinguishing characteristic of the new West. However, the perhaps naive faith in reason that defined the Enlightenment is being undermined. Americans are aware they are socialized into a society, which is only one of many cultures. They study the history of their society and learn how it has come into existence as a result of many human decisions over a long period of time. Learning about other cultures, they find some things they like, such as Chinese food, African music, Buddhism, Eskimo carvings. Their lifestyles become more cosmopolitan, as they take pleasure from exploring other cultures. Reading books by non-Americans or engaging in conversations with them, cosmopolitans know that each group believes in the value of its own culture. Such Americans may continue to prefer American culture but they also understand the impossibility of using reason to prove the superiority of their culture. Cosmopolitan people will tend to have relativist views.[17]

A Westerner might believe in individualism and thus defend the "obvious" need for human rights. However, classical Confucianism does not endorse the idea that an individual by virtue of simply existing should have any rights; conceivably, no amount of reasonable discussion might convince a Confucianist who uses only the classical contexts that there are such things as human rights. Again, a Westerner might believe that separating church and state is in the best interest of religion, but most Muslims will disagree, and reasoning together will not change that.

The loss of faith in reason has meant a legitimacy crisis for some people. Legitimacy refers to the extent that actions are perceived as consistent with rules or laws that are considered beyond human manipulation. There are two traditional sources of transcendent order: the natural and the supernatural (or will of God). Just as a god transcends us, so does nature. Neither a god nor nature is human-made or artificial. To the extent, then, that a person tries to bring his life into harmony with either the will of god(s) or the natural order, that person's life is legitimized. In the aftermath of the Enlightenment, it was also believed that rules for living could be justified – that is, placed beyond questioning – by reasoning. The late-modern loss of faith in reason means that people

---

17. Further analysis of the loss of faith in reason can be found in Anderson (1990), Jencks (1989), and Clifford (1988).

who have values not justified by religious sources or natural laws are unable to believe in the clear rightness of their commitments.

Consider the manner in which Arthur Schlesinger, Jr., (1995:228) justified a commitment to human rights:

> For our relative values are not a matter of whim and happenstance. History has given them to us. They are anchored in our national experience, in our great national documents, in our national heroes, in our folkways, traditions, standards. Some of these values seem to us so self-evident that even relativists think they have, or ought to have, universal application: the right to life, liberty and the pursuit of happiness, for example; the duty to treat persons as ends in themselves; the prohibition of slavery, torture, genocide. People with a different history will have different values. But we believe that our own are better for us. They work for us; and, for the reason, we live and die by them.

The rights mentioned by Schlesinger, which are the concretization of individualism, may seem near sacred to many people, yet he justifies them rather limply by saying "they work" for those who believe in them.

Among other universal desires that sometimes drive our choices is the desire to believe that what we are doing is right. Some people may find it hard to live thinking that what they are doing may be no better than if they had done the opposite. But living is often a messy business, and it is not known whether we all equally feel this need for legitimacy. It may be enough for some people to think that the choices they made, for now, seem better than the rejected options. For them, a late-modern type of religion would be fine.

However, if contemporary Americans do seek the comfort of legitimacy, they probably will turn to conservative religion. In providing legitimation, the conservative form of religion has the advantage, because conservative morality (i.e., rules for living) is more justifiable by references to the canonical texts. Consider some current issues for American Christians:

> Clergy in Middletown were asked their positions on eight public issues and what their reasons were for their attitudes (Johnson and Tamney 1986). Most of the reasons given by the clergy had nothing to do directly with religion, i.e., the responses did not include any mention of God, the Bible, or Christianity. It was found

that conservative clergy more often used religious justifications for their issue positions. Consistent with this finding, religious reasons were most frequently given to justify two traditional positions, support for school prayer and opposition to homosexuality. Two other questions asked about issues related to libertarianism [i.e., modernity], affirmative action and the equal rights amendment. A minority of reasons given in support of the libertarian position on these issues were religious, as were some of the reasons given for *opposing* the equal rights amendment (Tamney 1992b:123).

The defense of affirmative action and the women's movement is associated with modern Christianity, while support for school prayer and opposition to homosexuality are associated with conservative Christianity. The ministers' comments mean that the conservatives' rules for living are more easily legitimated in contemporary society using religious sources. This is true because the moral issues associated with modern religion are too new to have been sanctioned in the sacred texts of the existing world religions.

Conservative religious groups are presenting themselves as the needed replacement for a fallen reason (Keppel 1994:56–7). Here, then, we have a possible explanation for why people in a late-modern society would find conservative churches attractive. If people are longing for a sense of legitimacy, conservative religion would be appealing.

ANXIETY ABOUT THE FUTURE

As did Gress (1998), Robert Heilbroner (1995) emphasized the importance of a sense of confidence in our capacity to improve life as a defining trait of the new West. This faith in progress was rooted in new abilities resulting from technological developments and encouraged both by economic growth as a result of a free enterprise economy and by democratic movements that held out hope to the lower classes for a better life.

Today, however, Westerners are apprehensive about the future (Heilbroner 1995). People are anxious about new technologies such as nuclear power and genetic manipulation. The economy is creating increasing economic inequality, and more workers lack a sense of job security. Issues such as global warming call into question the basic idea of endless economic growth. Moreover, even democratic states seem to have given up on the task of closing the gap between social classes on incomes, political power, and quality of life. In addition, the inequality between rich and poor countries, which is becoming greater, is likely to increase acts of international terrorism.

People expect the state to deal with issues such as those raised by Heilbroner. The state should regulate new technologies and compensate for the inadequacies of capitalism. But one of the most profound changes occurring today is economic globalization, and one of the consequences of this process is a loss of power by national governments. Political leaders are increasingly at the mercy of economic forces beyond their control. As a result, the late-modern state is a weakened institution that is not able to alleviate the problems related to worldwide competition and new technologies.

The weakness of the state can be used by those who claim that the underlying cause of social problems is religious in nature. In the United States, the message of the Christian Right is "that born-again Christians are God's people, America is God's country, and if everyone would just become a conservative Christian, then everything would be all right again" (D'Antonio 1992:41). In the perspective of the religious right, all problems are basically religious in nature, and our anxiety about the future can be alleviated only by religious change. Such an analysis favors traditionalist religion because only this type of religion sees every issue as essentially religious, and the solution of every problem linked to the religious control of all institutions.

Appropriately, the Christian Coalition, a political movement based on conservative Protestantism, stands for eliminating national problems by means of moral reforms. Conceivably, people will be attracted to this movement, and thus to congregations supportive of this movement, because they have lost confidence that secular policies will solve national problems.

SUMMARY

Contemporary society has three religious forms. First, a traditionalist religion seeks to be a strong church (in Kelley's terms) and favors both the permeation of all culture by the group's beliefs and values and the use of the state to enforce the group's control of all institutions; moreover, the religion's members believe they must fight hostile, modern forces.[18]

---

18. In the Fundamentalism Project, Marty and Appleby (1991) defined "funda-
    mentalism" as a family of traits, not all of which need exist within a specific
    movement that the authors considered "fundamentalist." I find the result to

Second, a modern religion accepts a modern civic code, a fragmented culture, and the separation of church and state, yet expects to have a protected status and is ambivalent about being tolerant. Third, late-modern religion, while it accepts a modern civic code, a fragmented culture, and church-state separation, also puts the individual at the center of spirituality (each of us should form a personal religion, combining fragments from various traditions) and accepts doubt as a permanent condition; moreover, late-modern religion attacks religious groups that violate the modern civil morality.

The question is, why are conservative Protestant congregations, which at least approximate traditionalist religion, so popular in the late-modern United States? My approach is to use modernization theory to explain this phenomenon.

In the long term, modernization means technological development, societal expansion, structural differentiation, cultural fragmentation, and individuation. More specifically, Western modernity has meant the cultural acceptance of individualism, which has resulted in the transformation of all social institutions. Moreover, in the new West, people have become more dependent on the use of reason to solve problems, and because of impressive technical achievements and the use of science, they have developed a faith in reason and a belief in progress. In recent times, the self-actualization ethos has interpreted individualism in new ways, with consequences for all institutions. Late-modernity does not reject these traits, except perhaps the naive faith in reason. But, the late-modern period of history includes new problems: How does family life change to serve the self-realization of its individual members, how do people legitimate their lives when they no longer believe that reason in itself can establish what is right, and how can people eliminate the anxiety resulting from the diminished power of the state?

My argument is that while the basic modernization process weakens traditionalist religion, late-modern conditions may be stimulating an interest in just this form of religion. I suggest three reasons why

be the confusion of what I term "traditionalist religion" and what are simply religious revival movements. Overall, the Fundamentalism Project is about religious movements around the world that seek to revive traditional forms of religion. The Project published essays by scholars from around the world about the history, internal dynamics, and social consequences of such movements. In my opinion, the results would have been more useful if the many facts collected had been interpreted using one, or possibly more, theoretical frameworks consistently. Of course, my preference would have been to use modernization theory.

late-modern people may be attracted to traditionalist religion. First, people increasingly influenced by Third Force Psychology, yet also committed to traditional gender roles, may find conservative religions attractive because they favor neotraditional families. Second, because doubt is pervasive, making it difficult for people to think that their lives are based on legitimated rules, people may join religions that can use supernatural revelation to justify their morality. Third, the decline of the state may draw people toward religions that want to play a political role and that argue that problems can be solved if the nation returns to traditional values. Kelley's theory remains an alternative explanation for the appeal of traditionalist religion. People may need to assign ultimate significance to their lives and thus may choose a religion that people take seriously, as evidenced by the costliness of membership. In Chapter 7, I shall return to these hypotheses.[19]

The fact that traditionalist religion is inconsistent with the long-term modernization process suggests that even if my arguments about late-modernity are correct, we are not likely to witness a resurgence of true traditionalist religion in the United States. Current problems may favor only an approximation of this form of religion. The case studies of congregations in this book are meant to clarify what kinds of approximations are being made. In Chapters 3, 4, and 5, I discuss the appeal of specific conservative congregations. In Chapter 6, I will discuss why people joined a modern congregation and will return briefly to the topic of late-modern religion. However, the current appeal of conservative Protestantism is not only the result of unique late-modern problems. Such appeal must also express the fit of conservative religion with early-modern issues that continue to exist. In the next chapter, I discuss the appeal of conservative Protestantism during early-modernity.

---

19. Throughout the book, I highlight two theories of church growth: Kelley's theory and modernization theory. Christian Smith (1998:69–70, 83–84) has discussed the failure of "status discontent theory," that is, of trying to explain conservative Protestantism as a response to a perceived threat to people's social standing. Similarly, we found no support for this theory in our research. Although this book's introduction acknowledges the importance of resource mobilization theory and a general theory of individual change (e.g., Tamney, Powell, and Johnson 1989), these theories are not of concern in this book; such theories do not explain what makes the content of some religions appealing.

CHAPTER TWO

THE APPEAL OF

CONSERVATIVE

PROTESTANTISM IN

THE EARLY-MODERN

UNITED STATES

Although American Protestants live in late-modern times, most of the religious groups with which they identify originated in early-modernity, that is, between the Reformation and World War II. Moreover, since late-modernity is a stage in the modernization process, not a radical break with the past, we can assume that many of the reasons that people participated in such groups in the past continue to explain contemporary participation. In this chapter, I will use previous research that concerns early-modernity to understand the appeal of conservative Protestantism to Americans today. I will also comment on whether historical changes associated with Protestantism can be understood using modernization theory.

Three kinds of information will be used. First, I examine major historical developments in Protestantism to understand what it is people have wanted from this religion. Second, classical sociological studies of American communities are used to reveal something of the motivations for Protestant religiosity. Third, I utilize an earlier study I did about why people converted to the Church of the Nazarene, a conservative denomination. To begin, however, I present a brief overview of the development of early Protestantism in Europe.

MODERNIZATION AND PROTESTANTISM: THE PROTESTANT HERITAGE

The Protestant Reformation can be understood as part of the modernization process. Compared to medieval Catholicism, the new churches emphasized the importance of the individual and the basic spiritual equality of all individuals (Bruce 1995). Religiously, what mattered was not sacramental participation or priestly absolution of one's sins but only the degree to which an individual was committed to God. Spiritual equality was expressed in anticlericalism, reformers wanting to limit the rewards and privileges of the clergy and curtail its power over the laity (Collinson 1990:237–9).

Besides being more consistent with the modern value of individualism, Protestantism also broke with medieval Catholicism by placing greater importance on this world. In the old West, holiness was epitomized by the monk. Renaissance humanists were prominent in shifting the European way of seeing life. These intellectuals, such as Petrarch and Lorenzo de Medici, were critical of the church, but they were not unbelievers. Yet their culture can be labeled "secular" because it liberated people from guilt about worldly pleasures and activities. Renaissance culture "gave value to man's secular concerns and finally justified worldly endeavor not as a regrettable weakness, but as something fundamental to and glorious in human life" (Cantor 1994:558). Secular humanism was later evidenced in the belief in worldly progress that characterized the new West. Appropriately, Christianity ceased to idealize the monk. Protestants did not value celibacy over marriage, and they sanctified everyday, worldly jobs. They considered raising a family and doing such work as building homes or running a bank as ways of carrying out God's plan for the world.

However, while the reformers deserted the monasteries, they retained monkish ideals of piety. As Max Weber (1958:121) put it, ascetic Protestantism means being a monk in the world. It

> demanded of the believer, not celibacy, as in the case of the monk, but the avoidance of all erotic pleasure; not poverty, but the elimination of all idle and exploitative enjoyment of unearned wealth and income, and the avoidance of all feudalistic, sensuous ostentation of wealth; not the ascetic death-in-life of the cloister, but an alert, rationally controlled patterning of life, and the avoidance of all surrender to the beauty of the world, to art, or to one's own mood and emotions (Weber 1963:183).

Being a good Protestant differs from the traditional monk role in two ways. First, the goal of religious ecstasy is replaced by a work ethic: One does not seek union with God but strives to glorify God by carrying out His will in the world. A person is to be God's instrument for changing the world. Second, since the transition to a life in the world means that people have to relate with other humans, the ideal is to love God in others; generosity is to be accompanied by indifference to the actual people helped. In Ronald A. Knox's (1994:219) words, "If I give a birthday present to a child out of love for the child, and not explicitly out of love for God, then my motive is not charity (in the theological sense), and it must therefore be put down to some form of *cupidity*."

Initially Protestant groups retained the Catholic commitment to Christendom, that is, to create a society that was totally Christian – in its laws, institutions, and people. The Anglican Church (England), the Lutheran churches (Germany and Scandinavia), the Calvinistic Reformed churches (France, Switzerland, the Low Countries, and the Presbyterian Church in Scotland) originally accepted the Christendom model.

Protestantism, then, emphasized the individual's relationship to God, spiritual egalitarianism (anticlericalism), and a this-worldly orientation. At the same time, it retained characteristics of medieval Catholicism: an attitude of "holy indifference" (Saint Francis de Sales's phrase) to the things and people of the world, and a commitment to creating Christendom. These five traits are a strange mix if considered from the viewpoint of modernity. On the one hand, emphasizing the personal spiritual relationship and spiritual egalitarianism is clearly in line with the long-term modernization process. Moreover, a this-worldly orientation fits the general confidence of the new West that humans can make the world a better place, that social progress is possible. However, the ideal of Christendom is contrary to long-term modernization, and ascetic morality, which is based on a belief in the inherent sinful tendencies of human nature, would seem an uneasy bedfellow of individualism, which conveys a positive view of human nature. But overall, the success of the Protestant challenge to Catholicism is consistent with modernization theory (Tamney 1992a:14–5).

"CALVINISM" AND "DISSENT"

Since the story of American Protestantism is largely the result of influences from the churches of Great Britain, I will limit my remarks about changes in European Protestantism after the Reformation to developments in that society. The established churches in seventeenth-century Britain that came to the United States – and most especially the Presbyterian Church – expressed what I shall call "calvinism." Its distinguishing marks are the emphasis on the importance of the church, with its creed and rituals, and the belief that salvation is beyond an individual's control. John Calvin's doctrine of predestination epitomizes the latter aspect of calvinism. His ideas have been summarized thusly:

> God fully determines who will be the beneficiaries of his grace, and not because of any foreknowledge of any virtue in those whom he elects. This is because those ungifted with his grace have no virtues or merit. Thus, all humans in their natural capacity are sinful or depraved. Salvation is conditional on grace and the faith that results from the divine initiative. One can do nothing on one's own to merit salvation. But when God, working through the Word and the Spirit, chooses an individual, then his grace (his beauty) is simply irresistible. One is overwhelmed with a new insight, a new understanding, and new likes and dislikes. Finally, such a saving work by God is permanent. The saints, however much they may entertain doubts or fall into disobedience, will persevere – once in grace, always in grace (Conkin 1997:XIII).

Calvinism takes a belief in an all-powerful God to its logical conclusion.

Prior to the Protestant Reformation, various religious movements appeared that foreshadowed the end of Catholic dominance and represented a form of protesting quite different from calvinism (Collinson 1990:239). Noteworthy among them was the "English dissenting tradition," because its study "should be the first step in trying to understand the American Republic..." (Hall 1930:IX). Thomas Cuming Hall traced this tradition back to the fourteenth-century theologian John Wyclif. At the time, England was divided into a Norman, French-speaking nobility and a Saxon, English-speaking lower class. Wyclif taught that the church must be poor. He found support among the lower class, and he translated the Bible into the language of his constituency, English. Wyclif also trained "Poor Preachers" who were laypersons. Anti-elitism was basic to Wyclif's revolution. The essence of his legacy is that each individual can be saved as long as she or he allows the Spirit to lead her or him to a right understanding of Scripture. All that is needed is the Bible, the person, and the Spirit – no church, no sacraments, no pastor.

Such ideas were embroiled in the peasant's rising of 1381, which was a revolt against the land-owning class who were the aristocratic carriers of Norman culture. The Lollard movement, as the rebels were called, became a secret religious movement after its defeat. In England, "the oldest type of Protestantism became the distinct possession of a lower class, and under the Lollards took on the character of a more or less class-conscious protest against the whole traditional outlook upon life of the upper classes" (Hall 1930:30–1). The Lollards defined holiness in terms of not living like the ruling class, whose "worldly" lifestyle was epitomized by such things "as stage plays, public dances, gambling" (p. 48).

Hall actually divided English society into three classes: the lowest class, the rising lower class, and the ruling class. He believed that the Lollards appealed to the "hard-working, rising poor, dispossessed class, instinctively feeling its way to greater power and influence ..." (p. 34). The "very lowest classes," on the other hand, were often bitter foes of dissent because they were "dependent upon the upper aristocracy, and rejoiced in the shows, the dances, the tournaments, and display from which they in a small way often profited" (p. 34).

Although the Lollards emphasized the role of the individual, they also felt the need to band together and so developed the congregational form of religious organization. Generally, beliefs were relatively unimportant compared to conduct. However, congregations did develop their own creeds. But the main role of the congregation was to monitor the behavior of its members. The moral code sanctified the lifestyle of the rising lower class – "hard work, a primitive type of honesty, shrewdness, and temperance" (p. 217) – and prohibited the activities that embodied the luxurious and leisurely lifestyle of the ruling class.

Descendants of the Lollards included such seventeenth-century dissenting groups as the Baptists and the Quakers, who were part of a radical revolt that accompanied the Puritan revolution in England. The agenda of "the revolt within the revolution" was sweeping (Hill 1975). The radicals wanted to free the common person from dependence on specialists. For instance, the radicals simplified law codes and translated into English the medical texts, which at the time existed only in Latin. They wanted each person to be her or his own merchant, lawyer, parson, and doctor. The lasting legacy of the radical revolt within the revolution is libertarianism. This ideology asserts the value of the individual (individualism) *and* claims independence as an ideal.[1] In the radical

---

1. After traveling around the early-nineteenth-century United States, the Frenchman Alexis de Tocqueville defined a version of individualism espoused by Americans: an attitude that "disposes each member of the community to sever himself from the mass of his fellows and to draw apart with his family

utopia, each person would be free in the sense of being free from depending on others.

H. Richard Niebuhr (1957) called the radical religious groups, such as the early Quakers, "the churches of the disinherited." They were, however, forced to abandon their radicalness by "the superior power of the ruling classes while, at the same time, the ideal of a new social order was abandoned in favor of a sectarian organization of mutual aid and brotherhood" (pp. 52–3). But, while the specific denominations either disappeared or weakened their message, there remained a tradition of dissent, which I call "religious libertarianism." This tradition combines beliefs in the universal opportunity for salvation and individual spiritual self-sufficiency with an anti-elitism that resulted in equating sin with the lifestyle of the rich and powerful.

By the sixteenth century, reference to Lollards disappeared and people used labels such as "Anabaptists," or "sectaries," or "heretics" (Hall 1930:62). J. F. McGregor (1984) referred to "a popular heretical tradition" that included elements from Lollardy and Anabaptism (pp. 26, 35). Both movements were revolts of the lower class against established churches and in favor of voluntary religious commitment and the separation of church and state. The underlying theme was that no one should be forced into a church. Affiliation should be a personal choice.

The dissenting tradition was not a logically neat ideology but a set of beliefs and practices taking different shapes in different groups. The consequences are illustrated by the tensions within the English Baptist movement: "the effectiveness of the Baptists as a radical religious movement was always limited by the conflicting demands of egalitarian individualism and theocratic elitism, sectarian introversion and millennarian action, spiritual autonomy and collective discipline" (p. 62). The second set of demands expresses the perennial need for antisocietal movements to choose between the goals of separation or conquest. The other two sets evidence the strain between religious libertarianism – egalitarianism and spiritual autonomy – and the desire to form congregations, which leads to the development of internal hierarchies and the enforcement of behavioral conformity.

and friends, so that . . . he willingly leaves society at large to itself" (Tocqueville 1954:104). The individual who is valued is independent and self-reliant. To avoid confusing Tocqueville's "individualism" with "individualism" as I defined it in Chapter 1, I refer to the former as libertarianism.

English Baptists shared a commitment to autonomous congregations that were freely chosen by their members (p. 39). Such congregations, however, varied greatly in their beliefs. A few accepted predestination. In many cases, strict discipline was enforced, implying the importance of church doctrine. In effect, some Baptist congregations followed Calvin's theology of an all-powerful God and enforced congregational conformity. In such cases, the Baptist congregations differed from my calvinist type only in their rejection of church-state unity, which was rooted in their anti-elitism.

Thus, two versions of British Protestantism had an enduring impact on the United States. There was a shared core of beliefs. Both preached that salvation was a personal matter between God and the individual, that being saved did not require priestly forgiveness or receiving sacraments, that spirituality was to be expressed in worldly activity, that holiness required asceticism, and that a Christian society was the goal. However, the British Protestantism that was transplanted to the United States took two basic forms, which I call "calvinist" and "dissenting." By calvinism I mean a form of Protestantism with these traits: a belief in the spiritual helplessness of the individual (epitomized by predestination), a belief in the necessity of belonging to a church and accepting its tradition, and an acceptance of theocracy. In contrast, dissentism means religious libertarianism (spiritual self-sufficiency, everyone can be saved) and anti-elitism. Dissenters cannot accept a theocratic model since it is based on the unity of church and state elites; the goal is still a Christian society, but this has to be achieved without state coercion. Of the two forms, the dissenters are more compatible with the modernization process both because of their belief in church-state separation and because their theology empowered the individual more, which is consistent with the modern emphasis on the individual.

The Alternative Tradition and Methodism

A later development in Europe that significantly affected American religion was the success of Methodism. To understand the appeal of the Methodist Church, we must appreciate the continuing existence of an alternative religious tradition in Western Civilization.

THE "ALTERNATIVE TRADITION" AND "ENTHUSIASM"

Robert S. Ellwood, Jr. (1973a) divided Western religion into two traditions. The dominant one contains the various forms of Christianity and Judaism. The "alternative tradition" represents the continuing presence of premodern, shamanistic religion. Ellwood sees the alternative culture in such religions as Witchcraft, Rosicrucianism, Spiritualism, Theosophy, and Scientology.

The alternative tradition emphasizes the centrality of religious experience as a source of unexplainable wisdom. Religious people have direct experiences of the sacred, which are called ecstatic or mystical experiences. Religious ecstasy means being emotionally overcome, or entering a trance, because of contact with the supernatural. Mysticism implies a calm mood but also communion with the supernatural. The consequences of religious experiences include gaining not only wisdom but also such powers as healing, foretelling the future, or reading people's minds. While followers must seek to have the experiences themselves, until they do, they are dependent on charismatic figures who are more or less continuously in contact with the sacred. Alternative rituals using drugs, music, and dancing are designed to activate religious experiences.

The alternative tradition tends to be feminine both in the sense that women have been more prominent in this tradition and in the sense that the alternative culture includes values associated with women in the dominant culture, such as communion and intuitive knowledge (Ellwood 1973a:80).

In his book *Enthusiasm*, originally published in 1950, Ronald A. Knox (1994) analyzed alternative movements within Christianity. Such movements give primacy to experiencing the Holy Spirit personally. Ecstatic experiences are sometimes sought by performing rituals that might involve convulsions, trances, or visions. Practitioners are healers and prophets. Women are prominent in these schismatic movements. Knox considered the essence of enthusiastic religion to be "ultrasupernaturalism." Enthusiasts do not accept that grace (spiritual power gifted by God) perfects nature but believe that grace must replace nature. The human is replaced by the spiritual – reason by an inner light, human effort by God's will within (pp. 350–1). As implied by Knox, enthusiasm blends Christianity with what Ellwood called "the alternative tradition."

Knox believed such enthusiastic movements, which were often called heretical, originated in Eastern culture and appeared sporadically throughout Christian history but did not gain prominence and permanence until the seventeenth century. He described the manifestation of enthusiasm in, among other religious movements, Montanism (second century), Donatism (fourth century), Anabaptism (sixteenth century),

Quakerism (seventeenth century), Moravianism (eighteenth century), and lastly Methodism (eighteenth century).

John Wesley (1703–91) was Arminian, which fits the individualistic ethos of the dissenting tradition. But what characterized Methodism was that it expressed a peculiarly Protestant version of enthusiasm. Wesley distinguished between "the Christ of history and the Christ of experience" (Knox 1994:175). To be saved, it was necessary to experience Christ. Wesley accepted that conversion might be accompanied by convulsion, trances, or visions. He believed that the Spirit must be felt in experiences of peace and joy in "heart religion" (p. 537). Methodism presented life as a personal moral struggle that a person can end only by accepting Christ (the Spirit or grace) and rejecting worldly desires (nature). A person need have only one religious experience in which the roots of sin are destroyed. Thereafter, the convert is changed so that at the conscious level she or he can only serve God. Grace must replace nature; that is, the individual should achieve the ultrasupernaturalistic state.

Thus English Protestantism reflected three religious traditions: the calvinist, the dissenting, and the enthusiastic. In practice, congregations were either calvinist or dissenting, and the latter type were either enthusiastic or not.

AMERICAN PROTESTANTISM

The story of American Protestantism is largely that of denominations with roots in British history (Noll 1992:361). Table 1 shows the sizes of the major Christian groups in 1776, 1850, and 1990. All the Protestant groups originated in Great Britain.

Table 1. Percent of All Religious Adherents in Major Denominations

	Year		
Denomination	1776	1850	1990
Congregationalists	20.4	4.0	0.1
Episcopalians	15.7	3.5	2.2
Presbyterians	19.0	11.6	3.6
Baptists	16.9	20.5	19.6
Methodists	2.5	34.2	9.6
Catholics	1.8	13.9	26.3

Source: Finke and Stark (1992:55), Kosmin and Lachman (1993:15).

At the time of the American Revolution, four Protestant denominations – Episcopalians, Presbyterians, Congregationalists, and Baptists – dominated the new nation. The Revolution severely crippled the Episcopalians, then known as the Church of England (Butler 1990). The other three denominations were calvinist, but to different degrees. The Presbyterians most embodied calvinism. The Congregationalists (i.e., the New England Puritans) wanted a supportive state, but because they also emphasized congregational autonomy, the tie between state and congregation could not be binding. As today, Baptists included diverse types of congregations. They divided into those believing in predestination and those believing in the possibility of universal salvation, as well as those adhering to a confession of faith (i.e., a church creed) and those committed only to the Bible (Kroll-Smith 1982:358).

American religious history is the story of the decline of strongly calvinist churches (see Table 1). The success of dissenting Protestantism in a relatively modern society makes sense. But was compatibility with modernity the reason for the success of dissenting Protestantism?

Radical dissent was not born in the United States but this is where it gained cultural importance. Dissenters "had in America free room to develop along their own line, with the feeling of being masters in their own house" (Hall 1930:295). The colonists brought radical ideas with them into an environment lacking an established elite class. Their belief in independence and self-sufficiency was strengthened by frontier experience (Ammerman 1990:28). As a consequence, during the American Revolutionary period, "Restraint – whether political restraint from a corrupt Parliament, ecclesiastical restraint from denominational traditions, or professional restraint associated with the special prerogatives of lawyers, ministers, and physicians – was everywhere a cause for resentment" (Noll 1992:150). It seems obvious that at least part of the appeal of dissenting Protestantism was its modernity – that is, its relative emphasis on individual freedom.

Consistent with this interpretation, new religions were founded as expressions of libertarianism. The Restoration movement of the early nineteenth century wanted to restore the primitive New Testament church (Conkin 1997:1–56). Today, congregations that began as part of this movement call themselves "Christian," "Churches of Christ," or "Disciples of Christ." Restorationists tend to be Arminians – that is, they believe that Jesus died for everyone, not only a predetermined elite. Prominent aspects of the movement also include a rejection of denominationalism (there should be only one church) and the use of the Bible as the only creedal source. Alexander Campbell, an early leader in the Disciples of Christ/Christian Church movement of the nineteenth century, described this movement as "a great leveling institution, which brought down and raised up, and made the rich and the poor one, placing them on a common level" (quoted in Harrell 1995:110). The emphasis was on creating a movement that downplayed denominational traditions and clerical power. Such religious libertarianism was a defining characteristic of Restoration churches.

Yet the dissenting tradition has not one but two basic elements: not only religious libertarianism, but also anti-elitism. Stephen Kroll-Smith (1982) emphasized the latter element in explaining the growth of Baptist congregations in eighteenth-century Virginia. On the basis of his study of historical records, he claimed that it was upwardly mobile yeoman planters who joined the Baptist churches. Having achieved new wealth, they wanted greater social respectability to match their economic status. However, the gentry controlled the cultural order. With the conversion to the Baptist congregations, "New group boundaries were to be drawn, not on the worldly axis of gentleman-commoner, but on the sacred axis of saved-nonsaved" (p. 361). Redefining the social order freed the yeoman planters "from the deference demands and decision-making authority of the landed elite" (p. 362).

Kroll-Smith examined church minute books to determine what moral rules were being enforced within congregations. "Righteousness or moral conduct ... centered around a person's own initiative and responsibility in the work-a-day world. A virtuous person was honest, industrious, sober, prudent, and thrifty" (p. 366). In effect, this morality sanctified the kind of life practiced by the socially mobile planters. The consequences were twofold. First, the moral code, by reinforcing the need for industriousness and so forth, probably helped to ensure success. Second, by conforming to the new morality, the Baptists could perceive themselves as the true elite of Virginia society, thereby fracturing the traditional order (p. 368).

Kroll-Smith's analysis is similar to Hall's discussion of the Lollards: A new rising lower class wants to redefine the social order in such a way that not only frees them from their former inferior status but now establishes them as the true superior class. Kroll-Smith did not discuss the attraction of the libertarian aspects of Baptist belief and organization, although it is easy to believe that such aspects would have appealed to individual planters who had to depend very much on their own personal resources to achieve economic success. In any case, Kroll-Smith's analysis implies that at least in some cases, the anti-elitist element is as, or more, important than the libertarian one in explaining the success of non-calvinist churches in the United States.

Other historical evidence underlines the importance of the libertarian element in Baptist church history. This facet of the dissenting tradition had become especially strong during the nineteenth and twentieth centuries. E. Y. Mullins was an influential Southern Baptist. He was president of the Southern Baptist Theological Seminary, beginning in 1899, for twenty-nine years, and president of the Southern Baptist Convention during the period 1921–4. Mullins wrote in 1908, "Observe then that the idea of the competency of the soul in religion excludes at once all human interference, such as episcopacy, and infant baptism, and every form of religion by proxy. Religion is a personal matter between the soul and God" (quoted in Bloom 1993:200). Consequences of such theology include a commitment to the separation of church and state and a belief that "all believers have a right to equal privileges in the church" (quoted on p. 201). Mullins's resistance to creeds undermined the dominance of calvinist theology in this denomination. The importance given to the priesthood of the believer and the separation of church and state suggests that the libertarianism within the Baptist religion helps to explain its appeal.[2]

Thus, I argue that the major change occurring in the early-modern United States was the decline of calvinist Protestantism and the rise of dissenting Protestantism, and that the success of relatively libertarian churches is understandable using modernization theory. However, class conflict was also a factor that favored dissent. With economic change, the power of the old elite to control the culture waned, and dissenting congregations redefined the social order in their own favor. Because the new order placed more emphasis on individual effort, rather than family history or refined ways being taught in one's upbringing, the resulting

---

2. Dean M. Kelley's thesis about church growth is not supported by the history of the Methodist and Baptist churches in the South, where most of their members have lived. In the nineteenth century, the time of their greatest growth, these Protestant churches exercised less control over their members than in the previous century and conformed more to the culture (e.g., accepting slavery), investing "their energies in upholding the equality and honor of all white men" (Heyrman 1997:254–5; see also pp. 138–9, 159). Thus Protestant success in the South occurred when churches accommodated Southern culture, thereby making membership less costly for converts.

change in cultural values was also consistent with the modern emphasis on the individual.

THE METHODIST, HOLINESS, AND PENTECOSTAL MOVEMENTS

Another important part of the American Protestant story is the popularity of Methodism and other churches that compose the Holiness and Pentecostal movements. This episode cannot be explained solely in terms of religious dissent.

Enthusiasm pervaded early Methodism in the United States. Revivalists and laity, for instance, understood dreams to be messages from God, sometimes using them to predict the future (Butler 1990:222, 239). At evangelical gatherings, "there was much sighing, sobbing, and trembling, but there was much more shrieking, shouting, writhing, and falling – stricken souls collapsing on the floor under the weight of remorse and sometimes lapsing into trancelike states" (Heyrman 1997:35). Early Methodism was a heady mix of shamanism and Christian ultrasupernaturalism, of magical powers and experiences of God's indwelling.

During the nineteenth century, the upper class rejected enthusiasm under the influence of the Enlightenment, and enthusiasm became more clearly identified with the lower class (Butler 1990:83). Southern evangelical preachers, for instance, distanced themselves from elements of the alternative tradition such as believing in witches, the spiritual significance of dreams, and fortune-telling. Yet these preachers did at times claim miraculous powers such as the power to predict the future or heal the sick. Thus they

> sought at once to uphold their respectability among the learned without surrendering their influence over less skeptical members of the laity. The clergy wanted to have it both ways – to discount the sway of the demons and wonder-workers even as they played upon the susceptibilities of those who still inhabited a world shot through with marvel and mystery (Heyrman 1997:76).

During the nineteenth century, Methodism became a middle-class church, "guided by newfound prosperity, mammoth numbers, and a wider following among middling and affluent Americans . . ." (pp. 239–41). Methodists were influenced by the emphasis on rationality, which led them to avoid the emotional and magical aspects of enthusiasm, and this "purification" of Methodism lost the lower class. In the late nineteenth century, the Holiness (i. e., the enthusiastic) faction within Methodism had a higher proportion of lower-class members than there were in the denomination as a whole (Finke and Stark 1992:166). New churches sought to capture this segment by remaining true to enthusiasm.[3]

THE HOLINESS AND PENTECOSTAL MOVEMENTS

The Holiness movement includes several churches in the Church of God family, the Salvation Army, the Wesleyan Church, and the Church of the Nazarene. Holiness churches retained the goal of achieving the ultrasupernaturalistic state. Life is to be a process of rooting out sin and becoming more perfect in this world (hence the label "perfectionism"). In every person there is a sinful tendency or nature due to original sin; if we have faith in Christ – that is, believe He redeemed us on the cross, confess our sins to God, and ask His forgiveness – our sins will be forgiven. This is the "born again" experience or conversion. After this experience, there still exists in us the sinful tendency; our sins are forgiven but we are just going to commit more unless we root out our evil nature. When we realize this – that we are still not free from sin, and that we need God's help to be good – then we will be filled with the Holy Spirit, who will destroy our evil nature; now there is "no hankering to sin." This is the second work of grace or sanctification, which brings peace and joy to the hearts of men. The sanctified no longer desire evil.

Pentecostalism grew out of the Holiness movement. The distinguishing trait of the former is the belief that a sign of sanctification is speaking in tongues. This belief reflects the experience of Jesus's disciples on the day of Pentecost when "they were all filled with the Holy Spirit and began to speak in other tongues..." (Acts 2:4). Ecstatic speech was first made a normative part of an American religious group by the Shakers, who in turn were influenced by enthusiastic religious groups on the continent (Conkin 1997:290). Sister Aimee Semple McPherson, like all Pentecostalists, offered physical healing as a reward for holiness. At her own church, this leader of the Four Square Gospel movement

---

3. The creation of Holiness churches also expressed a dislike for the power of bishops in the Methodist Church. One reason people have left Methodism over the last two centuries is because they wanted a more decentralized, democratic church (Corn 1998:298).

"maintained a Miracle Room...where she displayed the abandoned crutches and other accoutrements of infirmity that her followers no longer needed" (Dumenil 1995:180). Other prominent gifts of the Spirit include prophecy and divination. The manifestation of such gifts is most prominent in the Pentecostal form of Protestantism.

Besides being influenced by enthusiastic practices used in eighteenth-century English and Scottish revivals, Pentecostalism was also affected by African American rituals. To this day, the largest Pentecostal church – the Church of God in Christ – is an African American church. More than the typical Holiness church, Pentecostal congregations use rhythmic music and speech to involve emotionally the participants, who are then encouraged to go with these emotions by "dancing in the Spirit," clapping, swaying, and singing. Participants feel empowered and joyful. Such responses are encouraged by song lyrics and the preachers' chant-like sermonizing.[4] Thus Harold Bloom believed that "Pentecostalism is American shamanism..." (Bloom 1993:175).

Holiness and especially Pentecostalism represent the continuing appeal of a Christianized version of the alternative tradition. Clearly, lower-class people continued to be attracted throughout early-modernity to religious groups that brought them communion with the sacred. To this day, the Holiness and Pentecostal churches have attracted the lowest class (Conkin 1997:285). Later in this chapter, I discuss why this social class has been drawn to Christianized enthusiasm.

PROTESTANT GROWTH IN PRE-TWENTIETH-CENTURY AMERICA

The early-modern history of American Protestantism is epitomized by the success of churches that appealed to the lower class. During the First Great Awakening (1730–50) and the Second Great Awakening (1795–1810), preachers and revivalists concentrated on the common people who were neglected by the established churches (Noll 1992:91). The successful message emphasized that God's grace was available to all ("free grace"), individuals could be saved if they repented

---

4. Dancing in the Spirit "refers to a spontaneous dancing by the congregation (usually in place and without partners) which is viewed as a form of biblically encouraged worship, much like singing or praying together. For others, particularly old-time Pentecostals, dancing in the Spirit implies that the Spirit takes over the person's body, leading him or her in dance" (Poloma 1989:85). The older view is closer to the alternative tradition.

(Arminianism), and individuals needed to strive for "perfection" or "holiness" (ceasing to desire to sin). Moreover, emotional rituals ("enthusiasm") were encouraged. The preachers were not well-educated. They accepted a larger role for the laity, who in turn claimed the right to interpret the Bible as they saw fit ("soul liberty") (Noll 1992; Hatch 1989; Finke and Stark 1992). As Mark A. Noll notes:

> The contrast with Revolutionary France could not have been greater. In France, liberty, the people, the Enlightenment, and the new sense of French national destiny stood over against the church. By contrast, in the United States, evangelicalism identified itself with the people, the Enlightenment, democracy, republicanism, economic liberalism, and the sense of American manifest destiny (Noll 1994:99).

As Noll goes on to write, had the Protestants not made these accommodations, "their fate would probably have been like the fate of Europe's established churches, which, as they continued to rely on tradition and hierarchy, increasingly lost touch with ordinary people and eventually forfeited their once-dominant place in Europe's intellectual life" (p. 105). As far as it goes, Noll's analysis seems valid. However, it is necessary to explain that Protestantism did not lose touch with the people, because this religion accommodated not only the Enlightenment (more precisely, its English dissenting version) but also enthusiasm.

During early-modernity, then, successful Protestant churches embodied dissent, enthusiasm, or both. Religious groups designed to appeal to the upper classes were unlikely to embrace either libertarianism, since this religious form included anti-elitism, or enthusiasm, since the elite was under the influence of the Enlightenment's valuing of rationality. As a consequence, these churches could not effectively compete for the allegiance of the lower class.

Among the heirs of the English dissenting tradition, there are important differences. Some gave primacy to the written word and thus emphasized biblical inerrancy (Baptist-type churches). Pentecostals and the Holiness groups have given primacy to religious experience, although they have been drawn toward the emphasis on inerrancy, making hard and fast distinctions among the diverse strands of dissentism difficult. But all of them embodied to varying degrees the ideals of religious libertarianism – no sacraments, no church, no pastor, and church-state separation. The lower class, given its British heritage, was attracted to churches that expressed principles rooted in anti-elitism and the ideal-ization of independence.

THE EMERGENCE OF CONSERVATIVE PROTESTANTISM

As previously discussed, Protestantism has been more modern than Catholicism, and within Protestantism, groups that rejected a state church, such as the Baptists, were yet more modern than other Protestant groups. Why, then, were most Baptists by the early twentieth century considered conservative?

Protestantism was reconfigured into "liberal" and "fundamentalist" movements when Protestantism lost its hegemonic control over American society. Early in the nineteenth century, Protestantism "was virtually a religious establishment" (Marsden 1980:6). "Few Protes-tants [then] doubted that theirs was a 'Christian nation.' Though religion in America was voluntary, a Protestant version of the me-dieval ideal of 'Christendom' still prevailed. American civilization, said Protestant leaders, was essentially 'Christian' " (Marsden 1991:10; Smith 1998: 3–5). "Liberals" accommodated the passing away of de facto Christendom. "Fundamentalists" refused to accept the secularization of American society; by the end of the nineteenth century, they saw them-selves as a "beleaguered minority" in a hostile world (Marsden 1980:7).

At this time, some more educated people were being swayed by new intellectual developments. Darwin's theory of evolution as well as bib-lical scholarship that questioned the authenticity of parts of the Bible were especially provocative developments symptomatic of a more gen-eral questioning attitude toward religious matters. Moreover, Darwin's idea that natural selection governs evolution implied that the idea of "god" as an explanation for natural events was no longer necessary. Critical studies of the Bible led some theologians to say that the reli-gious messages of the Old and New Testaments were different, under-mining the idea of a fixed, unchanging revelation. "Liberals" accepted that the meaning of the Bible is not always clear, while "fundamentalists" preached that the Bible is inerrant.

As Protestants lost their hold on American society, some of them be-came pessimists. The theology that gained popularity in the latter half of the nineteenth century claimed people were living in "the end times," just before Christ will return to earth and take the true believers to heaven. This is premillennial dispensationalism: Christ would have to return prior to the millennium, the one thousand years of theocratic rule on earth. Before 1850, Protestants tended to be postmillennialists, believing Christ was establishing His kingdom on earth and would return after the millennium. The switch in prophetic interpretation implied a growing pessimism about what was happening in society. Premillennialists believed they were living in "the last days" when Satan was running the world. This period ends with the miraculous removal of true Christians from the world (rapture) and a devastating end to this world (Armageddon). The underlying message of premillennial dispensationalism has been the apostasy of established churches, the decline of civilization, and the need for Christians to separate from worldly institutions (Noll 1994:119).

Why such pessimism? At least two reasons are probable. First, the Christian society model – that, is a society ruled according to God's laws – was fading as a realistic alternative. Protestants witnessed, for example, the secularizing of the public schools (epitomized in debates about Bible-reading in schools and teaching evolution). Second, urbanization and industrialization were exposing more people to slums, poverty, and the bitter fruit of class warfare. "By the turn of the century . . . , teeming, squalid cities and rapacious industrialists hardly looked like fixtures of a millennial kingdom" (Balmer 1993:172). What is most important for people who are theologically pessimistic is not a particular date for the end of the world but the conviction that God will overturn the world order and set things straight (Bainbridge 1997:93). Premillennial dispensationalism expresses a condemnation of "society" and defines the believers as a spiritual elite about to inherit the earth.

By the start of the twentieth century, American Protestantism was well on the way to a new reconfiguration. Previously calvinist but upper-class denominations (the "liberals"), such as the Presbyterians and the Congregationalists, were beginning to approximate what I call the modern type of religion. Dissenting churches, and some calvinist ones, became conservative religious groups; that is, they opposed what came to be identified as modern: the loss of even an approximation of Christendom and of confidence in the intelligibility of the Bible. One might say that the anger linked to the anti-elitist element in the dissenting tradition transformed into a pessimism about the future of society. By the end of the nineteenth century, religious groups that had been relatively modern fit my definition of traditionalist religion.

To flesh out what traditionalist Protestantism means, I will describe the congregation at Bob Jones University (BJU). This is an apt illustration for several reasons. First, this university defines itself as the representative of true "fundamentalism." It was founded in 1927 as a bastion of "ultrafundamentalism" (Dalhouse 1996:2). Second, the university continues to train pastors who serve congregations around the country to this very day. It "has produced scores of alumni who pastor churches, administer Christian day schools, span the globe as missionaries, teach in seminaries, and populate the business world" (p. 10). For example, as of 1995, "there were 1035 BJU graduates serving as full-time pastors in fundamentalist churches across the nation and abroad" (p. 151). Currently about 95 percent of BJU's ministerial students come from, and will return to, independent Baptist or "Baptistic" (e.g., "Bible") congregations, whose memberships are undoubtedly working class.[5] The Bob Jones University type of congregation will serve as a useful contrast to the congregations described later.

TRADITIONALIST PROTESTANTISM: BOB JONES UNIVERSITY

Bob Jones, Sr., and later his son and then his grandson, felt a need to battle against "modernism" or theological liberalism (Dalhouse 1996:10). The struggle has not been simply academic. As Bob Jones, Sr., and many other fundamentalists understood the world, cities are sites of moral decay because, in part, foreigners and Catholics have broken the hold of right-thinking Protestants (pp. 28–9). The crisis is both theological and social; only when the religious fundamentalists regain social control will the moral rot be eliminated.

The university, under the control of three generations of the Jones family, has sought to preserve theological purity. Its two main strategies have been to separate from all those who deny or compromise "true" Christianity and to create a Christian subculture for its own kind (p. 3).

BJU uses the Authorized Version of the Bible (i. e., the King James version), because some of the students are emotionally attached to it, not because the university believes it is the only acceptable version. The university teaches a literal interpretation; that is, if it sounds like the author is presenting something to be taken literally, it is to be so taken. For instance, the creation of the world in six days is to be taken literally.

5. Baptists, as a whole, have a very low social-status ranking in the United States (Kosmin and Lachman 1993:262); those at the independent Baptist and Bible congregations would rank lower yet if they were differentiated from denominational Baptists. The information about ministerial students, plus other facts mentioned without attribution in this section, came from BJU staff, who were always courteous and helpful.

School leaders tell followers what to believe. Ambiguity is nonexistent. The school values obedient students. "Bob Jones [the founder] recommended 'good, old-time ironhanded discipline' for young people..." (p. 34).

Separatism extends even to conservatives who remain in churches or religious alliances that include people who are considered religiously deviant. The Joneses justify their separatism with biblical references, such as when God told the nation of Israel that "I the Lord am holy, and have separated you from the peoples, that you should be mine" (Lev. 20:26 KJV). Again, Paul advised the church in Corinth not to be "mismatched with unbelievers. For what partnership has righteousness and inequity? Or what fellowship has light with darkness?" (2 Cor. 6:14). The church is to be a gathering of saints, of holy people. Sinners must be cast out. Only the fully committed should be let in.

The Joneses "constructed their own separatist society in Greenville [i. e., on the university campus]. In the lifestyle rules for faculty and students and in the educational philosophy governing the university, the Joneses demonstrated that they had already given much thought to what the ideal separatist society should resemble" (Dalhouse 1996:116). The school's subculture is defined by rules of conduct that separate followers from "worldly" things: no movie attendance, no rock or jazz music, no drinking, no smoking, no swearing, no gambling, no dancing, no intercourse outside of heterosexual marriage. Men are required to wear ties, and women skirts, to class (p. 141). At BJU, students are expected to report any rule violation by other students (p. 140). Moreover, the subculture requires extensive involvement in church life, not only on Sundays but weekdays.

No intellectual disciplines are thought of as secular since God's laws are revealed even in supposedly secular intellectual activities. In 1978, BJU faculty wrote *The Christian Teaching of History*. "Not only God's nature, but also the laws that He ordained for a stable social order can be found, according to the writers, in such diverse subject areas as economics, geography, social institutions, and history" (p. 125). Liberal arts subjects are justified because they reveal messages from God. Bob Jones, Jr., created a drama club that routinely performs Shakespeare's plays, an opera association that brings in professional singers, and an art gallery with an impressive collection of Baroque and Renaissance paintings. Such seemingly secular works are justified by their religious messages.

Separatism at BJU does not mean indifference to the "world." Evangelism is absolutely necessary, because eternal damnation is the consequence of not accepting Jesus as savior. The end is near; as many as possible must be saved.

The university does not advocate a theocratic government at this time. According to its dispensational theology, there are three historical periods: Israel during the time of the Old Testament, the era of the Christian church, and the millennium when Christ will return to rule the earth. Theocracy was the ideal during the first dispensation and will be the reality in the last. In the interval between, although the staff at BJU personally prefer a republican form of government, there is no biblically prescribed form.

In the History department at BJU, students learn that God blessed Americans with religious, civic, and economic freedoms. Yet politics and religion are not perceived as separate realms; thus national crises are understood to result from the nation disobeying God (Dalhouse 1996:130). BJU's students are to be "the hope of America" who "will save our civilization" (p. 147). To this end, the university has strong academic programs in film, accounting, and business administration. With the skills acquired in these programs, graduates can gain influence that will allow them to transform society. Similarly, political involvement on behalf of God is acceptable. Followers may work with others in secular organizations for moral purposes such as ending legalized abortion. Secular careers and political activity are encouraged, then, in order to make the United States a Christian civilization.

Protestantism as illustrated by Bob Jones University fits the definition of a traditionalist religion as one that absorbs individuals into a clearly defined group, that wants to orient all of culture around religious values, that seeks to control society, and that is hostile toward those identified with modernity. At BJU, enforced conformity to an unambiguous doctrine, as well as the many strict rules about worldly pleasures, symbolically separates its students from most Americans. Such symbolic differences lead to social separation, given that people prefer associating with like-minded others, and this separation is further encouraged and made easier by the Joneses' monitoring of official visitors to the campus and requiring frequent participation in church activities. In Dean Kelley's terms, authoritarianism, strictness, and separatism make BJU a strong group, the essence of which is clear, defended symbolic and social boundaries.

However, Bob Jones University has, in Dalhouse's words, a "split personality" (p. 199). On the one hand, the Joneses accept the pessimism about society characteristic of premillennialism, which makes them run

the campus as a separatist society. On the other hand, they strive to create a Christian society. Thus BJU approximates a strong group yet also
illustrates the second and third parts of my definition of traditionalist
religion. The ideal of religion permeating and shaping all of a society's culture is illustrated by BJU justifying its teaching of Shakespeare
because his plays reveal God's thinking. Finally, BJU is part of the religious right and exists to train individual warriors who will gain sufficient
political influence to create a Christian America.

Theologically, Bob Jones University combines the calvinist emphasis on church creed (congregational, not denominational) with
elements of the dissenting tradition, notably the rejection of predestination, the congregational form of organization, the commitment to
an America as the land of the free that BJU perceives as part of God's
plan, the enforcement of behavioral rules, and the desirability of a Christian society (i.e., one whose laws embody Christian morality). Absent
in BJU's theology is any hint of radical libertarianism; for example,
the dissenters' Arminianism is not accompanied by any notion of soul
liberty.

Since the controversy over modern ideas, all conservative Protestant
groups have been characterized as antimodern. In part, this is wrong –
at least to the degree that a group accepts religious libertarianism. In
part, such characterization is accurate. Bob Jones University reflects the
pessimism about American society that is a hallmark of what I call conservative Protestantism. Such theological pessimism results in rejection
of an underlying assumption of modernity: the belief that life is getting better. Not surprisingly, such theology was more popular among the
lower classes, many of whom were becoming part of a new working class
linked to urbanization. I will argue that the appeal of religious conservatism resulted from its fit with the new social conditions in the United
States.

Until this point in the analysis, I have not been able to use sociological
research carried out to understand why people were attracted to the
different forms of Protestantism, because such research was not done
prior to the twentieth century. People's motives were inferred from a
knowledge of what succeeded; for instance, because libertarian religion
appealed to people, I have assumed that it was the libertarian traits
that actually attracted them. However, beginning in the 1920s, social
scientists began studying what people liked about churches. In the next
section, then, I analyze what such studies tell us about why conservative
Protestantism appealed to Americans.

Industrial America and Protestantism

During the twentieth century, more detailed information about society has become available through the work of historians and sociologists. Two sociological classics studied the social history of small American towns during the period of industrialization (1870–1940). One is *Middletown* by Robert and Helen Lynd (1929). A follow-up volume was published that told the story of Middletown (Muncie, Indiana) through the depression (Lynd and Lynd 1937). The second classic is Liston Pope's (1942) *Millhands and Preachers*. Pope's book is about the churches and the economy in a southern county (Gaston County, North Carolina) dominated by textile mills. These three authors chose not to write about the "Negro" minorities. Both Middletown and Gaston County were overwhelmingly populated by whites who had been born in this country. I will use these classics plus other lesser works to discuss two issues. First, I discuss why, despite the abundance of religious groups catering to the lower class, this class was less involved in churches during the first part of the twentieth century. Second, I will discuss what has been learned about why the lower class did go to church, especially conservative Protestant churches.

H. Richard Niebuhr wrote in 1929, "the mass of the workers remain untouched; there is no effective religious movement among the disinherited today; as a result they are simply outside the pale of organized Christianity" (1957:76; see also Hollingshead 1949:248–51 and Demerath 1965). Why was this true?

Observers of working-class Catholics in New York City listed reasons why poverty-stricken people were not in the churches at the end of the nineteenth century:

... poverty tempted some to seek escape by routes condemned by the church, including crime and prostitution; the enforced idleness caused by unemployment sucked others into the saloon subculture, which in practice acted as one of the church's greatest rivals; the poor found it difficult to achieve the standards of respectability expected of churchgoers; and frequent moves led to a "lack of attachment to any particular church or priest" (McLeod 1996:132).

The Lynds also found that the difficulty of appearing respectable was one of the reasons that lower-class people in Middletown less often attended Sunday morning service. Said one woman, "It takes too much money to buy nice clothes for church, and if you aren't dressed up nice it's no place to go." Another said, "There's too much dressing up for church these days... [where they formerly lived, her husband] used to go to church in his overalls just as good as anybody. But now it won't do for people to go without being all dressed up and we just haven't got the clothes for that" (Lynd and Lynd 1929:365). Poverty and its consequences, then, help to explain why the lower class went unchurched.

Another reason was the class struggle. During the years 1870–1940, class conflict was a prominent part of life in towns and cities. Since religious leaders tended to be seen as part of the elite, class conflict meant lower-class hostility toward the churches (McLeod 1996). At the turn of the century, H. Francis Perry (1899) studied "the working-man's alienation from the church." Among others, he quoted Samuel Gompers, then president of the American Federation of Labor: "My associates have come to look upon the church and the ministry as the apologists and defenders of the wrong committed against the interests of the people... (p. 622).

On economic matters, American Protestantism has been strongly influenced by calvinism. Religious leaders in this tradition have criticized undue concern about material things (what is today called consumerism) and an excessive interest in making a profit. But on the whole, those influenced by calvinism judged capitalism to be the economic system most consistent with the Bible. Calvinists assumed that people were naturally prone to sloth, and so they needed to be encouraged to work hard by economic need and religious urging (Tamney, Burton, and Johnson 1989, and works cited therein). Moreover, conservative Protestant clergy, who were the pastors in lower-class Protestant congregations, defined all crises as essentially moral, and immorality meant especially smoking, drinking, and sexual licentiousness, sins which were supposedly encouraged by indecent female dress, dance halls, and the cinema. Thus at the turn of the century, the conservative movement did not perceive a structural crisis caused by industrialization but "a moral crisis brought forth by unbelief" (Riesèbrodt 1993:62).

The Social Gospel movement within Protestantism criticized the capitalist emphasis on making a profit. Each person was said to have a right to the resources necessary for self-development. The state must protect the weak. However, Protestant churches have never been united in support of such ideals and have never mounted a concerted campaign to change the American economy. As Martin Marty wrote of the religious reformers, "Few were Socialists and none of note favored Marxism or violent revolution. They were often vague about the reorganization of power in post-capitalist America and not many labor leaders or

Socialists turned to these mild progressives" (1990:410; see also Demerath 1965:51). Not surprisingly, the Lynds (1937:312) found that local congregations in Middletown were silent on public affairs, made only vague comments, or sided with the business class. On almost every controversial issue, "the local churches take over the causes and symbols of the local business control group."

Why, then, did the lower class stay away from churches? First, there were the consequences of being lower class: forced into crime, frequent moves to find jobs or affordable housing, and Sunday work; drawn to drinking; and unable to appear respectable enough for churchgoers. Second, while many in the lower class felt at war with the elite, most churches avoided the class struggle or denied it.

The second issue is, why did some in the lower class go to church? Pope's (1942) study included an extensive analysis of the appeal of lower-class churches. To begin with, successful preachers had to side with the people (p. 114). They could not be condescending or as out-of-touch with their audience as the preacher with a lower-class congregation who "used illustrations from the game of golf in his Sunday morning sermon (though none of his auditors could afford golf), and urged his congregation to be as regular and punctual in church attendance as directors of a corporation are at their meetings" (p. 114). The poor did not want to find in church a reenactment of the "world's" status hierarchy.

Indeed, the lower-class congregations empowered their people. Their members lived in a world full of signs of God's power, and signs of the strength of this power that the members could access. For instance, when a woman became ill, "she attributed her misfortune to her sin, saying that the Lord has brought it on her." Such an interpretation held out the hope that she could seek God's grace and be cured. Poor people turned to prayer for near-magical results – health, prosperity, and such. Church members could lean on God. Pope quoted from a testimony made during a church service: "When you have more than you can bear, cast it on Jesus, and He will always take it away." Another church member testified,

"In all my trials, Jesus is my refuge. I have been persecuted so much that I just smile now when somebody persecutes me, and cast it all on Jesus. I thank the Lord I'm sanctified. I ain't never seen a talking picture show; people who goes to such places can't save nobody if they want to – you got to be different from the World. You got to live Jesus! Me and Him lives alone and has a good time" (p. 88).

Being different from the world became a badge of honor. The poor in church became saints, allowing them to find in their rejection of the social world a sign of their spiritual elitism. It was the godly people of the working-class churches who would gain salvation in the next world. To ensure salvation, it was necessary to be "different from the world" (p. 88). The personal relationship with Jesus offered hope that His power would become available to these suffering people and, at the same time, this relationship was the core of their imagined world, their own "movies," in which they were the elite.

Ritually the churches encouraged the release of pent-up emotions, and the rhythmic music and singing were fun. Church meetings were as "one worker explained . . . the only entertainment we have" (p. 89). Congregations as social organizations were practically important. They served as community centers, offering everyone a "sense of belonging" and, to the more gifted, opportunities for leadership. The churches were also vehicles of welfare work, distributing money and food to the destitute (p. 29).

In Middletown, the Lynds found that the supernatural was much more a part of the lives of lower-class people (Lynd and Lynd 1929). They more often thought about heaven. People in this class more often said that *the* purpose of religion is to prepare people for the next life. As the Lynds wrote, "When an overwrought working-class woman, ill-dressed and unkempt, rose in a noisy Pentecostal church and cried, 'I'm tired of this ol' garlic and onions world! I'm going home to Jesus!' no simple description can convey the earnestness of her wailing words" (p. 390).

Lower-class women spoke about gaining courage from religion.

- "I used to cry when I was discouraged, but that didn't help any. Now I just git down on my knees and pray and that gives me strength."
- "Even though things are so unequal in this world and people that work hardest have the least, I know God will care for me somehow."
- "I just keep tellin' myself it was meant to be that way anyway. The Good Man up yonder knows what's best" (p. 324).

Despair was a lingering temptation. A Sunday School teacher at a lower-class church commented in between quotes from the Bible: "I know it's hard to see His guiding love with so much unemployment, but we must just continue to trust and know that He will bring us through" (p. 390).

The portrait of working-class religion given us by Pope and the Lynds is certainly clear. Socially, their congregations provided practical assistance, social activities, and opportunities for leadership. Theologically, the churches helped the poor resist despair: God is in control and in the end the good who reject the world will be rewarded, for they are the true elite. Jesus will take care of them. Moreover, God could use His power to produce seemingly magical results.

The research by Pope and the Lynds suggest that Karl Marx is a better guide than Kelley for understanding conservative Protestantism in industrial America. A Marxist view of religion is often equated with Marx's remark that religion is the opium of the people. Supposedly the upper class uses religion to justify the exploitation of the lower class. Suffering, the poor are told, is a just punishment for sins, or it is presented as God's way of testing the faithful. In either case, the preaching supposedly tells the lower class that suffering in this world matters little compared to eternal happiness in the next. Such an analysis overstates the passivity and the helplessness of the lower class. As McLeod (1996:136) wrote, "Religion did more than help people to accept their suffering: It frequently led into one or more of three ways of ameliorating the situation, which could be mutually exclusive, but were not necessarily so – individual self-help, neighborly support, and political action." American churches have helped lower-class individuals in practical ways, such as by organizing charity drives and running soup kitchens.

Yet there is also truth in the Marxist perspective. The poor stayed away from churches, in part, because religious leaders were perceived as siding with the elite. Moreover, when the poor went to church it was not to hear about the need to create a just society but to find ways of surviving despite their worldly suffering. Religion offered solace to beaten-down people. Lower-class people went to church to find help for coping with poverty and powerlessness. In their despair, they could trust in Jesus. In Pope's (1942) work: "cast it all on Jesus" (p. 88). In the Lynds' (1929) book: "I'm going home to Jesus" (p. 390), and "I know God will care for me somehow" (p. 324). In addition, some churches encouraged the magical use of prayer. More generally, lower-class conservative churches conferred elite status on those who were different from the world.

The people described by Pope and the Lynds do not at all remind us of the rising ruling class as exemplified by Hall's Lollards, or the radical libertarians who enacted the English "revolt within the revolution," or Kroll-Smith's Virginian yeoman planters. The Protestants described by Pope and the Lynds were pessimistic. Premillennial dispensationalism fit.

THE HOLINESS TRADITION

While the research by Pope and the Lynds is useful for understanding the appeal of Protestant conservatism generally, it does little to explain the impressive popularity of churches in the Holiness-Pentecostal tradition. To fill this gap, I will summarize my analysis of material I collected some years ago about why people joined Church of the Nazarene congregations.

Phineas Bresee in Los Angeles founded an independent church, called the Church of the Nazarene, in 1895 in order to preserve the Methodist tradition "in purity, sobriety, and honor" (Kosmin and Lachman 1993:79). At the turn of the century, numerous splinter groups had appeared who were devoted to preaching holiness. In 1907, many of them united to form the national Church of the Nazarene. Initially the church had .08 members per one thousand people in the United States; in 1986, the figure was 2.2 (Finke and Stark 1992:165). Nazarenes have remained lower in the class structure than Episcopalians, Presbyterians, Lutherans, and Methodists (Kosmin and Lachman 1993:253).[6] During the years 1959 and 1960, I talked with people who had converted to the Church of the Nazarene to find out why they had done so and to study the conversion process. These stories included events during the period 1930–60.

Holiness doctrine – the need to experience conversion and sanctification – strongly appealed to the Nazarenes. The doctrine that the human being is born a sinner but can be saved by accepting Christ appeals to people even when it does not solve their problems. To people who are suffering, who view living as an excruciating experience, the Nazarene assertion that the human being is naturally evil must seem so true, so real. It explains how people can continually hurt others, and why people are being hurt. The main appeal of this doctrine, however, is that it offers salvation. Holiness doctrine allows people to be reborn without desires and attitudes that are being frustrated. By accepting Christ, they find the peace on earth that comes from surrendering the self.

The more dramatic stories involved extreme poverty, a tormenting husband, abandonment, and racial discrimination. These converts struggled to control erotic and aggressive feelings. A convert to the Church

---

6. For instance, according to a national survey done in 1990, the percentages of denominational members who were college graduates were as follows: Episcopalians, 39%; Presbyterians, 34%; Methodists, 21%; Lutherans, 18%; and Nazarenes, 12% (Kosmin and Lachman 1993:258).

of the Nazarene, Edna, described to me a life of poverty and frustrated sexual desire. She called herself flirtatious. Her husband had deserted her. A major event in her life story was an invitation from a casual friend to go away for a weekend. As Edna said, "Let's face it, I missed my husband." In our talk, Edna spoke of wondering if she had been drawn to two ministers because she had been falling in love with them. A revealing story concerned a missionary for whom Edna had worked. She thought he liked her. As an April fool joke, Edna wrote him a letter asking him to preach in an isolated place. He took it seriously and began looking over maps, planning the trip. Edna loved it. Then she told him the truth and was fired. Edna's action could be interpreted as signifying a desire to get this man alone, yet by allowing the minister to continue believing the message was real after he first received it, her silence seems indicative of some anger as well toward the missionary.

Edna spoke directly about anger. In fact, she described what it meant to be sanctified this way: Before sanctification, she would get angry, but not express it. After sanctification, she does not have angry feelings. Edna illustrated the change with this story. Shortly before the interview, on the day prior to payday when Edna had no money left from the last paycheck, she tripped and scattered the only food she had on the floor; it meant no dinner that night. Before sanctification, she would have become hysterical, but at that moment she felt nothing.

Several Nazarene people with whom I talked emphasized the control they gained over their tempers. For example, an African American woman, Minnie, was sanctified and lost her prejudice toward whites, which had been partially fueled by the "accidental" killing of her boyfriend by a fellow soldier during the Second World War. In all, three Nazarenes claimed a radical break with their former angry selves. "After sanctification, I lost my temper troubles"; "Now, I don't get angry"; "I was the kind of person who thought he knew it all, always ready for a fight; but all that changed; I changed my attitude, spirit toward other people."

One of the converts compared her experience – appropriately, I believe – to therapy: Both may be ways by which people try to gain control over feelings that threaten to overwhelm them. Our case studies suggest that controlling sensuous desires *and* anger was important. Because lower-class people, and especially the women in this class, are likely to experience a great deal of frustration and anger, self-control is both harder and more urgent. People raised in a subculture that attributes all problems to personal moral failure are especially likely, when frustrated or angry, to solve whatever problems they have by rejecting the world and exerting greater self-control. For some of the people I interviewed, sanctification "eliminated" anger and eros, which meant a sense of peace.

Lillian emphasized that a sanctified Christian trusts completely in God. She illustrated what such trust means with this story. Shortly before our talk, Lillian's ten-year-old son was late coming home. This was a cause of concern since they lived near a dangerous body of water. Lillian told me, "He is a problem child, but we love him. . . . I was concerned – if I could have done something to save him from harm, I would have." What Lillian did do was give her son into God's hands. Her attitude was that if God wanted her son, that was that; yet if her son came home, she would be gladdened. Her son arrived home at 7 P.M. This incident illustrates that, in some cases, sanctification can result in a state approaching detachment or emotional numbness.

The calmness in seemingly frustrating or tragic circumstances is an important part of enthusiasm. The diaries and autobiographies of early Pentecostals reveal "that even officially sanctioned satisfactions such as family, children, and marital sex often lost all appeal" (Wacker 1995:145):

If Pentecostals discountenanced the routine pleasures of life, they were equally prepared to forego the bonds that tethered them to earth. This helps explain why believers could dismiss digging a storm cellar, an act that surely seems prudent enough today, as a "habit of the flesh." It also helps explain why a sister who claimed to be heaven bound, yet worried about the eternal fate of her children, could become a target of ridicule. If a mother were *truly* heaven bound, the argument ran, she would not be compromised by any earthly interest, even a concern for the souls of her offspring.

Night after night enthusiasts lustily sang, "Take the world, but give me Jesus." But there really was not much to take. They were already living on that distant shore (p. 147).

Another theme in the Nazarene stories was the importance of their personal relationships with Jesus. One of the people I interviewed, Margie, had been in an unhappy marriage for decades. She talked to me about having lived under a dark cloud; Margie was so depressed, she thought of suicide. After meeting a kindly minister, Margie was saved and, soon after, sanctified. She told me that subsequently she had no desire for things of the world. While Margie continued going to church, after being sanctified, she emphasized that what was important was the personal relationship with God. Margie had conversations with Christ, directly at home, indirectly during church services through the preacher. Her spiritual relationship was a very real one, and others confirmed its reality. Yet it lacked a visual dimension (except indirectly when Christ talked to her through the minister). As if to diminish the importance of visual contact, Margie stressed listening. When she attended services, Margie closed her eyes and listened to the singing. She preferred radio to television. Margie continued to live with an uncaring husband, sustained by her talks with Christ.

Sociologists have tended to perceive religion as a set of beliefs and practices associated with formal organizations. Spiritual involvement has been neglected. But the theology and ritual of a church may allow members to develop a personal relationship with Jesus, which they may experience as not so different from "normal" personal ties. "The Deity is less immediate than many social encounters, but not significantly less than with a pen pal; the Deity is less visible, but no less than kings often were for peasants . . ." (Tamney 1966:147). Moreover, in the right congregational context, the reality of this spiritual relationship is routinely confirmed, and explanations of inner changes or worldly experiences as signs of Christ being there for the person are widely supported. While Pope's analysis emphasized the power to be gained from the spiritual relationship, I would stress the sense of being loved in the spiritual relationship.

Within the Holiness context, peace is accompanied by joy in relating to a loving Jesus. I asked a convert, Noola, if it bothered her to lose friends because she joined the Church of the Nazarene. She said, "No," and I asked why. "I guess because I had found God." Churches such as the Church of the Nazarene emphasize the personal relationship with Jesus and have rituals that allow the emotional expression of such a relationship, as well as the personal experiences that seem to confirm Jesus's love and attentiveness. For Margie, Holiness doctrine and a personal relationship with Jesus allowed her to die to this world and thereby to avoid the suicide she once thought of committing.

Others told less dramatic stories, but they also emphasized gaining self-control. They defined a sinner as someone who drinks, smokes, dances, and goes to the movies, and being saved as meaning that you did not do these things.[7] Several men were attracted to the Church of the Nazarene because they knew male members who had quit drinking and smoking, and they wanted to emulate them. The sense of breaking with the world stands out in the comments of several interviewees: "I abhor them [drinking and smoking] now"; "I lost desires for things of the world"; "I no longer have a taste for such things [dances, parties]." "I am no longer a part of the world." Ten Nazarenes explicitly mentioned withdrawal from such worldly activities.

Losing desire or simply gaining control of feelings was possible in the Nazarene churches in part because of their ritual. One convert, Bret, compared his experience at a Catholic Mass and at a Holiness service. The Catholic Mass, he said, is an occasion for establishing a relationship with God, but if you feel that you have fallen out of grace and are unworthy of God, the appeal of this ritual is lost. The repetitiousness of the Mass, to a person like Bret, symbolized lack of change, whereas the Protestant service, with its constant freshness and its stress on the need for dramatic conversion, symbolized change. Catholics have confession, but Bret could not take it seriously. People he knew did not use it as a breaking point between a life of sin and a life of holiness but only to gain forgiveness for past sins. Confession seemed to have little power, because afterward the confessors committed the same sins again.

As Bret's case suggests, Holiness rituals are suited to people unhappy with themselves and seeking to become new persons. Such profound personal changes are more likely in Holiness and Pentecostal churches because the ritual encourages personal transformation. The friendly people in the churches support and recognize the emergence of new personal identities. The pastors encourage people to answer the altar call or to testify, when they would share their problems with others. In such an atmosphere, people seeking to change themselves can feel supported and can receive affirmation that they have changed. In effect, rituals may allow people to destroy their old selves symbolically and publicly (Tamney 1962, 1970).

What, then, have we learned from these Nazarenes? Their stories emphasize the importance of a loving Jesus. The Nazarenes also make us realize the importance of rituals evoking personal change as support for a

---

7. Between five and seven people (out of the nineteen converts I interviewed) mentioned each of these sins. Two people mentioned lying. The following sins were each mentioned once: getting ahead at others' expense, stealing, swearing, "sexual things," card playing, and dirty-joke telling.

theology of rebirth. But most importantly the Nazarene stories emphasize the role of doctrine, especially sanctification. Holiness (and Pentecostal) doctrine and ritual encourage people to be reborn seemingly without troubling feelings or sinful habits.

I suggest that Marx presented primarily a masculine view of the lower-class situation. For some, perhaps many, women in that class, economic problems were indirect and only partial causes of family-related problems such as sexual frustration, desertion, and unhappy marriages – and it was these problems that brought such women into the churches.[8] Even though poverty was implicated in their suffering, they perceived their problems as personal, such as an unfaithful husband. For these people, religious change was a solution to sexual frustration, shyness, loneliness, and desertion – as well as to prejudice and poverty.

Neither Kelley nor Marx appreciated the rewards of ultrasupernaturalism. Churches preaching a Holiness or Pentecostal message can be especially helpful to the lower class. The doctrine and ritual are useful to people who need to be reborn into a more peaceful life without physically escaping their social situation. For some, being sanctified may mean ultrasupernaturalism: One is emotionally dead to the world, especially to desires for sensual pleasures or to feelings of anger. The renunciation of desire is a surrender of self that results in a sense of peace. For others, being sanctified may mean breaking bad habits, which for the Nazarene converts most frequently include such things as drinking or smoking. At the same time, the converts throw off the old self and are alive to Jesus, who provides comfort and love. The beliefs allow unhappy people to deny feelings of anger, sexual desire, jealousy, and such while experiencing the joy of feeling loved by God.

CONCLUSION ABOUT RELIGIOUS POPULARITY IN EARLY-MODERNITY

Conservative Protestantism in the United States reflects three religious traditions. The calvinist one emphasizes the spiritual helplessness of the individual, denominational tradition, and theocracy. The dissenting

---

8. Appropriately for religious groups with some roots in the alternative tradition, women have been leaders in the Holiness and Pentecostal movements (see Conkin's [1997] discussion of American churches). Given that more women than men have attended church, female leadership no doubt also aided the success of enthusiastic churches early in their development, that is, before female leaders were eliminated or marginalized.

one embodies religious libertarianism, anti-elitism, and a commitment to create a Christian society. The enthusiastic tradition gives priority to personal attainment of the ultrasupernaturalistic condition and of spiritual powers. All three reject theological modernism.[9]

In Chapter 1, I defined a traditionalist religion as one that favors a situation in which the individual is absorbed into a clearly defined group, the group's religion is diffused throughout the society's culture, the state is controlled by the religious group, and there is a sense of hostility toward the modernizing elite. My calvinist type most clearly resembles traditionalist religion. Within dissenting groups, libertarian tendencies undermine the dominance of the group and the desirability of church-state entanglement. Enthusiasts are least committed to the religious group because they continually seek to be, in Weber's words, "spiritually suffused" by their god(s). As a Nazarene that I interviewed told me, church was no longer important, as salvation "is a personal thing between God and man."[10] However, even among enthusiasts, the religious groups are important because the group affirms the reality of the spiritual relationship and the group's ritual stimulates the occurrence of ultrasupernaturalistic experiences. Moreover, in contrast to modern religion, all three types of conservatism are committed to creating a Christian society – a society in which all institutions and all of culture are shaped by Christian beliefs and values.

The question is why relatively traditionalist forms of religion – or, to be more specific, conservative Protestantism – gained in popularity during the early-modern phase of American history. My first answer is that because the churches that eventually became designated as conservative led the way in embodying libertarianism, they attracted participants.

9. The calvinist and dissenting types resemble Weber's inner-worldly ascetic, whereas the enthusiast resembles Weber's inner-worldly mystic. Weber's ascetic seeks salvation as an instrument of God's will for the transformation of the world (Weber 1978:544). The ascetic is "a warrior in behalf of God." In contrast, Weber's mystic is God's vessel rather than God's instrument (p. 546). The mystic's goal is union with the divine: What is important is maintaining communion with God while carrying out practical activities (Weber 1963:174).

10. The individualistic bias of enthusiasm expresses itself in Pentecostal rituals, which combine communal activities with periods of social disintegration. Anne Parsons noticed this in a Pentecostal service: "Prayer-period was so individualistic that one's first impression was of a babel of sounds, each voice uttering its own pattern of lament, vehemence, or supplication with no attempt to harmonize with the whole" (1965:190).

Successful American churches during early-modernity were those groups that rejected calvinism and tended to limit clerical authority. Such libertarianism is the opposite of what Kelley associated with his "strong church." Indeed, the importance of the British legacy of dissent is a major reason for the failure of Kelley's analysis.

But have I overestimated the significance of libertarianism? Nathan O. Hatch argued that "the theme of democratization is central to understanding the development of American Christianity" (Hatch 1989:3). Yet Hatch also pointed out that people supposedly desirous of democracy supported religious demagogues and joined nondemocratic religions (e.g., Mormons). I suggest a somewhat different analysis. The churches that succeeded during early-modernity were more clearly libertarian than democratic. Freedom has diverse connotations. It may mean being able to do what one wants, free of control by others; it may mean being part of a democratic group (Tamney 1992a:101). Libertarianism emphasizes independence, the absence of other people telling the individual what to believe or how to act. Democracy refers to a set of shared rules for equalizing everyone's power to shape society. Democracy can be seen as preventing complete independence, the libertarian goal. Demagogues may control people who believe they are freely following someone who thinks just as they do – especially if the demagogues embody the anti-elitism that is central to the American tradition of dissent. That is, demagogues may run clearly nondemocratic organizations, yet create the illusion of a libertarian experience. Thus, the absence of democratic religious organizations, in itself, does not mean that Americans were not attracted by religions seemingly consistent with libertarian goals.

However, it is also true that the analyses of lower-class religion by Pope and the Lynds, as well as my case studies, do not raise the issue of libertarianism. That is, the appeal of churches was not related to their espousal of soul liberty or to congregational autonomy. Rather, people praised religion for helping them to cope with their poverty and powerlessness. It seems likely that when basic needs are not met and strong feelings torment their victims, matters of church organization recede into the background or fade away altogether. Among the truly down and out, issues of freedom and authority may not be salient.[11] The

11. It is true that authoritarian churches have succeeded in the United States. Kelley frequently referred to the Jehovah's Witnesses as an example of a strong church, and it made sense for him to do so (see Penton 1997). But it remains unclear why some people have been attracted to an organizational form so

appeal of conservative Protestantism, then, must also be seen as a consequence of enforcing ascetic rules, advocating a pessimistic theology, and practicing an enthusiastic form of religion.

My analysis suggests three reasons for the importance of ascetic rules. First, at least since the days of the Lollard movement, such rules have been defined in a way that holiness implies the sinfulness of the lifestyle of the rich. For the lower class, specific ascetic rules have been important because they express hostility toward the elite. Second, these rules symbolize breaking with "the world." The poor can compensate for lack of worldly success by rejecting the things of this world. Third, some rules – notably the one against drinking – were seen as necessary aids for frustrated people who had turned to drink or other vices as "solutions" to their problems and who came to think that regaining control of their desires might lead to more satisfying "solutions." Thus I argue that among the lower class, traditional asceticism is important as an expression of anti-elitism, as a symbolic rejection of the desirability of worldly success, and as a useful aid for achieving greater self-control. The evidence does not support Kelley's contention that strict rules are important because they are costly and therefore connote religious seriousness.

The suffering of the lower class during the industrialization phase of American history is certainly an important reason for the appeal of a pessimistic theology and of enthusiasm. The rewards from joining congregations with these traits would be:

• Feeling justified in being part of a spiritual elite
• Gaining magical powers
• Gaining relief by being in Jesus's hands
• Having fun in church
• Escaping frustration by a loss of worldly desires (in Knox's terms, "ultrasupernaturalism"; in Weber's terms, "inner-worldly mysticism")

contrary to the libertarian tradition. Of course, African Americans are at least one-third of the current membership (Conkin 1997:159; Kosmin and Lachman 1993:131), and they come from a heritage in which the libertarian tradition did not exist. It is also possible that what members like is not the authoritarian nature of the church but the rewards of espousing a millennarian theology: the promise of eventual life in paradise, a new identity and self-respect as a spiritual elite, and hope of victory over satanic (worldly) forces (Curry 1992:168). Given the lower-class constituency of the church – in 1990 the Witnesses were last in a social-status ranking of American religious groups (Kosmin and Lachman 1993:262) – the latter explanation certainly makes sense.

It is true that my reference to magical powers is not precisely correct. Technically, in the enthusiastic tradition, magic does not exist. Those in need cannot control the gods through the recitation of formulas or the performance of rites. But enthusiasts can believe that there is a God who wants to help them and that He will answer heartfelt requests addressed to Him if they are not morally inappropriate.

The decline of calvinist churches and the appeal of the dissenting tradition are understandable using modernization theory. But this theory cannot explain the appeal of enforcing strict ascetic rules, of a pessimistic theology, and of enthusiasm. The importance of these traits must be understood as a result of the overwhelmingly working-class composition of the American population. However, to anticipate later arguments briefly, I believe that the appeal of strict rules, pessimistic theology, and enthusiasm is not a long-term trend and that, consistent with modernization theory, these characteristics are now declining in importance.

THE PRESENT STUDY

The period of industrialization in the United States was dominated by a continual struggle, often violent, between workers and owners. The language of class war was apt and was used. However, post–World War II America was a new country. For the first time ever, an affluent nation existed. Moreover, the average American had at least completed high school. Newly enriched people formed a massive migration to the suburbs, while rural areas shrunk in population. Workers unionized and the language of class warfare became passé.

Religion did not remain unchanged in this late-modern period. Less-educated people more often went to church, while the percentage of those claiming religious affiliation and of those attending church declined among the *better* educated (Roozen 1980:437; Condran and Tamney 1985; Wuthnow 1988:170). Given the general affluence, the memberships of conservative Protestant churches became better off (Roof and McKinney 1987:111). I am interested in how these churches are appealing to members of the first affluent modern society ever to exist. The assumption is that congregations for relatively affluent conservatives would not fit the classic traditionalist model, for which the congregation at Bob Jones University is the prototype. This matter will be discussed in Chapter 5.

THE SAMPLE

In 1996, we chose local consultants to select four popular churches. This seemed an adequate number of congregations to test our hypotheses. Three of the churches were chosen because they were theologically conservative and not lower-class congregations. At the same time, the three represented different kinds of Protestant conservatism – a charismatic Methodist congregation, a calvinistic Presbyterian church, and a Church of God (Anderson) congregation (a Holiness group). The fourth congregation was a mainline Presbyterian one; it was selected so that by comparing the four churches we could get a better understanding of what distinguishes conservatism. What these religious categories (e.g., calvinistic Presbyterian, mainline Presbyterian) mean will become clearer as we proceed. The four churches are called "Spirited Church," "Truth Church," "Caring Church," and "Open Church" in this study.

Lists of people who started to attend the churches recently were given to us by pastors at the four churches. In three cases, the lists seemed to be exhaustive of the population. I do not believe that the names we were given were preselected in any systematically biased manner. Peggy J. Shaffer, Susan M. Ryan, and I then called people on the lists to arrange interviews until we achieved the desired number of interviews.[12] Usually the meeting took place in the interviewee's home. Sixty-nine people were interviewed, twenty-seven by myself and forty-two by Shaffer and Ryan. See Table 2 for details about the sample.

The interviews were open-ended, that is, the questions did not have predetermined possible responses and the discussion followed the flow of the conversation. The interviewer began by asking the person when she or he first learned about the congregation and what happened between then and when the person decided to commit to the church. An interview schedule provided a list of topics to cover during the meeting (see Appendix 1). If the interviewee agreed, the discussion was taped. All but six of the interviews were recorded.

12. Peggy J. Shaffer had a master's of science in sociology. Susan M. Ryan was a candidate for a master of arts in counseling psychology. They used the following procedure. After a few interviews, the interviewer gave me the interview tapes (or written digests), a brief analysis of why each person attended the sampled church, and suggested follow-up questions. I studied this material and then met with the interviewer to give feedback on the interview process and to give the interviewer follow-up questions. The case was closed when answers to these questions were given to me.

Table 2. Interviewees

Characteristics	Congregation				
	Spirited (17)	Truth (20)	Open (15)	Communal (17)	Total Sample (69)
Gender					
• Female	10	12	10	13	45
Education					
• High school or less	3	2		3	8
• Some schooling beyond high school	10	4	4	1	19
• College graduate	4	9	3	5	21
• Postgraduate education		5	8	8	21
Age					
• 18–34	7	8	5	4	24
• 35–49	8	8	9	9	34
• 50–64	2	1		4	7
• 65 or older		3	1		4

I listened to these tapes, or read the interviewers' reports in the few cases in which the discussion was not recorded, in order to determine what the interviewees liked about their congregations and what the selected traits meant to the interviewees. In the following chapters, the congregational characteristics that are discussed are the ones picked out by the interviewees. I am presenting their views of the four congregations in the study. In addition, I use their comments to understand the meaning of the traits that were salient to those with whom we spoke. The question is whether the motivations revealed in the congregational traits selected and in the meaning of these traits to the interviewees fit any of the hypotheses presented in Chapter 1. As will become evident, the interviews forced me to change my initial theoretical ideas about the popularity of conservative Protestantism.

After writing draft versions of the chapters about the four congregations in the study, I met with a member of the pastoral staff from each of the four churches. These representatives had read the relevant chapter and corrected any misrepresentations of their congregations. Following their advice, I made the necessary changes. I am confident that the four congregational portraits in this book are valid.

Each interviewee was asked about the appeal of church services (rituals), church programs, the people at the church, the leaders, the way the church is run, and church teachings. For the most part, our respondents were little concerned about church polity. Programs such as religious education and Bible study groups were very important considerations for some people; in addition, some respondents thought churches should engage in missionary or charitable activities, but such programs were of secondary importance to our respondents. In contrast, church beliefs, characteristics of the pastors, and the nature of the rituals were centrally important.

The interviewees at Spirited Church, judging by their education, were lower-middle class. Those in the other three congregations were more representative of the upper-middle class. In the next chapter, I discuss Spirited Church, the congregation most similar to those analyzed in this chapter; it illustrates a current movement, supported by a minority within Methodism, to reintroduce enthusiastic elements within this denomination. Chapter 4 is about a congregation in a relatively new conservative denomination that was created during late-modernity. In Chapter 5, besides discussing Caring Church, which is part of a Holiness denomination dating back to the nineteenth century, I compare all three conservative congregations with the Bob Jones model.

CHAPTER THREE

SPIRITED CHURCH

Spirited Church ballooned during the 1980s and early 1990s. Some fifteen years ago, it was a small, rural church. After the present pastor arrived, and after the church service became contemporary, Sunday worship attendance went from eighty in 1981 to eight hundred in 1988, and was about fourteen hundred (in two services) in 1996. Although the last figure was down several hundred from Spirited's peak size earlier in the decade, Spirited still had the largest Sunday morning attendance among Protestant churches in Middletown. Appropriately, this congregation exemplifies the "new paradigm" Protestant church (Miller 1997), whose nature I will discuss throughout this chapter. Because the church's Sunday service is so popular, I begin my analysis of Spirited's appeal with a description of its Sunday morning ritual.

THE RITUAL[1]

The streetside sign says "Spirited Church" but does not mention that it is a United Methodist Church. You enter what had been a car dealer's salesroom. Even now that it has been converted to a church, the building does not display much religious symbolism, except for a large, empty cross in the front. A platform runs across the front of the room. An altar table is at the rear of the platform with vases of flowers and a large book – neither table nor book is used during the service.

Before the service begins, people are milling around, talking. The congregation tends to dress casually. There are no traditional pews,

1. Part of this description of a church service was written by Stacy Harbaugh, who at the time was a student at my university.

hymnals, or Bibles available. Church members bring their own Bibles, sit on padded folding chairs, and read the lyrics of contemporary Christian songs off of transparencies projected on a large screen. In the front of the sanctuary, a traditional organist is replaced by a full band complete with electric guitars, an electric bass, a keyboardist, a rock-style drummer, and sometimes extra percussionists. About five to six church members stand in the front of the sanctuary with cordless microphones to lead the congregation in the contemporary songs.

These choral leaders not only provide leadership in how the melodies and harmonies are sung, but they also set the standard for the level of expressiveness that is acceptable during songs. When choral leaders raise their hands in worship, some in the congregation follow. When choral leaders clap and dance in particularly upbeat pieces, a few in the congregation follow. As the singing proceeds, some (a minority) sway with the music. The choral leaders are led by one male associate pastor. He calls the congregation to order by starting the singing, which comprises at least the first half-hour of a service in which five, six, seven, or more songs are sung in a row broken only by the prayers of the main choral leader. Special musical performances are applauded.

In each service, attendance and a collection are taken. The attendance sheets are tucked into each program and ask about names, addresses, whether the congregant is a regular or first-time attendee, names of spouses and children, requests for family/marriage/personal/financial help or counseling, or requests for information on social groups. After the offering is called for, people applaud as a sign of joyful giving.

While music serves as an important part of each service and while everyone participates and seems to enjoy the music, not everyone arrives on time. Church members stream in at all times during the singing, but people rarely come in so late as to interrupt the sermon. After the singing, the performers leave the platform, as the minister and his wife step up onto it. They stand behind a lectern that is front and center. The pastor wears suit and tie. After he makes some announcements, his wife rejoins the congregation. The people stand while the pastor reads from Scripture, then all sit and the sermon begins. About one hour later, after the sermon ends, the pastor asks those needing the help of prayer to come forward. The congregation sings softly. The preacher asks laypastors and friends to join those in front to pray for them, or if requested by those who answered the altar call, to pray with them. After about ten minutes, the pastor ends the service with a prayer. Everyone is calm; all are focused on the minister.

Not a Bob Jones University–Type of Congregation

Irene was a convert who came to appreciate Spirited Church, in part because it did not fit the traditionalist Protestant model. (Throughout this and subsequent chapters, most indented material is my paraphrasing of the interviewee's comments unless the material is in quotation marks.)

Irene was raised in a Baptist church in another state.[2] When she and her husband came to Middletown, they at first joined an independent Baptist church. They were unhappy there. For one thing, the new church had a more traditional service than she was accustomed to. For another thing, the church was new and small; it demanded a lot from its members. Finally, Irene and her husband did not like the pastor as a person.

While church-shopping, Irene and her husband visited Spirited Church. Raised as a Baptist, Irene held certain doctrines that initially prevented her from joining the church. She believed in eternal security – that is, once saved, always saved. Moreover, Irene believed immersion in water was necessary for baptism; at Spirited Church, people choose between immersion and being sprinkled with water.

What shaped her search? At the independent Baptist church in Middletown, Irene learned what she did not like. The church was legalistic. For example, women had to wear dresses on Sunday, which puts too much emphasis on outward appearance. The Bible teaches us to be modest, and a woman can wear pants without violating this requirement. Moreover, the pastor was a separatist, refusing even to join other pastors in any activity; he lived in his own little world. Finally, the sermons were doctrinal lessons without any evident relevance to living in today's world.

Irene did not want to join a "social club," where you are told to be nice to your neighbor but the Truth is not taught. The new church had to have a pastor who taught the Truth, the Word of God. He should be willing to challenge people, to step on their toes. This makes the sermons interesting.

2. For each interviewee, I note whether the person was younger or older than forty years of age at the time of the interview; in addition, if the person is a college graduate, I describe the interviewee as "highly educated." Irene was younger than forty at the time of the interview.

Irene and her husband kept returning to Spirited Church. Irene liked the praise and worship, as well as the preaching. The pastor at Spirited Church is led by the Spirit. He tries to "get himself out of the way." The turning point for her husband was a sermon about witnessing. The preacher approved of different styles, each appropriate for people of a certain personality. Not everyone has to go door to door. "Lifestyle witnessing" also appealed to Irene. A Christian does not have to tell people that if they are not saved, they will go to hell. You can witness with your life. If people see that you have something they want, such as peacefulness even in troubled times, they will want it and ask about it. Then you can talk about religion. After hearing the sermon on witnessing, Irene and her husband joined a Sunday School class in which the people were friendly; in this group they received personal attention and felt "at home."

Irene liked the music because it was contemporary but not too emotional. A church can go too far by trying to give participants an emotional high. The music can make you feel good, but "have you really met God?" The pastor warned against this in a sermon. People are free to worship as they want, up to a point. If you want to lift your hands or do a little dance during the singing, it is okay. But order is maintained. The service is not too charismatic, not too wild.

Baptists may believe in the gifts of speaking in tongues, healing, and prophecy, but their churches are not open to them in the services. Irene has seen the gifts displayed at Spirited Church and she has enjoyed the experience. People have spoken in tongues. The pastor makes sure all is done by the Word. For instance, only one person may speak at a time. If many do it simultaneously, the result would not be edifying, just confusing. At Spirited Church, prophetic utterances have been made, always by the same man. He speaks what the Lord tells him. Each speech in tongues is interpreted in a way true to Scripture. The pastor makes sure that such remarks are uplifting and encouraging, not condemning.

Irene believes she is being drawn closer to God. In her daily walk with God, she is becoming more obedient. Each day she prays and reads the Bible, listening to God. The Wednesday night Bible study class is the uplifting point of her week between Sundays. Irene feels a little guilty that she is not ministering to others. She wants to find an area of ministry that God wants her to do;

she believes in His time He will make it known to her. Irene lives to please God, to obey Him in every area of life. By daily Bible study, Irene maintains her relationship with God.

Coming from a Baptist background, Irene was hesitant to join a relatively enthusiastic church, that is, a church where the ritual approximated a Pentecostal one and where her theological beliefs in eternal security and full-immersion baptism were not held as sacred. While church-shopping, Irene came to understand what was really important. The pastor has to believe the Bible is true and has to challenge Irene. She grew up with a religion that does not feel right if it is not stepping on her toes. The "pain" is necessary.

Irene also came to appreciate the lively church ritual – the music and the display of gifts. But like others with whom we talked, what was important was that the service was enthusiastic yet orderly. They appreciated the control exercised over the use of Pentecostal gifts such as speaking in tongues and prophesying. Church service is not "too wild." The pastors are expected to weed out behavior that is not genuine and keep the ritual from becoming a show.

The mix of expressiveness and restraint is a popular aspect of Spirited Church. For instance, some men believed the praise and worship to be a welcome opportunity to extend themselves. They found themselves being stretched by clapping or raising their hands during the singing, because they were showing emotion. One of the men had visited an Assemblies of God church. He felt uncomfortable because he was not raising his hands during the singing, while almost everyone else was. At Spirited Church one does not feel compelled to raise hands. You can worship as you want, although people at Spirited Church do not have the "freedom to get out of hand." A "spiritual balance" is what distinguishes a neo-Pentecostal or "charismatic ritual" from a classic Pentecostal one (Harder 1985). I shall use the term "charismatic ritual" to refer to a controlled enthusiastic service.

Creating such a worship experience is official policy. As a church document (*Spirited Church: Story of Renewal*) reads,

An ongoing struggle is in *maintaining spiritual balance* in the worship services. We allow the Spirit freedom to move and work in our midst, and yet maintain an orderly service, full of integrity and sincere worship. The emotionalism which so easily overtakes is not encouraged, yet we want to allow freedom to express heartfelt sentiments. The issue of speaking in tongues has been resolved in love by encouraging all believers to seek spiritual gifts, but not to make this one gift an issue of the "haves" and "have nots." The key to maintaining spiritual balance in the worship services is in the pastor maintaining control and staying in authority during the worship services. When spiritual gifts are in operation, an explanation is always given by [the pastor], so that newcomers understand what has taken place. This alleviates any fear, and answers questions in the minds of those unfamiliar with the spiritual gifts and their operation.

One respondent compared the praise and worship to a rock concert. Interestingly, premodern religious rituals, revivalist camp meetings, and contemporary rock concerts have been called examples of the same ritual type, "communitas" (Martin 1978; Myerhoff 1975; Turner and Turner 1978:241). Supposedly in these situations there "is a loss of self, a fusion of the individual with the group . . ." (Myerhoff 1975:43). Everyday social roles are forgotten, as everyone feels part of a temporary collectivity based on a shared ecstatic experience. While to some extent this description fits Spirited's ritual, the difference is equally significant. The individual is unlikely to be absorbed because of the emphasis given to having a balanced ritual. Moreover, at church each is to be herself or himself; you dress to suit yourself; you raise your hands if it feels right to you. Uniformity and conformity are minimal. At Spirited Church, while a sense of closeness to others develops during the praise and worship, there is no "loss of self."

On the contrary, I came to understand that what the people with whom we talked liked about Spirited Church was its implicit respect for them as individuals. Irene had been turned off by the "legalistic" requirement at a Baptist church she had attended that women must wear dresses. Such a rule emphasizes appearance, but spiritually what is important is an inner attitude. Others we talked with complained that at many churches in Middletown, men are expected to attend Sunday service wearing a coat and tie, women in a nice dress and high heels. If you are not dressed that way, such churches do not want you. One respondent had thought, "I'll just send my suit." At Spirited Church, the pastors do not have such dress codes.

The importance of the individual person is also implicitly recognized by the pastoral effort to create enjoyable services. Irene, as others, liked the church service. Going to a ritual that you enjoy means not feeling you are doing what others want you to do. A respondent described a traditional service as follows:

". . . other churches have these things where, 'Okay, stand up, sing Hymn 141, sit down, sing this,' you know, 'Do responsive reading' . . . all these set rituals . . . sometimes they sing songs they know, songs they like," said the respondent, "but a lot of times, I think the person who wrote the program just thought 'Well let's see. Lets go through the index and find out what matches vaguely what the pastor is talking about, and let's sing that.' "

The traditional service was perceived as a structure, a thing, to which church attendees were obligated to conform. At Spirited Church, the ritual fits the desires of the congregation.

An important aspect of the balanced ritual is that individuals have options. They may clap, they may speak in tongues. Ritual freedom extends to choosing not to participate in the praise service. As a respondent told me, "you can choose not to come that first half an hour and slip in . . . right before he starts speaking and some opt to do that."

Similarly, individuals can choose a way to evangelize that suits them. The mission statement of Spirited Church includes evangelism as a necessary activity: "We believe it is the responsibility of every believer to carry the message of the gospel to others." Newcomers frequently mentioned outreach programs as an important part of Spirited Church. But individuals can practice lifestyle evangelism, as already discussed, or choose from a variety of other programs. Some of them are old-fashioned evangelism. Forty-two teenagers went to the 1996 Olympics in Atlanta for street evangelism. Once or twice a year, smaller groups have been going to Eastern Europe, bringing medical skills and teaching English using biblical material. Spirited Church also supports individuals and couples involved in missionary work overseas.

Evangelism is also linked with charitable work. Blood-N-Fire is a multichurch group that delivers bags of groceries and prays for the recipients who live in a downtown public housing project. Spirited Church strongly supports this group. A member of Blood-N-Fire who attends Spirited told this story: Once while walking through a public housing project, some member of the group met an alcoholic; every week they went back to see how he was. The alcoholic turned his life around, gave his life to the Lord, and now participates in the Blood-N-Fire program.

The church also practices servant evangelism. Serf Club members show God's love for people in varied ways, such as walking a neighborhood praying for the residents or washing car windows at a street intersection. The club one day visited a neighborhood, freely handing out carnations to women and batteries to men. Club members told those they chanced upon that the group wanted to show everybody that God loves them, and the members asked each person if she or he needed prayers; some people opened up to the Serfers, saying they had not thought that anybody cared about them. The systematic development of the servant style is a recent event and reveals the nature of new paradigm congregations such as Spirited Church.

"SERVANT EVANGELISM"

Steve Sjogren pastors a new paradigm church and has developed the servant evangelism that is practiced by Spirited Church. Sjogren (1993:61–3) accepts that there is a place for all kinds of evangelism, although he is critical of the door-to-door type as very demanding on the evangelists with little payoff, that is, with very few people accepting Jesus Christ.

On the cover of Sjogren's book, beneath the title, we read that he is offering a new approach with "no guilt [i.e., without laying guilt 'trips' on outsiders], no stress, low risks, and high grace." The last needs some explanation. Servant evangelism is "demonstrating the kindness of God by offering to do some act of humble service with no strings attached" (pp. 17–8). Sjogren says that showing love is *the* sign of a Christian (p. 29), so being a servant maximizes the probability that God will add His grace to the effort, which is the meaning of "high grace."

Sjogren wants people to enjoy ministry:

If children observe their parents serving out of duty or sheer commitment, they will get a bad taste in their mouths for church, ministry, and perhaps even for God. I am convinced that duty-oriented Christianity has turned many more children off the Lord than any recognized enemy of the faith such as secular humanism (p. 181).

Thus Sjogren suggests congregations should accommodate people with different levels of commitment: Some will be servants weekly, some monthly, some quarterly, some yearly. He asks people to be servants monthly for two hours (pp. 150–1, 195–6).

The purpose of servant evangelism is somewhat complex. Clearly it is to win converts to Christ. In addition, servant evangelism is supposedly linked to congregational growth and to the servant's spiritual health (p. 148). In any case, such evangelism is not to be simply a duty. Sjogren concludes his book by wishing the reader could join him and his group washing the windshields of strangers' cars: "We'd have great fun!" (p. 236).

The respect for the individual that can be discerned in the ritual appears in the evangelistic options available from street evangelism to lifestyle evangelism. Moreover, this form of evangelism implicitly respects the privacy of others. Servant evangelism is especially interesting because it allows individuals to choose a comfortable level of involvement. Moreover, showing love is also basic to servant evangelism. Sjogren advocates evangelism that is not insensitive (p. 36). "For years I loved the lost in obedience to God and His Word. In recent years something has shifted in my heart. Now I don't just love the lost, I even like them" (p. 99). He illustrates not being a monk in the world, but getting involved with others, and in a way that evidences respect for others, just as does lifestyle evangelism.

Thus, an attractive aspect of Spirited Church is that the ritual implies the importance of the individual: Each decides how to participate during the praise and worship, each decides how to dress, each decides how to evangelize, and each likes coming to church on Sunday. Religious activities such as praise and worship as well as evangelism are to be enjoyable, so that individuals participate not because they have to but because they want to. To develop these ideas further, I turn to a discussion of the pastor, who was very popular among the people with whom we spoke.

THE PASTOR

The image of the pastor that came across in the interviews was as follows. He is led by the Spirit and he challenges people. The pastor says what he wants because he believes that God works through him. He might abruptly stop a sermon and do something different because he feels that is what God wanted him to do. For example, the congregation may shift to singing or the pastor may call people to the altar to be prayed with. The pastor doesn't hold back, he is not afraid to offend people. If it is the Truth, he is going to say it. For example, one Sunday he confronted the congregation over being involved in the Life Chain (prolife activism); he implied some people would not go because they were afraid of being seen and thus hurting their reputation.

A respondent compared a woman pastor at a Presbyterian church he once attended and Spirited's leader. The woman tried to give the congregation a "warm fuzzy." The Sunday service was a social occasion when members of the congregation could feel good about being together. In contrast, Spirited's pastor wants people to be hot for God, to be more aggressive in sharing the faith. This respondent could not be in a church that uses gender-neutral language in discussing God, that is prochoice, or that accepts homosexuals as pastors. Spirited Church is not such a church; it is not "wimping out." The church changes nothing to accommodate an audience. The male imagery is obvious. The fact that the pastors (at the time of our study) were tall, handsome, athletic men reinforced the masculine quality of this congregation.[3]

Yet other aspects of the pastor's performance were also important. Consider the following excerpt from a sermon given in 1996. As usual, the pastor began by announcing he had good news: "Jesus Christ is alive!" The text was Romans 6:1–11. The topic was baptism:

Reasonable people have come to a point of disagreement over this subject throughout the past twenty centuries. I do not pretend today to have the definitive answer on baptism. I will say that there are approximately three major streams when it comes to the subject of water baptism; reasonable, loving, God-loving, spirit-filled people disagree about this, but there are some three streams. One is a Baptist stream. If you're a Baptist, say "Amen." There is a – well, their numbers are decreasing. There is also a sacramental stream; there is also a reformed stream in the subject of baptism. There are some folks who believe that when you are baptized in water, regardless of your age, that somehow saving grace is imputed upon your life at that time and that God takes possession of your life. There are others who believe that baptism is simply an extenuation of an ongoing work of salvation in the life of a person who embraces the Christian faith. There are still others who believe that only folks who have come to personal faith in Christ become candidates for water baptism, so believer's baptism

---

3. This point was made by the Reverend George Saunders.

only. You have this whole spectrum of things. I just want you to know that as I begin this relatively short talk this morning that I have no energy to fight with you about any aspect regarding baptism, only if you try to convince me that it is not necessary or not important.

The pastor then told the following story:

I heard the story of two guys who died, got to the gates of heaven. Their names were Bob and Ray. Bob stepped up to the gatekeeper and said: "My name is Bob." The gatekeeper checked the names, and said: "Oh, well there is a bit of a problem." Bob said: "What kind of problem are you referring to?" The gatekeeper said: "Well, you were quite a character, weren't you? You got some serious sins piled up here, in fact your sins are so serious, we are not sure even the grace of God can cover these things. We are going to let you into heaven but there's one condition." "Well," Bob said: "What is that?"

"Well, the one condition is you're going to have to spend eternity with this woman." Around the corner came this creature, you know, knuckles dragging on the ground. It was this hulk of a woman, and I mean horrible, horrible woman. This woman walked right over to Bob, took him by the arm, and began to escort him through the gates. It was a rather disappointing, discouraging, frustrating, frightening moment for Bob.

Bob stopped and looked back and there was Ray, who stepped up to the gatekeeper and gave his name and the gatekeeper said, "Well, there is a bit of a requirement being placed on you as well," and he said, "Well, okay, what is it?" "Well, you're going to have to spend eternity with a certain person as well," and around the corner came the most drop-dead gorgeous woman that you have ever seen in your life. I mean exquisite in every conceivable way, and walked right over and took Ray by the arm and started to escort him away, and Ray said, "Now I have to spend eternity with this person?" "Yes."

So Bob got a few steps and started to complain. He said, "Now, what is the deal? I have to spend eternity, all eternity with this creature, and he gets to spend eternity with her." To which the gatekeeper responded, "Well, yes, this young woman has to pay for *her* sins as well." [laughter]

The whole gatekeeper story includes not a word about baptism. But then the pastor returned to his theme: "Good people argue about the meaning and method of baptism. Do we immerse? Do we sprinkle? We don't get uptight about it." What is important, the pastor went on, is the inner reality of a person. Baptism occurs when you're dead to your old life and you are born anew so that you can say, "Christ lives in me." You must get dead to yourselves to belong to Jesus. Your life must no longer be your own. You must cast the shadow of Jesus.

Being reborn, the pastor said, you are united to a new community of those who share your faith and with whom you form the body of Christ. You are baptized into a body of people who love each other unconditionally. "When I place my hands on a baby, there is no magic." What does happen is that the baptized person gains power from being in a supportive, loving community. Ultimately, of course, it is Jesus who gives love, power, and joy.

I want to emphasize three aspects of this sermon. First, it was funny, which is the usual case. Six people volunteered how much they liked the pastor's sense of humor. The joke I quoted might be considered sexist. But the fact that the pastor (whose name happened to be Bob) seemed to be poking fun at himself made it a good-natured, relaxing, entertaining moment.

Second, the pastor spotlighted Jesus and each person's relationship with Him. As the pastor said that day, "Jesus is appealing to a lot of people in our world today. The church is not." The message is good. Churches do not get it across. They are not doing a very good job, in part because they get preoccupied with theological disputes such as debates about correct baptism. This brings me to the third point: People at Spirited Church are free to differ on theological matters such as the nature and role of baptism. Appropriately the pastoral staff is theologically diverse. The pastor sees himself as a true Wesleyan. Yet two staff members are true Calvinists. Within limits, Spirited practices a philosophy of *vive la différence*.

However, Spirited is a conservative church built on the belief that the Bible is true. Of the nine people who revealed their views of the Bible, seven interpreted it quite literally, one person definitely did not, and one interviewee has begun to rethink his previously literal approach in favor of a somewhat more metaphorical interpretation of the Bible. An associate pastor told me that the church teaches a literal interpretation of the Bible – that is, in the creation story, a "day" is what we mean by "day."

"NEW PARADIGM CHURCHES"

Donald E. Miller (1997) in *Reinventing American Protestantism* studied popular religious movements that began during the 1960s and 1970s in California – Calvary Chapel, Vineyard Christian Fellowship, and Hope Chapel. The three movements have over one thousand congregations. Both Calvary Chapel and Hope Chapel have roots in the Foursquare Gospel denomination. The movements are middle class, but many of their congregants have blue-collar jobs. Perhaps a third are college graduates. Almost all participants are white. This constituency is similar to the people we interviewed at Spirited Church (see Table 2), except that the college-educated are a smaller part of the Spirited congregation. Throughout this chapter, I will comment on the fit between Spirited Church and the new paradigm.

Several of the attractive features of Spirited Church that I have already mentioned are part of the new paradigm church. First, they have balanced rituals that feature lively contemporary music (pp. 85–6). Second, dress regulations are minimal. Third, the focus is on the spiritual relationship: "new paradigm Christianity is not primarily a matter of cognitive assent; it is an attitude and a relationship between the individual and God" (p. 128).[4]

Miller wrote that

> New paradigm Christians ... are *doctrinal minimalists*. Their emphasis is on one's relationship with Jesus, not on whether one believes in predestination, or whether one believes that Christ will return before or after the great "tribulation" of the "end times." New paradigm Christians view doctrine as being of human origin and see it as something that too often divides the church (p. 121).

The pastor's comments on baptism and the importance of the inner person, as well as the theological diversity of the pastoral staff, are consistent with Miller's description.

---

4. Charles Trueheart toured the United States visiting congregations that supposedly illustrated "the next church." Some were in the religious movements studied by Miller. Others belonged to denominations, but they more or less hid this fact (as does Spirited Church): "what they are concealing in the names they have chosen is at the heart of the great convulsion going on in American Church life: the challenge to denominations" (Trueheart 1996:57).

New paradigm congregations are quite different from the Bob Jones University type, although not completely. They are similarly conservative: There is a commitment to the truth of the Bible and a desire to challenge the world. In Miller's understanding, the new paradigm congregations retain the message of the BJU type, although they have changed the medium, such as by using contemporary music. Unlike Miller, I believe congregations such as Spirited Church not only use a new medium but also offer a new message, one that fits late-modernity.

My own understanding is caught in Marshall McLuhan's (1964) famous pronouncement: "the medium is the message." Spirited Church shows how much it values the individual by providing enjoyable religious activities as well as by allowing options in how people participate in the Sunday service, how they dress, how they spread the good news, and, on some theological matters, what they believe. Central to new paradigm congregations – in stark contrast to BJU-type churches – is the respect and choices given to individual members. Individualism is more in evidence in new paradigm congregations.

Now I will consider in more detail another important aspect of Spirited Church that has already been noted: the personal relationship with the Lord. People are Spirit-filled. I asked one respondent how she knew the people on Sunday were experiencing the Spirit:

> "Coming to the altar. I mean tears, laughing, crying together. . . . I've experienced that a few times . . . in our old church, but not like this! Like I say, it's addicting. It's like 'Go!' You end up feeling so much more in touch with God. You can feel His presence through the people."

Both the pastoral message and the nature of the ritual emphasize the centrality and reality of experiencing the sacred. In his sermon, the pastor told his audience they must cast the shadow of Jesus, an image appropriate for enthusiasm. I want to develop these ideas further by discussing the more dramatic stories we were told.

Most of the interviewees had been attending either other conservative churches (eleven people) or other Methodist churches (four people); two people had been unchurched but had been raised Methodists. Most either had recently moved to Middletown and had been shopping for an appropriate conservative church or had switched from another local congregation with which they were unhappy.

Interviewees were dissatisfied with the old churches because of bickering over petty issues such as how many hymns to sing, or because of conflict over substantive theological issues. Six of the people at Spirited Church had undergone the stereotypical conversion story: a sense that one's personal life is intolerable followed by a spiritual rebirth. I will discuss their stories.

Ultrasupernaturalism and a Therapeutic Culture

Among all the people with whom we talked, only a minority were seeking relief from deeply disturbing personal problems, and most of those were attending Spirited Church. Churches such as Spirited Church expect people to be personally troubled. Their rituals and services encourage and support personal change. The altar calls on Sunday beckon to people wanting to transform themselves. Moreover, it was at Spirited Church that personally troubled people would hear consoling sermons.

One such sermon was about "delay." If God does not answer prayers right away, we should not lose heart. We must wait on God. He is more interested in shaping our character than in giving us what we want. Christ wants us to be holy, not necessarily happy. God will give you the blessing when you are ready. The pastor told about a church member who prayed thirty years before her husband finally joined the church. (The sermon also contained practical advice: If you pay interest on a credit card, the pastor said, get rid of it.)

Another sermon was about "troubles." The biblical references were Joshua 7:20–6 and Hosea 2:14–5. Sin is a primary source of personal troubles. Disobeying God, being rebellious, brings trouble. Today Americans avoid blaming problems on sin. They have created a god that suits them, who is tolerant. But God is righteous. He has standards. However, Satan also causes much of the pain that people suffer. In any case, "stuff happens": Good people get hurt. The pastor advised his people to trust in God and keep their eyes on the next world. He ended with good news: God will help you. These sermons conveyed to the listeners the need to stick with God no matter what. Regardless of what frustration or suffering is experienced, maintain the spiritual relationship.

A theme in Irene's comments, which I have not yet discussed, is the importance of her personal relationship with God. She is being drawn closer to Him, and her life is increasingly being organized around this spiritual relationship. The best part of the week is Wednesday night

Bible study. Irene said she lives to please God. Such comments are more central to Jill's story:

Jill and her family had recently moved to Middletown.[5] They had been attending a Pentecostal church. Jill spelled out what she believes. She is an Arminian. She believes in the literal truth of everything in the Bible, including the miracle stories, and that biblical prophecies will be fulfilled. She follows the dietary rules found in the Old Testament. For Jill, Jesus is the bridge to God. Jesus died for us and rose again; if you accept Him, Jesus's blood covers your sins. But the Spirit must come and dwell inside of you – that is, you must be born again, be empowered by the Spirit. Jill believes everyone can be empowered by the indwelling of the Holy Spirit, that is, we can all walk in the power of God – healing, speaking in tongues, prophesying.

As a college student, Jill entered a life of partying. However, a relative got her to attend a Pentecostal church. God empowered her to stop the worldly lifestyle. Ending such a lifestyle is a joy. "I love to be in His presence. There is nothing like it. ... It is almost like a high that you can never get with the other stuff."

Jill met the man she would marry at this church. Even before she met her boyfriend, she knew this was the guy she was going to marry. On their second date, he asked her to marry him, because he felt the Lord was telling him to do that. She said yes. They have had problems like everybody, but, "We have seen God work in our marriage so much."

After Jill moved to Middletown, she prayed to God asking where He wanted them to be. After walking into Spirited Church the very first time, "I knew right away this was the church God wanted us [her family] to be in." When the service started, her feeling was confirmed. "I felt the presence of God."

Jill likes the style of worship – contemporary. You feel free: "If you want to lift your hands in worship, that is fine; if you don't, that is fine." Likewise, if you want to wear shorts, that is fine. The church is not lofty. You can come as you are.

Jill was a full-time housewife at the time of the interview. Her parents were divorced when she was a child. They had stopped

5. Jill was younger than forty.

attending church. Jill believes that if they had continued to go to church, they would have stayed together. God is using Spirited Church to help her family.

When asked if she has changed, Jill responded that she has asked God for wisdom and received some. (When you ask God for something, you must believe it will happen.) Jill has sought counsel from one of the pastors and a friend in the Women's Bible Study group. God uses them to help her with her problems. "I think I am more patient, loving with my husband. I don't think I nag him as bad. I think I accept him more .... ." She had wanted to change his ways that bugged her, but she no longer wants to do that. "Let God deal with him."

Jill and her husband do the things God says in order to build a strong marriage. They read the Bible daily and watch Christian TV, such as The 700 Club. She has stopped watching secular TV, such as soap operas. "I want my marriage to be strong and grow." She does not watch programs about adultery and murder.

Jill is excited that Spirited Church is involved in evangelism. We must be extensions of God, because otherwise the congregation would be just a social club.

Jill and her family are not official members of the church. However, Jill believes that since they are born-again Christians, they qualify as members.

Jill was a full-time housewife. The family was a basic part of her life and a source of worry. She seems concerned about following in her divorced parents' footsteps. Jill's worries are probably less painful because she has her relationship with God. Sunday church service is an occasion to feel God's presence. At church she can be herself – be as expressive as she wants to be, dress as she wants to appear. Churchgoing means developing her personal relationship with the Spirit. Jill has given up partying because of the joy she feels in His presence. She depends on God's guidance – to pick a husband, to choose a church, to grow spiritually. Jill seems to follow biblical rules to an unusual extent, even in choosing foods to eat. She no longer tries to change her husband; she is more patient. The counselors at church are God's instruments, just as all church members must be as evangelists. It is God who will save her marriage. Her family watches only Christian television, as a way to keep her marriage strong. Yet this change does not mean Jill is satisfied with her husband, for she still hopes God will change him. Jill works on deepening her spiritual relationship, leaving her family in God's hands. She reminds me of the Nazarene women discussed in the last chapter. Her family life is her worldly life, and it is a source of worry. In response, Jill is reorienting her life around her spiritual world.

As discussed in the last chapter, Ronald A. Knox's (1994) ultrasuper-naturalist is someone who does not socially leave this world, yet who does live in such a way as to maximize involvement with the sacred. These mystics seek not to change the world but to become one with God. The person surrenders the self to God's will. Both Irene and Jill emphasized their personal relationships with God. However, Christians vary in the degree they try to be in this world but not of it, leaving aside entering a monastery. Jill is more extreme than Irene, in that Jill more clearly approximates the ultrasupernaturalist.

A consequence of emphasizing the spiritual relationship is less commitment to the religious institution. Jill believes that because her family members are born again, they are automatically "members." Another interviewee played down the importance of a church: "I am who I am spiritually no matter what church I am going to." Lois, whose story will soon be told, is not a church member. "God knows where I am." Having the membership, your name on a piece of paper, is not important. For Lois's parents, "paper is important," but for Lois, "your heart has to be in the right place."

The first sermon Lois heard touched her heart.[6] The topic was depression. Lois had been unhappy. During the sermon she came to understand that she had been foolishly trying to find happiness through material things. Lois had been concerned about living in an impressive house, having the right kind of car. She had sought praise from other people. Lois thought you could buy happiness. The pastor's sermon convinced her to seek happiness by focusing on Jesus.

When asked how her life has changed, Lois replied that it has in every way because now God is her focus. All she cares about is serving and obeying God. People trick you, mislead you. "The Bible is the only Truth you can find in this world." Lois takes the Bible quite literally.

When she comes to Sunday service, Lois likes the singing because it allows her to connect with God. Lois asserted strongly,

---

6. Lois was younger than forty.

"the Spirit is there." She knows this is true because she can feel the presence of the Spirit.

When asked to sum up the appeal of Spirited Church, Lois spoke about the pastors. They know God, are in tune with God. The leaders make decisions on the basis of what God tells them. They have turned themselves over to God so He can speak through them. When the pastor preaches, God speaks to him, and through the pastor, to the congregation. For example, when Lois was trying to decide whether she should get a paying job, she had been praying for divine guidance. During a Sunday sermon, the pastor pointed in her direction while praising mothers who choose to stay at home. Lois was sure God had spoken to her through the sermon.

Lois does not automatically do whatever the pastor suggests. His advice must be consistent with what Lois knows in her heart is true from her reading of the Bible.

When Lois was asked about her beliefs, her only response was that "we need to let God control our lives." She is now happy.

Lois's depression came from numerous unfulfilled desires. She had been expecting happiness from material things and the praise of others. But she now concentrates on the spiritual. Spirited's ritual is ideal because it allows her to feel the Spirit. The pastors are conduits for God; through them, God speaks to her. Now God is in control. He relieved her of the need to get paid work, which of course was acceptable to Lois because she no longer seeks to buy happiness. People cannot be trusted. She cares only about serving God. Lois's story, as Irene's, has the coloring of ultrasupernaturalism.

Unlike Lois, however, Irene mentioned seeking counseling at Spirited Church. This practice was quite important to others at church:

As a teenager, Kathy had attended a Methodist church in Middletown.[7] Then she dropped out. After Kathy married, she felt a need to be part of a church. She had an attitude problem, being too selfish. The Spirit revealed to her that if she were going to be a true Christian she would need to go weekly. She needed the fellowship.

Kathy believes that the Spirit works though the pastor at Spirited Church and that the people want to center their lives on

7. Kathy was younger than forty.

God. She is part of a community, being involved with other church members throughout the week. Kathy has also used the counseling service and the marriage enrichment class available at Spirited Church.

Kathy's story illustrates how marriage brings people back into churches. Being married requires making sacrifices, and Spirited Church provided a moral community that actively encourages the kind of behavior Kathy believes marriage requires. Kathy referred to centering life on God but she also has received more specialized help through the marriage enrichment class and the counseling service. Spirited Church is helping keep her marriage together. Kathy's story illustrated an important theme that ran through our stories: the appeal of Spirited's counseling program.

A long-time friend asked Lily to visit Spirited Church.[8] Like Lily, the friend had been having personal problems, but she had found help at church. Lily was depressed because of familial financial problems and because of dysfunctional interpersonal relationships involving herself and her family. Lily visited Spirited Church and became deeply involved.

Soon after her first visit, Lily used the counseling service. She really values the counseling program because you can open up without fear of being criticized for your thoughts and because the counselor helps you work out your problems. Lily has used the service several different times.

In a similar vein, Lily has gotten help from others at church. Most friends do not like to open up; they keep their problems hidden. But there are some people in the Women's Bible Study group with whom she feels comfortable being open about her problems. She has been ill recently, and people have called to ask if they could be of help. Lily has also participated in the Prayer Chain. Her experience made her realize that her life could be worse; some people have problems such as serious illnesses that are worse than hers.

Lily likes the Sunday services. The pastor reassures people that if they have fallen short, the Lord will forgive them their sins. The pastor has increased the frequency of altar calls at the conclusions

8. Lily was over forty.

of his sermons. He asks those in need to come forward, and they are joined by the Prayer Team, who pray with the people.[9] Lily and her husband have come forward several times and she has felt the Lord speaking to her on these occasions.

At her old church, the services were routine; she felt like a robot, and people did not participate. At Spirited Church, the people are "on fire for the Lord," raising their hands, moving with the music, sometimes prophesying.

Lily likes the casual dress code. What you wear is not important. Churchgoers are interested in what kind of person you are.

At Spirited Church, if you miss one of a series of talks that are being given, you would not feel looked down on. You are expected to make your own choice; if you miss a session, no one will ask why. If you have financial problems, whatever you can give is okay. Spirited's leaders are friendly; they address you by your first name, you feel like they are on the same level and that they have the same problems as you, and you feel you can speak with them.

Her child had a bad experience in Sunday School at her former church. He was asked a question, did not know the answer, and was "put on the spot." "At Spirited Church, they just want to help them [i.e., the children] grow. If he didn't know the answer, it's okay."

On Sunday evenings, Lily and her husband participate in a Life Group where they study the Bible, pray, and have fellowship. A congregation should be like a family. People should be warm. If people love the Lord and want to express love, they should be loving toward each other in the church.

Lily was depressed over money and family problems. Living seems an ongoing struggle for her. Lily uses friends in the Women's Bible Study group *and* the church counselor with whom she can be open without fear of condemnation. She needs a loving environment, which she finds through Spirited Church. The pastor and people at church accept her as she is. People are open and loving. They just want to help people to grow.

9. The prayer team is composed of thirty to fifty people trained to listen well and to pray with feeling, yet also with sensitivity to the prayer style of those seeking help. It was described by a church leader as a "healing" ministry.

Teri's story also makes the point that the church atmosphere is not guilt-ridden.[10] Rather, people feel accepted.

Teri was raised a Baptist at a separatist conservative church. After dropping out for awhile, she began looking for a church. She was invited to go to Spirited Church. Her friends called it a weird church, and when Teri attended Spirited Church, she did find their practices – praising, clapping, raising hands – to be weird.

It was the singles ministry that brought Teri into the church. She attended a singles event, "and that's when I felt why they do that [i.e., the "weird" things], because it [the occasion and the attandees' emotions] overwhelms you, and that's when I started coming."

At the event, people were singing and having a good time, "and it felt like the Holy Spirit just came over me, my whole body. And I started crying, weeping, really felt like I was in the presence of the Lord!" After that experience, Teri began attending Sunday service. She slowly made a few friends – "they had that same kind of peace and that same excitement. And so I'd sit with them [in church] . . . but for awhile I was by myself. I wouldn't allow people to get that close." She sat in the back because the ritual was strange. But she got into it. "I just really started falling in love with the people here."

Teri's decision to try Spirited Church had been influenced by a man she knew who had been a member of the church. "He smiled all the time, he was happy, he had peace inside, and I said 'That's what I want! I want that peace.'" She found that a majority of people at church had that same peace.

Teri's friends told her about the support and unconditional love to be found in church. As she said, "even though we make mistakes, there are things out of our control such as divorce and bad choices we make in our lives that Spirited Church doesn't condemn you for the rest of your life. They still allow you to get your life right and participate and serve the Lord in His church. And so that was a big plus in my life, because at [my parents' church] I could never do anything. I couldn't teach, I couldn't teach a Sunday School class. I had been divorced. So automatically, I felt an opening of love for the church because of that."

10. Teri was younger than forty.

Church leaders have been divorced. One of them runs a group for divorced people: "She is able to feel the pain of the people sitting there in front of her – and I'm thinking, 'Yes, Lord, you can use us that are making mistakes.'" Teri felt that the people at the Baptist church saw themselves as superior, as people who had not made mistakes. "I guess I am still bitter about this."

Teri enjoyed church so much, she started bringing her children to the children's program on Wednesday night. "I'd get off from work, come straight home and get the kids and come to church. I thought this is crazy – why am I doing this – but I was so hungry that I wanted to be here. I wanted to be around the people that loved me."

When Susan asked Teri how going to Spirited Church has changed her, she said, "I feel that I have more peace about me. I'm able to be more empathetic and loving towards others, not so judgmental. I was more of a judgmental person even though I didn't want to be, because I was judged so much that I just turned it around and judged you, because you're going to judge me first so I might as well get you first."

Prior to attending Spirited Church, Teri didn't feel loved. She has not always done good, so she wondered how God could love her. It "was hard for me to love my kids when they were bad." She has used the counselor at church. Counseling has allowed her to forgive herself for some of the things she has done in the past. Forgiving herself and others brings peace. "You're happy; you feel loved."

Being loved has made Teri stronger. For instance, put-down, negative comments from a cousin don't make her feel bad about herself. She now seeks the Lord's help in making decisions, because she knows He cares about her. Teri's "spiritual walk" involves spreading the word about her church and "being loving and giving, which is Christlike."

When Teri moved back to Middletown, at first she returned to the conservative church she was raised in and which her parents still attended. But she was not content and began visiting other churches. Her mom accused her of "just church-shopping." Said Teri, "I quit pleasing my parents. I please me."

When asked what it was about the church she had attended that wasn't for her, Teri said, "I felt dead. I felt every time I walked into the church I felt I was a horrible sinner, which we are all sinners, but I felt like I didn't deserve to be in God's presence at God's church. And from the preaching, that's how it always felt – guilt-ridden, guilt-ridden, guilt-ridden. I got tired of being condemned. That's how I felt. . . . You need some hugs. I felt like it was too negative." In her old church, "Every service was like I needed to go down in front and just fall on my face and say, 'God, I am so sorry.' You just need to do that one time."

Teri feels more free. "If you want to wear a pair of shorts, that's okay." At her former church, if a woman wore dressy pants or shorts to church on Sunday, fifty people would be staring at her. Spirited Church has no formal or informal dress code, as long as you dress decently. At her former church, men wore pants and women wore dresses. "No one bucks the system." Teri wears pants during the winter to church.

Teri returned for a service at the old church. "I felt so dead." The singing lacked life. "It was decaffeinated coffee." At Spirited Church, you feel alive. "Not that you're supposed to focus on the feeling of what you get when you sing, you're there praising the Lord. What you feel is God loves you."

In Teri's mind, her former church was destructive. As a divorced person, she was spiritually inferior. She felt "dead" there. The dress code symbolized that the individual had to conform to "the system" to be respected. Going to Spirited Church meant having a good time, being accepted by others, and being at peace. Her divorce did not stigmatize her in the eyes of church members. Teri found people who loved her, and now she feels capable of loving others. Counseling has also helped by encouraging her to forgive herself. In Spirited's loving environment, Teri has come alive.

Pauline's story also emphasizes the less judgmental attitude at Spirited Church.[11] Pauline was recently divorced, and she was hurting when we talked with her. Pauline repeatedly said she does not feel that she fits in with anyone, in or out of church. Many times she described herself as a loner. Pauline especially had problems relating to married people, because they made her feel inferior and guilty. When she was a child, her parents had divorced. The people at the Pentecostal church she had been attending at the time did not accept divorce and gossiped about her parents, making Pauline feel like an outcast. Understandably she is involved in Spirited's singles group

11. Pauline was over forty.

as well as the Women's Bible Study group. The pastor gave a sermon on divorce that led her to believe he accepted divorced people. Pauline does not seem to have benefited from going to Spiritual Church as has Teri, but Pauline's story again emphasizes the need divorced conservative women have to find a church where they feel accepted.

Other people with whom we talked also appreciated the accepting attitude at Spirited Church. In a church document, the pastor stated his views:

> ...people are not perfect, and for the most part are very much aware of that fact. Therefore, people respond to being loved and lifted into shape rather than pounded. I am discovering that people will give you their best when they are affirmed and accepted for who they are. This does not exclude the challenges of the gospel and the high expectations of Christ to lead an exemplary life. I am simply saying that every person should clearly understand they are loved, accepted, and forgiven in the Spirit of Christ. When this truth becomes real to people, they will gladly give their lives in grateful service to Christ and His church.

The social environment at Spirited Church is therapeutic. That is, people do not emphasize judgment and guilt. One respondent complained to me about a Baptist church she had tried out where the minister yelled a lot: "that is almost like I'm getting punished, and I don't want to feel that way." Put positively, therapeutic means people offer unconditional love. They create a situation where people feel trust for others, which allows an unusual degree of openness. The resulting communication process is meant to help troubled people accept themselves and to grow, using a loving Jesus as a model.

THE SIGNIFICANCE OF COUNSELING

Counseling is done informally by staff members and in the small groups and formally by mental health specialists. In all, five people appreciated the counseling classes or private counseling available in the church. I have already discussed the stories of Jill, Kathy, Lilly, and Teri. Leslie attended a Sunday School class on anger that was taught by a member of the counseling staff.[12] She then sought personal help, which is changing

---

12. Leslie was over forty and is highly educated.

her life. At the end of the interview, Leslie returned to the availability of counseling at Spirited Church, emphasizing its importance. Then Leslie praised the six-month marriage preparation course at Spirited Church. People need to understand that marriage "is a covenant, not just a contract you can break."

Jill, Kathy, and Lilly had marriage problems. Teri had suffered the consequences of divorce. I do not know the source of Leslie's anger, although her linking of counseling and preparation for marriage suggests that Leslie's anger might have been related to her marriage. In all, these women had problems similar to the female Nazarenes discussed in the last chapter, except the situations of the women at Spirited Church were less severe. The difference between the Church of the Nazarene in the 1950s and Spirited Church is the availability of a therapeutic environment, and more specifically of a counseling program. I suggest that this program allows seriously troubled people to deal directly with their problems, thereby avoiding the need to deny their inner desires (e.g., the Nazarene women) or to pass responsibility for solving the problem to God (e.g., Jill).

The presence of a counseling program is significant. After World War II, "the public's fascination with psychology led to an increased interest in personal counseling . . ." (Hudnut-Beumler 1994:10). During the 1950s, numerous theological schools offered classes in such counseling. These classes emphasized Carl Rogers' "client-centered" form of therapy, which sought the full realization of the client's potential. Moreover, clients wanted to be happy, and this was accepted as a worthy goal (pp. 10–1). It took longer for conservatives to accept counseling. Given that the traditionalist type seeks to have a culture completely dominated by his or her form of religion, the existence of clinical psychology as a differentiated expertise is troubling to conservatives, which explains Larry Crabb's Institute of Biblical Counseling in Morrison, Colorado (Miller 1995). Crabb perceives humans to be composed of body and spirit (soul). All nonorganic psychological problems are spiritual problems that should be handled within a Christian community by church people advanced in biblical wisdom, personal godliness, and personal compassion. As Crabb said about the claim that professional counseling is necessary, "Ultimately, we're saying the Scriptures and Christianity don't meaningfully address the core concerns of our lives" (p. 16). At Spirited Church, humans are body, spirit, and mind, and both the first and last can be medically treated. The church's perspective accepts the usefulness of psychological counseling while keeping it subordinate to religion.[13]

The accommodation of the counseling profession, I suggest, is resulting in a significant change in the nature of enthusiastic Christianity. Ultrasupernaturalism continues to have appeal. Irene and Lois reacted to personal problems by detaching from this world and devoting themselves almost totally to their relationships with God. But I suggest that the creation of a therapeutic environment lessens the need for the ultrasupernaturalistic lifestyle; people can find in therapy ways of coping with problems that do not require the degree of emotional withdrawal from the world that is required by ultrasupernaturalism. In this sense, the counseling program allows seriously troubled people not to choose ultrasupernaturalism as an escape from problems. Thus a significant difference between enthusiasm and the charismatic movement is that charismatics are more deeply and emotionally involved with others. Mystical tendencies are more tempered by social engagement – being loved by God by being loved by others. This change, in turn, allows congregations in the enthusiastic tradition to encourage personal growth and worldly happiness.

LIFE GROUPS

Spirited Church was successful, in part, because it was a well-run organization seemingly devoid of major internal conflicts. But while these conditions are necessary for success, they are not sufficient. Spirited Church has many programs that are popular. Seven people voiced approval of the childcare and youth programs. The 9 A.M. Sunday School had thirteen different classes for children and youth, as well as six adult classes. Three people made use of the singles group. But two programs stood out in the interviews: the Life Groups (small Bible study groups) and the missionary-oriented service programs. The former program contributes to making Spirited Church a therapeutic environment.

13. As a Christian counselor wrote, "the Christian therapist is not one who practices a certain type of therapy but one who views himself in God's services in and through his profession and who sees his primary allegiance and accountability to his God, and only secondarily to his profession or discipline" (Benner 1988:274).

Numerous small groups meet weekly for worship, Bible study, and fellowship. The actual mix of these activities seems to vary from one group to the next. Leslie chose Spirited Church over another charismatic church because of Spirited's Life Groups. As Leslie said, it is in the Life Groups, as in other small groups, that the most important ministry occurs. There, people show concern for each other and spend time sharing and praying for each other.

Max gave the greatest importance to his participation in a Life Group.[14] Six couples, similar in age, meet weekly for three hours. To begin with, they have supper, and chitchat about kids or other aspects of their lives; men talk with other men, the women with each other. Then they come together as a group. They announce prayer requests or report some good experiences. Then everyone stands, holds hands, and prays for the needs of the members. All sit, and the study leader begins an open discussion of some biblical passage. Max has made close friends in the group. They eat together, play golf together, and so forth. They have become a family. For the first time in his life, Max has trusted friends with whom he can discuss personal, spiritual issues openly.

Small groups also require accountability. Faith is strengthened through group participation. An individual submits himself or herself to the others for correction. Accountability means if you are struggling with yourself you can discuss it with the others and ask for their help, which might mean praying together, receiving phone calls from others in the group, or meeting others.

A church document sets forth the policy for Life Groups: "The number one emphasis of this small group ministry is outreach and evangelism. Secondly, the emphasis is on pastoral care through the small groups." Our interviews suggest that in fact pastoral care is the primary purpose for Life Groups. In the small groups, people receive personal attention and, as one member put it, "feel at home." A church leader told me that the pastoral staff was concerned that the Life Groups were becoming too self-centered; the staff wants these groups to balance caring for each other and doing mission work.

Donald E. Miller wrote that members at new paradigm churches frequently said the home-based groups were "the family they never had as children and teenagers" (Miller 1997:16). Participants in such groups share burdens, give comfort, celebrate victories, and reinforce standards (p. 137). A pastor at a Vineyard church told his congregation, "Come

14. Max was younger than forty.

as you are, you'll be loved." It is not just Jesus who will love you but also the congregation. Generally in new paradigm congregations, people like the openness and honesty among the members. They can be themselves and admit their problems, knowing they will be accepted and not judged (p. 21). While being accountable is no doubt important in the Bible study groups, based on our interviews I believe their more important aspect is to function as we *now* expect families to be, which is to embody what I call therapeutic values (unconditional love, trust, openness, and personal growth).

Spirited Church appeals to people because through its counseling program, Life Groups, and general atmosphere, its leaders have created a therapeutic environment, which represents another significant accommodation of late-modernity.

WHAT DID NOT EXPLAIN SPIRITED'S APPEAL

The fact that the interviewees who were attracted to Spirited Church failed to emphasize some of the theoretical ideas presented in Chapter 1 is interesting.

AUTHORITARIAN STRUCTURE

As the pastor wrote, "In the United Methodist Church, pastors are looking for bigger churches while the people are looking for bigger leaders." He expressed his philosophy as follows:

> Every pastor should catch a vision for that local church, share it with the trusted leaders (Amos 3:3, Nehemiah 2:17), write it down (Habakkuk 2:2), and be willing to assume responsibility for leadership. The pastor must take the steering wheel. You cannot direct the church from the back seat. If the church is not going in the right direction, it is the fault of the pastor.

Like new paradigm congregations, Spirited is run by the pastor, who, however, has created small groups within which the laity have considerable autonomy (Miller 1997:ch. 6). The point, however, is that the interviewees neither praised nor condemned the authoritarian structure of Spirited Church. Why, then, the lack of reference to the authoritarian structure? Two reasons seem likely. First, the people perceived the pastor as God's conduit and therefore did not experience the congregation as run by the pastor. What was important about the pastor was the belief that he is led by the Spirit. Second, given the diffusion of power, because of the many relatively autonomous small groups in the congregation, the church was not seen to be a truly authoritarian organization.

MEMBERSHIP CRITERIA

If people wish to join the congregation formally, they must take a six-week course that covers church history and doctrine as well as the story of Spirited Church itself. Then they must sign a "Certificate of Commitment in Membership," a procedure that is to be repeated annually. Among the ten listed statements on the form are:

- I have written my testimony, a summary of how I came to know Christ as my savior, and presented it to the leadership . . . as a statement of my faith and commitment.
- I participate in a Small Group (Life Group, Sunday School Class). . . .
- I am committed to discover, develop, and deploy talents, abilities, and Spiritual Gifts in effective ministry and service for Christ. I have a ministry.
- I hold the conviction that the tithe (10% of my income) is the minimum biblical standard of giving for disciples of Jesus Christ.

Yearly the leaders give a sermon on stewardship, in which tithing is emphasized. The certificate also contains pledges by the member to nurture the relationship with God, to cooperate with the church leaders, and to make sacrifices "in the building up of this church."

It is noteworthy that after listening to all the interviews, I did not know that the certificate existed. A member of the pastoral staff told me about it. But no interviewee said, "I was attracted to Spirited Church because it demands high commitment by expecting you to sign a demanding agreement annually." What people did talk about was that because membership itself is not a big issue in the church, you can participate in programs or be a church officer without being a member. Similarly, new paradigm churches have "permeable boundaries," inviting nonbelievers into many programs. They avoid segregation from "the world" (Miller 1997:152).

CHURCH AND POLITICS[15]

None of our interviewees said the church's involvement in politics was important in their choosing Spirited Church. Yet such involvement is important to the pastor. Formerly he eschewed politics and was almost separatist. He has changed. A sermon in October 1996 was a Bible study on Romans 5:12–7. On that particular Sunday, a citywide anti-abortion demonstration was planned. The Life Chain is an annual event organized by local churches to provide a peaceful, prayerful demonstration of religious concern for the abortion debate and the moral state of America. Spirited Church was one of the participating churches.

The pastor gave a personal story about his interest in the event:

> For seven years I have had a hesitancy of getting involved in public protest. I always felt that I was exercising my convictions through counseling and preaching to people in need. But then I felt provoked by the Holy Spirit to act in a secular, public way. I found the Life Chain to be a valuable event that I looked forward to participating in with my wife and family each year. I want to talk about how abortion kills children and that adoption is the optimal choice.
>
> The Life Chain is a silent, peaceful, prayerful way to take a stand for life. Evil will triumph when good men do nothing.
>
> I am making it my mission this morning to make you upset. I'm serious. For all of you who rationalize and justify your not going today; for you who are going to stay home and watch football and putter around the house; I hope you have a bad afternoon. (laughter from the congregation)
>
> Are you sufficiently uncomfortable?

The pastor went on to announce that shuttle buses would be available to depart from the church parking lot for those who could not drive or who wanted to carpool. A table outside the sanctuary provided stacks of anti-abortion signs with messages of "Jesus Forgives and Heals," "Abortion Hurts Women," "Adoption the Loving Option," and "Lord Forgive Us and Our Nation."

Abortion was not the only public issue that interested the pastor. Shortly before our study began, he had become involved in a multi-church effort to save inner-city community centers from being closed

15. Part of this section was written by Stacy Harbaugh.

by the city for financial reasons. A group of twenty pastors, "black and white together," met and decided to work together to run the centers. The pastor discussed the matter in a sermon given in 1996:

> So during the meeting . . . this combined group of clergy basically said, "We propose to take over all three of these centers. The Church of Middletown, The Church (there is just one church) in Middletown. There is just one. We propose as The Church of Middletown." "Who are you people?" "We are The Church. We're black and white, Methodists, Baptists, Pentecostal, confused. We're everyone. We propose to take the directorship of these centers and to run the program."
>
> . . . Local government shouldn't be in the community center business to begin with. If the last thirty years have taught us anything, it is that the welfare state does not work. We find ourselves with greater problems than we had thirty years ago. Something has got to give.
>
> Let me tell you what needs to give – the church. The financial crises that the local community is facing in my interpretation [are] a given and providential opportunity that God is setting before us as the people of God to assume responsibility that we should have been assuming all along. Someone say, "Amen."

The sermon combined with dissentist elements the calvinist trait of charging churches to redeem society. The audience is asked to participate through personal prayers to be God's instrument for redeeming the city – denomination or race is to be ignored. The Church of Middletown must act because government is bankrupt. The welfare state has failed. Churchgoing people must assume responsibility for charity. These remarks express the dissentist's devaluing of denominational boundaries and the distrust of government. However, the pastor did not express the anti-elitist call to redistribute wealth.[16]

16. As an aside, I want to call attention to the interracial composition of the group that discussed the community centers. Three people mentioned with great approval that Spirited Church is open to all races. When one respondent and her family were checking out churches, her nonwhite children would ask if a church had all white people. A Presbyterian church was not appealing to them because the all-white community made her feel that the congregation was not welcoming. While I noticed only a few African Americans at Sunday service, the people we talked with believed that there were no racial barriers at Spirited Church.

To return to the pastor's community involvement, it is clear that he is in sympathy with some of the goals of the Christian Right. He firmly supports abortion activism. Moreover, shortly before the presidential election in 1996, voter guides sponsored by the Christian Coalition were available in the lobby, and their availability was mentioned in the "announcements" section of the Sunday program. The guide, sponsored by the Christian Coalition, covered the presidential, governor, and district congressional races. Finally, the pastor wants the church in Middletown to replace the public welfare program.

But none of the people with whom we talked at Spirited Church were drawn to it by social activism or support for the Christian Right. In fact, our interviewees had quite diverse opinions on the religious right. Some people we talked with either did not know what the Christian Coalition is or were against the organization.

I will briefly present responses to our question about the religious right made by Leslie, Lily, and Teri – people we have already met. Leslie likes the Christian Right. She favors religious groups getting involved in politics by running soup kitchens, homes for unwed mothers, and so forth. We do not need so much government. In her opinion, when Christians pulled out, society was hurt. But Leslie was not representative of the people with whom we talked. Lily has watched the 700 Club. But she does not believe pastors should enter politics. They should not force religion on anyone; that should be a free choice. Finally, Teri is quite clearly not a stereotypical Christian Rightist:

> "There are so many needy people out there, there are so many people out there crying, 'nobody loves me,' . . . [and who need to know] there is so much love to be given, and it's okay if you make a mistake . . . . I volunteered for AIM. AIM is Abortion Alternatives in Middletown . . . some of the people who walked in there [i.e., into the organization's office] didn't realize there was a choice . . . but it's still your choice" said Teri. "We're not going to say, 'don't believe in abortion.' But 'I want you to know what you could go through.' So getting involved in community, you don't have to push your beliefs on others. It's just loving others. It's still their choice."

Teri illustrates how being compassionate and valuing the freedom to choose run counter to the Christian Right program to use the law to enforce abortion beliefs.

In sum, three traits of Spirited Church fit the Bob Jones University model: authoritarian structure, strict membership criteria, and pastoral sympathy for the religious right. Significantly, none of them were important in explaining the congregation's appeal to the people with whom we spoke.

CONCLUSION

The success of Spirited Church, in part, is an old story. The church embodies enthusiastic Christianity, as well as libertarian themes, in appealing to a largely working-class constituency. Enthusiasm is evidenced in the lively, enjoyable praise and worship, the display of spiritual gifts, the Spirit-led pastor, and the primacy of the spiritual relationship. The church has Spirit-filled people who quite visibly display their holiness, at times coming to the altar, laughing, and crying. Personal transformation is expected and encouraged by the pastoral message and by the rituals. Becoming Jesus's shadow (ultrasupernaturalism) is the ideal. Pleasing God, and not representatives of the world, is the essence of religion, so it is critical that pastor and congregation establish boundaries between themselves and the world.

The libertarian themes at Spirited Church are downplaying denominational differences (thereby undercutting the power of denominational officials and their creeds and rules), offering many opportunities for lay leadership, ignoring racial identity, and imposing minimal religious dogma and imagery. Spirited Church's success, then, results from its embodiment of enduring and popular religious themes. But the presence of libertarian elements and of religious practices with roots in the alternative tradition does not sufficiently explain Spirited's success.

What is newsworthy about Spirited Church's success is how it has accommodated late-modernity. Elsewhere I have analyzed the disparate elements that have been labeled "the counterculture" (Tamney 1992a: 71–82). Two were the alternative tradition and radical libertarianism, both long present in Western culture. Two other countercultural themes were relatively new. First, there was an emphasis on self-realization that included valuing relationships and organizations that encourage personal growth, that is, Third Force Psychology. Second, there was what I called "the affluence ethic": "a set of beliefs and values that are guides to leading an elegant life" (p. 81). The norms within this new ethic are based on valuing pleasure and beauty. The relatively new ideas affirmed the need for others, but within open relationships, and criticized the prevailing puritanic asceticism. The self-realization ethos and the affluence ethic are the late-modern cultural developments that Spirited Church has accommodated.

The accommodation of the self-realization theme is evidenced in the balanced nature of the Sunday ritual, the various options given participants to find a religiosity that suits them individually, and the general therapeutic congregational environment. The ideal is unconditional love. Passing judgments on specific people or inflaming guilt feelings is considered counterproductive. Interpersonal openness is believed necessary for personal spiritual growth. The nature of the small groups as well as the pastor's philosophy evidence the influence of the self-realization ethos.

What about Spirited Church and the affluence ethic? Again, I believe accommodation has occurred. The underlying issue is the attitude toward the world. While Spirited's pastor emphasizes opposition to the world, the message is different from enthusiastic churches earlier in the century. As Mark Shibley (1996:109) correctly noted, new paradigm churches do not emphasize the sinfulness of such activities as drinking and dancing. Rather, abortion and homosexuality have become the defining issues. This is also true at Spirited Church. This shift in moral concern implies a moving away from ascetic morality by allowing the enjoyment of worldly pleasures. I shall return to this change in Chapter 7.

The affluence ethic can also be discerned in the importance of fun. For instance, servant evangelists are supposed to enjoy their activities. Similarly, people come to Sunday services because they enjoy them. Of course, as Liston Pope (1942) observed, people had gone to church to have fun before late-modernity. What I suggest is new is the conscious use of pleasure as a norm to evaluate religious activities. Sunday service is to be fun, evangelism is to be fun, and I imagine the Life Groups are to be fun as well. As Donald E. Miller (1997:185) wrote, "one of the draws of new paradigm religion is that it is fun!"[17]

17. A colleague received from an Apostolic church a newsletter that included the following comment: "Studying the Bible doesn't have to be a tedious process agonizing over places with names you could never pronounce right, but it can be a fun uplifting time of fellowship with one another. [Brother Bill] is training some of us in how simple and fun it can be to study the Bible with someone."

In sum, Spirited Church is appealing because it embodies the alternative tradition (in the form of religious enthusiasm), as well as libertarianism, and accommodates important aspects of late-modern culture (the self-realization ethos and the affluence ethic). I call such congregations "charismatic."[18]

As we saw in Chapter 2, conservative Protestants define themselves in opposition to "the world," motivated by their frustration at the loss of a de facto Protestant society and by the suffering of ordinary people brought on by industrialization. The pessimistic theology of the conservatives requires separation from the world. Spirited Church sees itself as part of a religious counterculture, as standing in opposition to the world. Yet the church has also accommodated late-modernity. So, the church has succeeded by subtly accommodating the 1960s' secular counterculture while defiantly proclaiming itself a fighter for a religious counterculture.

During 1998 and 1999, I asked pastors at the four congregations described in this book why they thought their churches have been popular. An associate pastor at Spirited Church began by saying that the pastoral staff does not ascribe success to any one theory about church growth (and, I might add, the associate pastor seems to have read widely on the subject). Success has come from God's grace, he told me. The staff has made mistakes, yet the church has continued to grow. Of course, he said, it helps to have highly skilled people. Yet, in the end, the staff is puzzled by the church's success.

However, the associate pastor also said that popularity comes from catching God's wave, implying that there is a role for pastoral insight and planning. Later in our discussion, the pastor described a recent spurt of growth that he ascribed to the arrival of a new youth minister and the new facilities and programs developed by this person. The new youth minister is a woman. She now runs a youth center that contains computer games as well as a place to have cappuccino and other types of coffee.

In addition, the pastor told me that the staff will shortly begin offering a Saturday evening celebration service. It is believed this will aid growth

18. The term "charismatic" is often used to denote the introduction of enthusiasm into elitist churches (Yamane 1998). Such usage overlooks significant changes taking place within some congregations in Holiness and Pentecostal denominations. Thus I prefer to use "charismatic" to refer to a form of religiosity that may appear in any denomination.

Table 3. New Paradigm Traits and Corresponding Theoretical Meanings

Church Trait	Theoretical Meaning
A. The focus is on deepening the spiritual relationship; the people are doctrinal minimalists.	Enthusiasm
B. The congregation has rituals that encourage and confirm personal transformation.	Enthusiasm
C. The congregation defends a religious counterculture.	Enthusiasm
D. Dress codes are out; a casual atmosphere is encouraged.	Accommodates libertarianism and self-realization ethos
E. The congregation is a loving environment; small groups are "the families" that attendees always wanted, with openness, trust, and acceptance paramount.	Accommodates self-realization ethos
F. The congregation has "permeable boundaries"; it is not a church of saints.	Accommodates self-realization ethos
G. Contemporary lively music is used.	Accommodates alternative tradition, libertarianism, and affluence ethic
H. Servant and lifestyle forms of evangelism are acceptable.	Accommodates libertarianism and affluence ethic
I. Religion is fun.	Accommodates affluence ethic

in two ways. First, the sanctuary has been 80 to 90 percent full at the more popular, later Sunday morning service, and church growth experts say that such crowding inhibits growth; conceivably some people now attending the later Sunday service will switch to the Saturday service, thereby opening up space for newcomers at a popular time on Sunday. Second, the staff believes the new time slot will tap a different population that likes to do something other than go to church on Sunday morning.

The associate pastor's comments made two points. First, the staff at Spirited Church is trying to market its congregation by discerning the needs of potential members and by changing their practices to fit these needs. Second, the congregation is accommodating late-modern developments – cappuccino bars and the breakdown of the association of churchgoing with Sunday. Not only is church to be a place to have fun, but Sunday is being freed up for various activities, some of which undoubtedly will be fun. These developments witness to the declining influence of a puritan ethic.

The left column in Table 3 lists the traits that made Spirited Church appealing. All of them are consistent with Miller's new paradigm.[19] The right column in Table 3 lists the meaning of these traits in terms of my analytic framework.

In Chapter 1, I suggested that the success of conservative Protestantism might be the result of compensating for late-modernity. The case of Spirited Church suggests that success results from accommodating late-modern developments. Shibley (1996) studied the new paradigm religious movement. He ascribed its success to helping effectively people both experiencing personal crises (e.g., financial problems, alcoholism, and divorce) *and* lacking adequate social support (pp. 120–32), an analysis with which I can certainly agree. In addition, Shibley ascribed new paradigm success to the accommodation of the dominant culture (p. 84). A difference between Miller and Shibley is that the latter believes the new paradigm churches have accommodated not only their style but also their message to the dominant culture, a conclusion with which I agree. Unlike Shibley, however, I interpret the accommodation using modernization theory: Congregations such as Spirited Church fit a late-modern society in which Third Force Psychology and an affluence ethic are gaining importance.

19. Miller's (1997) new paradigm checklist would also include something like this: "the congregation is run by the pastor, but laypeople exercise leadership in the small group." This describes Spirited Church but was not emphasized by the people with whom we talked.

CHAPTER FOUR

TRUTH CHURCH

In this chapter, I want to make evident, among other things, the differences between two forms of Protestant conservatism: the enthusiastic tradition (Spirited Church) and one centered on doctrine (Truth Church). Average attendance at Truth Church for 1995 was about five hundred people, attending two Sunday morning worship services in a sanctuary that comfortably seats about 370 people. Several years ago, Truth Church had created a new congregation, seeded by its own members. The church, as shall become clear, is not an example of the new paradigm. Why, then, has it been successful?

SPIRITED AND TRUTH CHURCHES

Truth Church is part of the Presbyterian Church in America (PCA), which was formed in 1973, although its roots are in the Protestant Reformation. The founders of the denomination believed that mainline churches, such as the Presbyterian Church (USA), were compromising basic Christian doctrine. To quote their brochure, "We believe that the Bible is the written word of God, inspired by the Holy Spirit and without error in the original manuscripts. The Bible is our infallible and divine authority in all matters of faith and life." The first line of the "Statement of Faith" printed in the weekly bulletin is, "We believe that the Bible is God's true and holy word." A national study of Presbyterian clergy in the 1960s found that only 19 percent agreed with the statement, "I believe in a literal or nearly literal interpretation of the Bible" (Hadden 1970:44). Many of them formed the PCA in the 1970s.

Spirited and Truth churches share a belief that the Bible is true and that it should be used as a guide in all important matters. However, in three ways Truth Church better fits my description of the calvinist type. First, the pastors at Truth Church preach predestination. To quote the denominational brochure, "all men are sinners and are totally unable to save themselves. . . . " Again: "salvation is by God's action alone, who sovereignly chooses out of the fallen race of mankind those whom He will save."

Second, Truth Church also ascribes more importance to denominational tradition. The PCA had ties with the conservative Christian Reformed Church. In 1997, the former voted to terminate recognition of the Christian Reformed Church "as a church in ecclesiastical fellowship" because the latter had given its regional bodies the option of ordaining women ministers. The PCA said the Reformed Church was ceasing to follow Scripture. A spokesperson for the PCA said the issue is not just the ordination of women. It "is also the authority of Scripture" (*Christianity Today*, 11 August 1997). To ordain women is to believe Scripture is not authoritative. In contrast, Spirited Church chose a woman to be its youth minister subsequent to our interviews with people at the church.

The importance of tradition is also evident in the way Truth Church presents itself to the public. The weekly bulletin at Truth Church has a cover picture of the building, which is clearly a church. Spirited Church meets in a building that was originally used for a secular purpose, and the new owners have modified the building very little. Whereas Truth's street side carries its name, which includes "Presbyterian," Spirited's sign has no reference to its denomination. Truth Church's presentation to outsiders connotes greater commitment to a creedal heritage.

Third, whereas Spirited Church practices a charismatic ritual, Truth Church conducts what I call a "solemn ritual." The difference between the two congregations is evident in the contrasting nature of the rituals at the two churches. An interviewee from Spirited Church told us that some people left that church because of scenes such as the following. (I remind the reader that all indented material is my paraphrasing of the interviewees' comments unless the material is in quotation marks.)

". . . sometimes people seem to faint or pass out and then they just lie on the floor, and after awhile they wake up, and it's obvious that something has changed them," said the respondent. "It is obvious that they have much more peace, inner peace, you know, and sound strange. Other people just start laughing, seemingly uncontrollably, but they're just so – God changes lives, you know,

God changes lives, and who are we to say that the way He does it is not, I don't know, is not the way God works? You know what I mean? How can we say how God works? And I understand a lot of people are, you know, they read the Bible a lot, they study the Bible a lot, but they just haven't come to the point where they can accept... miracles or something. Maybe they just don't quite believe in the supernatural. Maybe structure and maybe just reading something is good enough for them."

Three respondents at Truth Church were repelled by the enthusiastic style they had experienced at other churches, including Spirited Church. The one who had visited Spirited Church liked the teaching but not the "rock-n-roll relaxed setting." She prefers traditional music and worship, which reflect "reverence of God." Whereas the charismatic style is "distracting," Truth's service is "quieter" – it's a lot easier to focus, pray, and worship God. The others were disturbed by the emotional expressiveness at charismatic rituals. They wanted more structured events in which people do not get carried away by what is happening around them. Truth Church attracts people who go to a church service to express their reverence for God. What this means can be better appreciated if I describe the Sunday morning ritual.

A SOLEMN RITUAL

The church is full. The people are white. All ages are there. The sanctuary is fairly bare. The back wall is wood, at its center is a bare cross. When people enter, the lights are already dimmed, and quieting music is being played on the organ. The women are dressed up; among men the attire is more varied, although most are wearing jackets, with or without ties. The chattering dies down. The twenty-five member choir, wearing white robes and red sashes, sits underneath the cross on the raised platform that runs the width of the front of the sanctuary. The musicians and soloists stand on the left side of the platform, where there is an organ and a piano.

The lights go up, and the pastor, wearing a suit and tie, enters from the back of the sanctuary, walking down the center aisle. He stands behind a lectern, center-stage, facing the congregation. He announces a few upcoming events. As the service begins, people sign and pass the attendance pads found in each pew (the pad enables the attendee to indicate name, address, telephone number, status [e.g., visitor], and whether the attendee wants to be called). The pastor may ask people to greet each other. During the opening prayer, the preacher discusses specific people such as the birth of a new baby and a member's return home from the hospital.

Soft music is played on the organ; all are silent. Everyone stands. The pastor and people recite a prayer in that Sunday's church bulletin. The choir sings a slow, traditional hymn, while tithes and offerings are collected. Some of the congregation sing along, as does the pastor, who stands with his arms folded across his chest. He is a model of composure; as one respondent told me, his posture sets the appropriate tone for a worshipful service.

The congregation sits to listen to "worship through music." One Sunday there was a brass and woodwind ensemble complete with percussion; on another occasion there was a separate men's choir, as well as the regular choir, and a large group of women playing the hand-bells. Another time the choir director took her place in front of the choir to lead it in song, accompanied by a piano and two clarinets. The pastor sits to the side. When the music ends, there is no applause, and the choir and musicians join the congregation.

Whether or not applause is appropriate during worship service was discussed by the church board, who decided on the following policy.

The Session . . . wishes to reaffirm the policy of discouraging people from applauding during worship services, especially after offerings of worship through music.

The primary reason is theological: Biblically, worship is a dialogue between God and man, and is always initiated by God. God acts, through creation, providence, redemption and all His other activities, and man responds through worship. . . . Man's response includes praise, prayer, commitment to creeds, vows, and also musical expressions of praise.

God, therefore, is the only legitimate recipient for our responses. Applause, on the other hand, is a response to the person who is offering praise to God, and therefore is inappropriate no matter how beautiful the musical praise.

In another sense, worship is our offering to God, making God the audience of our worship. We as a congregation are often participants in worship, but we are never the audience; only God is the audience. Therefore the only Being who may rightfully applaud is God Himself.

On a more practical level, the applause for one form of praise without similar applause for every other form of praise would indicate that one was more pleasing than another. But with God being the audience, it is impossible for us to tell which is more pleasing to God. The result of one musician receiving more adulation than another can be very discouraging to those who don't receive such praise.

The main event is a thirty-minute sermon containing much information and delivered with feeling. The pastor reads the key text, says a prayer for illumination, and then gives the sermon. On one occasion, he sought responses three times from the congregation – once there were scattered "amens," twice a few people called out the key word desired by the pastor. The mood is relaxed from time to time, as the pastor tells personal stories with both humor and a relevant point. The sermon contains information about, and explanation of, the text. At its conclusion, all stand and sing. This is followed by the pastor's benediction. The organ plays softly, and the pastor walks down the center aisle. The music picks up, and people leave by various doors. Many of those going out the front door stop to talk briefly with the preacher.

In my conversation with Bart, he was critical of church services that are billed as "celebrations."[1] "Are we genuinely worshiping an almighty God or are we just here to make ourselves feel better?" As Bart told me,

"Truth Church has some extraordinary musicians and extraordinary singers, but you're never center stage.... You're always on the side, and with rare exceptions, you don't hold the microphone [as do pop singers]. You just stand there [no animation]. We don't clap for them," said Bart. "... it's a very, I hate to say, solemn, because it's so uplifting to be there, and yet, they're making a clear statement, 'We're doing this for God.'"

Elsewhere I defined a solemn ritual as one that creates a sense of unity among the participants through actions that express respect for a powerful being (Tamney 1965). Characteristics of a solemn ritual emphasize the exceptional nature of the event (wearing unique costumes, moving slowly as in processions) and the subordination of the self (periods of

---

1. Bart was over forty.

silence, absence of emotional display). Such a ritual creates feelings of reverence and deference.

Sunday service at Truth Church approximates the solemn type. The initial quiet time signals a transition from a profane to a sacred event. The ritual is not meant to make participants feel good or to feel God. Rather, the purpose is to express reverence for an almighty God. The ritual plays down the individual self – no applause or self-expression, a uniformed choir, the controlled composure of those on the platform and in the pews. In contrast to enthusiastic rituals, Truth's service was labeled formal, reserved, and staid. The enthusiastic style gives participants more freedom to be themselves, and thus allows them to express how they feel about what is going on; the quiet, structured ritual encourages self-control and provides a sense of security. The solemn style evokes a worshipful, reverential attitude, which is what some people want to experience in church.

To sum up the differences between Truth and Spirited Churches, the former more clearly deemphasizes the individual. Predestination portrays the individual as powerless to achieve salvation. The solemn ritual favors self-control and more generally reverence for God and His church. In Truth Church, serving God means accepting denominational restraints; a member's life is to be founded on the Bible, as understood within the denominational history. Thus calvinist churches more clearly approximate the traditionalist type than do charismatic ones.

Most of the respondents who attended Truth Church came from conservative churches such as Southern Baptist, Christian and Missionary Alliance, or the Evangelical Free Church. Four had been reared as Methodists, one had been an American Baptist, and another a mainline Presbyterian; in all these six cases, the people themselves had been religiously conservative. One respondent who had been unchurched became disillusioned with his lifestyle and wanted to create a new life. For most of the people interviewed, joining Truth Church followed from moving into the area. The people we talked with were almost all predisposed to conservative religion, but not just any kind of conservatism. My question was, why do people affiliate with a calvinist Protestant congregation? Or to put it another way, why do people attend a congregation that seems to be less accommodating of modernity than Spirited Church?

TEACHING THEOLOGY AT TRUTH CHURCH

Church growth or at least Protestant church growth is affected by the quality of the pastor. The respondents consistently praised their pastor.

He is a reason that Truth Church is popular. The pastor is admired as a teacher, because his sermons are organized, informative, and delivered with feeling. He is also liked as a person, as an approachable, caring leader. This image is aided by his use of personal stories during sermons and by his compassionate remarks during the Sunday service announcements about members of the congregation who are undergoing unusual, sad, or happy experiences. But above all, he is admired as a biblical scholar.

Bart was sweeping in his criticism of "liberal churches."

"To me, it's the preacher's not preaching with the Bible laying on the pulpit," said Bart. "Where's he getting his inspiration from? Where, you know, if he's just up there speaking his opinion, our opinion, my opinion, anybody's opinion will do; we're not going to get anywhere doing this. I, we're trying to seek God's will, we need to find the way to do that, and we believe the Bible is God's inspired word.... I don't disagree that things change, and churches change; but if you don't have a basis, if you don't have something to mount from, if you don't have a guidebook, you're in trouble...."

Like others with whom we talked, Bart admired Truth's pastor because his sermons were very informative lessons on the meaning of biblical passages.

While church-shopping, Sarah and her husband visited a Methodist church.[2] They attended the Sunday School class and found they were the only ones who had a Bible. The class discussed

"some book they were reading," said Sarah. "... it was a lovely discussion about something wonderful but it had nothing to do at all with the Bible.... My husband asked the teacher, 'Where's the Bible? Why aren't you studying the Bible?' Well, he kind of shuffled around a bit and said, 'Sometimes we study the Bible, but not all the time. We study books or whatever people want to talk about.' I'm not interested in talking about a book. If I want to talk about a book, I'll go to the university and talk about a book.... If I'm going to a church, then I intend to go to study the Bible."

---

2. Sarah was over forty and is highly educated.

As Sarah said, "Here's the deal – when I go to church I don't go but for one reason. I am an extraordinarily busy person, and when I go to the grocery store, I go to buy food, that's all." When she goes to church, it is to study the Bible.

Important to the respondents, then, is that the pastor sticks to the Bible. He begins with a biblical verse, then reveals its meaning, using other verses. His effectiveness is enhanced by his expository style. He gives series of sermons, each series focusing on a particular biblical book. The continuity of messages increases learning and understanding.

The pastor is scholarly, and the congregants seem somewhat like students. The preacher gives biblical references for what he says, so that one can note the references and go back through them at home, doing even more in-depth study. People are awed by the pastor's interpretative ability, revealing new meanings in analyses that sometimes proceed word by word through a text. People come to Truth Church because they want to hear authoritative analyses of a document they believe contains the truths by which they need to live. People do not go to Truth Church just to hear interesting ideas, no matter how profound. They do not go to hear a preacher conveying some personal inspiration. They believe God has made known His unchanging will in the Bible and they come to church to learn from an expert what God expects of them.

As discussed in Chapter 1, nothing is sacred in late-modern culture, and having doubts about all important beliefs is normal. The culture at Truth Church seems starkly different. Why are people drawn to a congregation that defines itself as the antithesis of late-modern culture?

WHY PEOPLE DESIRE AUTHORITATIVENESS

One image of a "liberal church" held by people at Truth Church is that of a place that tolerates all beliefs, the only important thing being the acceptance of each other. The crucial thing, for our respondents, was the commitment to the belief that the authority in all important matters must be the Bible. People are not so much committed to certain beliefs but to the existence of an unquestionable authority. I examined the interview material trying to understand why people want such an authority. Many people desire an authoritative religion simply because they were raised to value such a religion. I was interested in other reasons. Elinor was one of the interviewees upset by the "distracting" ritual at Spirited Church.[3] As she said, "I'm the type of person I want to know, you know, I want to make a decision as far as what I believe, and then . . . have the evidence there." She was also troubled by, as she perceived Spirited Church, the absence of theological structure and by its "unstable" membership. She liked the membership class at Truth Church because it made the doctrine "clearer in my mind." Several times she referred to the church providing structure and a foundation. Because of their personalities, some people such as Elinor can feel comfortable only in structured social environments and thus would appreciate an authoritative congregation.

But there are other reasons that people like authoritativeness. After briefly considering the stories of eight people who were attending Truth Church, I shall return to the subject of the appeal of authoritative religion.

A CONSERVATIVE INTELLECTUAL

I hesitatingly asked Allen a question, which he kindly paraphrased for me as, "How can I as an intelligent person believe this stuff?"[4] He continued, "That's the question I've been waiting for, hoping for." Allen's answer was lengthy. A key to his thinking is the comment, "My view is this: If you believe in a God . . . there has got to be a sense in which that God is limitless, and you are limited."

Regarding the Bible,

"there are some things in it that don't quite add up, but it's mostly true. Well, then when do you decide what is true and what is not? And, then how can you trust the Bible for anything? . . . To me the alternatives are to believe it or to just ignore it. . . . I have a really hard time understanding intellectually . . . the so-called liberal position of sort of selecting which parts of the Bible to believe. . . . "

" . . . And so sometimes you know there are things that make you wonder. I mean, I'm not just mindlessly saying, 'My pastor says it's God's Word and I believe it. It's true.' I'm not mindlessly saying that." Sometimes Allen questions the pastor's biblical interpretations, but he concludes eventually that the pastor is right. "One of

3. Elinor was younger than forty and is highly educated.
4. Allen was younger than forty and is highly educated.

the things I appreciate is that more and more and more questions are being answered. . . . It takes time, but my attitude is how dare I operate from the assumption that I as a human mortal man can know all this, that I can challenge God."

Allen is prepared to be patient. It is amazing to him how much the Bible holds together given that it was written over a long time by dozens of authors. Moreover, his belief is shored up by his conviction that God has provided for him, for example, by having gotten him into an elite university. "Why did they let me in? I asked my advisor that once, he didn't really have a good answer. I got a full ride and money. Now, that's God." Allen has "experiential confidence."

Allen is deeply disturbed by the American culture of convenience. Abortion often expresses the sentiment, "'I don't want this baby now because it will intrude upon what I want to do with my life.'" Allen believes that "to get to where we want to be on abortion, what you've got to do is you've got to create a culture that is less addicted to convenience. . . . There are limits to freedom, and one of the real problems with our society . . . [is] we no longer have a clear sense of what the limits of freedom are, and that is one of the perils of democracy that we live with. . . . I believe in parameters for what I do, and sometimes there comes the point at which I say, 'Okay, God, I'll get this answer from you when I get there.'"

Allen dislikes church-shopping because you are requiring a church to live up to *your* standards. For him, "you're not going to church to find what you want. You're going to church to find the ways you can serve God."

Raised in a "fundamentalist subculture," Allen has joined a more intellectual religious environment. Not surprisingly, he is not comfortable when he visits the church in which he grew up. "I see myself as an immigrant," he said, and described himself as having the kind of experiences portrayed in Thomas Wolfe's *Homeward Bound*. "I was raised on country and western music; I listen to classical music now." At Truth Church, he is intellectually challenged, and he really likes that. Church members include university professors, doctors, and many other professionals. As Allen said, it is a classy but not "high-falutin" church. Allen finds Truth Church "quite liberating." "My experience is that Truth Church is the most freeing place I've ever been in." For instance, church members put on a skit at a congregational dinner that poked fun at some church rules.

Again, if he wanted to drink moderately, he could. While Truth Church allows Allen greater freedom, its commitment to the authority of the Bible provides stability in an otherwise change-filled life.

MORAL CONSERVATISM

Phylis summed up the religious situation in the United States[5]:

> "The United States is not a well-churched society . . . ," said Phylis, "there's basically two types of churches. There's the types that are not as strong biblically, and when the world moves away from the Bible standards, to appeal to the world, they also move . . . a little bit away from Bible standards, and . . . they accept social drink-ing . . . premarital sex or marrying divorcees or all these different things that are not really staying true to the Bible, but because of the way the nineties is going, and they don't want to lose their membership, maybe tend to move a little closer and accept things. And then there's the churches that stay true to the Word of God regardless of where the world is. . . . "

"Conservative churches" stay true to God's standards; "liberal churches" vacillate, depending on what society's standards dictate.

Many conservative congregations would fit Phylis's good type of church. Why Truth Church? For Phylis and her husband, the youth pro-gram was the deciding factor. For them, a good youth program affirms the biblical stands on issues about which they have strong feelings, such as drinking, smoking, abortion, and premarital sex. Moreover, classes are tailor-made for diverse age groups. Ideally the program balances "preachy stuff" with fun like ski trips. The program would create friendship groups, within which peer pressure would keep the children out of trouble. In all these ways, Truth Church had a good youth program. As Phylis told me,

> "So the youth group in a large sense replaces, I think, in your children's lives things that are not wholesome that you kind of want to keep them away from," commented Phylis, "and when they develop and get close with these kids, they go to school with them, then they see them twice a week in church and youth groups, and

5. Phylis was younger than forty.

they do a lot of activities together, they bond so closely that . . . they would prefer to be with those types of kids rather than . . . you know, maybe some of the kids that aren't such good influence . . . and they all have parents and families that believe the same things, and so you just, you don't worry as much as a parent. . . . "

The kids in the youth group keep each other accountable. Peer pressure, she said, keeps them right on track. The youth program is an alternative social world where the environment supports traditional moral norms. Phylis does not isolate her children from their peers who have different values. She depends on the sophisticated youth program to win over her children, in part by making religious instruction part of a program that includes fun activities.

Sarah defined herself as a "liberal conservative." Her comments revealed more uncertainty than Phylis's, yet Sarah also wanted a conservative moral environment for her children:

"I am very straight in my morals, there are things I feel very strongly about, you know, I think that you should wait to have sex after marriage. . . . I take the Bible very seriously. . . . " She does not believe women should be teaching leaders in church. Yet she has a "modern relationship" with her husband; for instance, he has sacrificed so that she could advance her career. She concluded that there is probably no church that fits them exactly – "my husband and I are too questioning . . . we do too much intellectualizing and discussing of these issues to ever find a place that does exactly what we think it should."

While these parents have strict norms for their teenage children, she is less conservative on other matters, such as literalness. "I feel very strongly that a text and a reader come together and that meaning is made when those two come together, that there is not an inherent meaning in that text. . . . when I read the Bible and I interpret the Bible, I think there is something in that text, but there is also stuff that I bring and that together we make meaning."

Sarah wants to be part of a conservative church, because she wants to be in a church that holds the line on matters such as abortion, homosexuality, and sexual matters generally. Not that biblical norms are so clear: Even in the case of abortion, she told me, its prohibition is not clearly commanded in the

Bible. However, Sarah is committed to conservative norms on such matters and wants to be in a church that confirms her choices.

Because Sarah and her husband have children, when they moved to Middletown and were visiting churches, they were very interested in a church's youth program. Sarah would talk with the directors of such programs at churches they visited. Virginity before marriage and condemnation of abortion were important moral stands for her. When she spoke to the woman at a mainline church who was in charge of the youth program, Sarah asked about how that church approached such moral issues: "her response was that what they try to do is just reinforce whatever the kids believe, that they don't try to push anything on them but just sort of uphold and uplift whatever they believe." Needless to say, this response upset Sarah.

When I asked why her family returned to Truth Church after checking out other congregations, Sarah said, "One of the main reasons is because they had a good youth program. We have two . . . children, and one of the things that we are very interested in is them staying committed to what we believe in."

Sarah is a mix of traditional and modern. She thinks for herself. Sarah does not believe, as is the position of Truth Church's leaders, that their policies on abortion and homosexuality are clearly justifiable using the Bible. However, she is committed to old-fashioned sexual morality and wants to be in a religious environment that supports such a moral code.

MALE LEADERSHIP

For Nora, obeying God is the crux of religion, and she learns His will by studying the Bible.[6] At Truth Church, she is learning so much about the Bible. She is more sure of her faith, and this gives Nora confidence. "I know I belong to the Lord. Unhuh. Absolutely. I'm assured of a future, and that future has already started, eternally. It's really a big difference. Now, He's close to me. . . ." It is a joy to go to church.

6. Nora was over forty and is highly educated.

In Nora's case, gender itself was an issue. Her first impression of Truth Church was very satisfying:

"Here were families worshipping," noted Nora, "but not only that, the men, the fathers in those homes, were taking a leadership role. [In her family's old, small church] . . . we used to laugh and say, 'If a woman didn't do it, it didn't get done,' because the men were so busy in their jobs . . . and the contrast of that was so great."

In Truth Church, men were singing, ushering, serving communion:

"It was just so obvious that men were taking a real leadership role, and that is – that's wonderful to see" said Nora. "I mean, I probably had a feeling, as I do now, men need to have that leadership role in the family. You can't both – there can't be two bosses, and we saw real families."

Male leadership signaled a rightly ordered universe. For Nora, the spiritual relationship might almost literally be a fatherly bond.

Janet believes the strength of the church is in the men.[7] Men should lead families and churches. It is God's design. I asked her, since she seemed a capable woman, how she felt about submitting to her husband's authority:

" . . . to me, being under authority and being under submission to those under authority is a very freeing experience. . . . I'm going to get very practical" said Janet. "The car needed new tires. . . . I can make an appeal and say . . . it's his responsibility. . . . I can just be free. I related back to when I was a little girl in my parent's home, and . . . my mom and dad were the authorities, and it was so freeing."

Women raised in traditional homes can find conservative churches where men lead to be comforting, freeing them from anxieties. Both Nora and Janet learned that women are to be obedient. Understandably they feel more comfortable in congregations that resemble the family in

7. Janet was younger than forty and is highly educated.

which they were raised, where they learned that to be a woman is to put oneself in the capable hands of a man.

A person with whom I talked was attracted by several aspects of Truth Church, but one seemed especially important and relates to a source of appeal I have not yet discussed:

> Raised a Methodist, Iris eventually joined Truth Church.[8] I asked her if she switched because she changed or because the Methodist Church had changed. While both were probably true, she gave more importance to changes in the Church. Methodism has shifted away from the Bible. Sermons are about everyday things such as how to deal with stress. Iris strongly disagrees with the acceptance of homosexual pastors.
>
> An incident that happened not too long before the switch seemed especially important, as I listened to her story. Iris was contemplating divorce and went to see the Methodist minister. The message she received was that if that was what she wanted to do, then she needed to do it. Upon reflection, Iris realizes that she needed to get a divorce but that it was also true that she never got good counseling. She contrasted that experience with a discussion with the pastor at Truth Church. After attending that church for awhile, Iris was bothered by remarks in several sermons that made her feel different from everyone else because of her divorce. She met with the pastor and told him why she got divorced. He explained that he believes we should try to avoid divorce, but that there are biblically acceptable reasons for divorce, such as her reason. The Methodist minister did not explain that there were acceptable and unacceptable reasons, and never helped Iris think through her options; he just accepted what she was doing.

Iris needed a conservative congregation that would allow her to accept her divorce and therefore herself. The Methodist minister tried to empower Iris to decide what is right, but she could not assume such responsibility. The pastor at Truth Church judged Iris's action using not

---

8. Iris was younger than forty and is highly educated.

his own frame of reference, but a biblical one. Iris needed to feel forgiven by God, which to her meant being forgiven according to rules not of her own devising.[9]

A PERSONAL RELATIONSHIP WITH GOD

I asked Ruth what she liked about the pastor's sermons[10]:

"Well, I think one very important thing to me is that I think he has placed a great emphasis on the sovereignty of God, and even though we might not be able to understand everything, that we don't question God, that God is in control of our lives and in control of all things" remarked Ruth. "And so the sovereignty of God is one really important thing that he has stressed, I feel. Another thing that he has, that I feel he has stressed, is the joy that you feel as a Christian not based on the circumstances around you, but in spite of the circumstances around you, that happiness – some people are only happy when everything is going their way, and God is good, and He is wonderful, and praise the Lord, but when the hard times come, then, 'where is God,' or, 'I curse God for this,' or, 'I blame Him for that,' or, 'I question Him'. . . I think that is one of the very, very precious truths that He has impacted my life with, has been that your life – life is not fair, and it's not always going to be dependent, your happiness is not going to be dependent on all the good things that are happening to you, but that when you really walk close to the Lord and you study His Word, and you talk to Him in prayer, etcetera, that you can feel that inner peace and confidence in knowing that this is part of His plan for your life. You might not understand it until the very last day. You may have some questions that you'd like to ask Him when you get there. But you can experience real Christian joy in spite of the circumstances that you have to go through."

Ruth's conviction that God is in control allows her to remain joyous no matter what happens. Talking with God, she feels inner peace. In

9. Biblical grounds for divorce at Truth Church are adultery, abandonment, and physical or emotional abuse. The innocent party may remarry. The offending party might remarry if the divorce occurred before the person became a Christian. Again, if reconciliation is not possible, and the offending party is repentant, remarriage is possible.
10. Ruth was over forty.

church, you learn what God expects of you; as Ruth said, "real happiness comes from adhering to the guidelines set in the Word of God." Gaining biblical knowledge means understanding how to make the spiritual relationship concrete in daily life. Without biblical instruction, Ruth would not know how to make the spiritual bond a lived reality. Her concluding remark was, "it's the personal relationship with Jesus Christ as your savior and the one that controls your life that really is what religion is – the relationship."

Edy also talked about her spiritual relationship:

What was important to Edy was not a denomination but her relationship to the Lord.[11] The worship service at church brings her closer to God, it makes her want to worship "this God that you have an intimate relationship with." Her goal: "to grow in my relationship and my intimacy with God." Truth Church has aided her spiritual growth. The pastor's sermons reveal the Word of God and spell out what God expects of her.

Edy asked Christ into her life when she was a high school student, but it was only last year that she told the Lord she loved Him. She had told people in her life that she loved them, but she had kept Him "on a shelf in a sense. But my heart has become more receptive to His Word and Him." She has become "more open to giving Him control." "I think he gives us free choice, yet He is sovereign and will work in the hearts that He chooses, and so He began to work in my heart, and I was receptive, and . . . I believe that His word – He was real in Abraham's, Isaac's, and Jacob's lives, and I believe He is real in my life today and in His desire to work in and through my life as He was in their lives." She now sees what God is doing in her life, and she can "freely say, I love you, God. Thank you."

Edy realizes "that He wants to have control of my life instead of me wanting to control it." It is hard to give up self-control. In the future, "I hope that I would be more yielding and more willing to be of service to Him." She wants "to have a yielding heart" to God's wishes for her. She wants to be God's "servant." She has been a homemaker, a "servant" to her family.

One change in her life is a new freedom to acknowledge the role God plays in her daily life. She is more open about her relationship with God: "I share my thoughts about what God is

11. Edy was over forty.

doing or what I am asking." She goes to church to get together with God.

I asked Edy if no longer having children at home resulted in a renewed interest in religion. She said, you mean "the empty nest syndrome." She did not believe there was a connection. The timing was coincidental. "I have poured myself into my children and loved doing that, but I feel like kids grow up. It's time for them to move on. I look forward to when they are gone . . . because then I'll be – my husband and I can be just us again. No, I think it's a natural process, so I didn't grieve. . . . I was melancholy for a little bit, but I don't think it did."

Interestingly, the two people who emphasized the personal relationship with God were women. Their beliefs and attitudes were similar to the Nazarene women in Chapter 2 and some of the women in Chapter 3 who illustrated ultrasupernaturalism. This is especially true of Edy. Neither of these women had experienced the hurt felt by the Nazarene women. Yet Ruth and Edy now belong to the Lord. They emphasized biblical study as the way they deepened their spiritual relationship.

Ruth learned a lesson similar to that of a number of women with whom we talked: Happiness comes from surrendering the self to God. This is not an intellectual matter. You feel peace and joy in God's embrace. Edy referred several times to Christ working in her heart. She seems to be depending more on her personal relationship with Christ rather than on her church. Denominationalism is not important to her. Her spiritual relationship seems to be filling a void resulting from her children leaving home. Although Edy denied any connection, the timing of her new love for Christ suggests a connection, as does her describing the change in her life as going from being a servant to her family to being God's servant. Edy is growing in "intimacy" with God. Increasingly, God controls her life. I would not be surprised if Edy someday joined a congregation similar to Spirited Church.

THE DESIRE FOR AUTHORITATIVE RELIGION

Authoritativeness appeals for a variety of reasons. Some people need structure and clear rules in every aspect of their lives. The appeal of authoritativeness results from their type of personality. Others, such as Allen, believe our society suffers because the culture does not sufficiently emphasize the necessity for limits on freedom. They need to be anchored in an institution that requires individuals to acknowledge their inferiority before God and to accept the obligation to serve the Almighty. The Allens of the world cannot accept intellectually a human-designed world.

For people like Phylis and Sarah, what is important is being part of an institution that legitimates conservative sexual morality. Given the lack of support for her views in society, Sarah wants to be part of a community that strongly affirms her moral code. Yet other women want to be in a congregation that, contrary to social trends, supports patriarchy.

Iris was different. Above all she needed to feel forgiven. Iris could not decide that God forgave her divorce; for Iris to accept that this had occurred, her divorce had to be justified using rules not of her design but ones identified with God because they are found in the Bible. What allowed her to gain this sense of being forgiven was the confidence she had in the pastor as an interpreter of the Bible. His expertise, combined with his analysis, allowed Iris to free herself from her guilt.

For others, the pastor's confidence in the truth of the Bible serves to assure them of the truth of Jesus, and his expositions on biblical statements make clear what they must do to get closer to God. This type of person shades into the women we met in Chapter 3, for whom a congregation was important because of its support for their personal relationships with Jesus.

Two types of people seem ideally suited for Truth Church: those who fear a culture of convenience, and those who are committed to a traditional morality that is losing its acceptability within the society. In a society whose culture is based on convenience, some believe that no effective moral code can exist because, on their own, people define moral norms arbitrarily. Others perceive moral decline more concretely as the failure of society to support traditional sexual morality or patriarchy. Regardless of whether moral decline is understood as the ascendancy of convenience or as the decline of a specific set of moral norms, some people are in church because they perceive it to be the guardian of values that should be the foundation of society. I suggest such people are the ideal market for calvinist churches.

In contrast, some of the people with whom I talked at Truth Church did sound like those who had chosen to go to Spirited Church. Ruth and Edy valued an authoritative church because it confirmed the reality of the deep personal bond they felt with God. Iris, unlike Allen and Sarah especially, did need personal redemption: She could not forgive herself for being divorced, and only God (through a conservative pastor) could relieve her guilt. The presence of such people makes clear that a calvinist congregation may attract people who could be equally or more comfortable elsewhere.

Thus the audiences for calvinist and charismatic congregations are different. People are attracted to the former out of a concern for society, to the latter because of personal troubles. These types of audiences probably differ by social class. A pastor at Spirited Church identified the congregation as "working class." The members are certainly lower in the hierarchy than those at Truth Church, whose members are highly educated and thus probably more influenced by the Enlightenment valuing of reason with the goal of reaching truth. For this reason, the people at Truth Church appreciated the scholarly approach of the pastor. Moreover, given the hardships associated with poverty and powerlessness, it is probable that upper-class people will less often experience the personal troubles that bring people into charismatic churches.

The desire for authoritativeness, then, has a variety of sources, but it is this desire that evidences the fact that conservative congregations struggle against modernity. However, even Truth Church shows the positive influence of the modernization process.

TRUTH CHURCH IS NOT A BOB JONES UNIVERSITY TYPE OF CONGREGATION

While authoritativeness is important, Truth Church is not an authoritarian congregation. Respondents were routinely asked for their thoughts on how the church is run. Three of them appreciated that the pastor and his staff were accountable for their actions to church members and to the presbytery. The denomination has three levels of authority: the congregational board of elders, the presbytery, and the general assembly. Each level includes pastors and elders. The pastor is authoritative, but the congregation is not an authoritarian organization.

Regarding biblical inerrancy, we found more diverse views at Truth Church than at Spirited Church. Staying true to the word of God implies for many conservatives a commitment to biblical inerrancy. Of the sixteen people I specifically asked about inerrancy, eleven gave unqualified support to a strict literal interpretation, believing for instance that a "day" in the creation story means what "day" denotes to us (twenty-four hours). As one interviewee told me, you cannot start questioning the literal truth of the Bible, because once started, the process may not be stoppable, leading to the rejection of the entire Bible. As another person put it, if you question the meaning of "day" in the creation story, may you not also question whether Christ died and rose from the dead? But the resurrection story is the crux of Christianity.

While all the respondents emphasized the importance of the church's commitment to the unquestioned truth of the Bible, differences existed about what this commitment means. I asked another respondent whether in the creation story six days means literally six days:

> "That's a tough question.... There was not time until creation happened, and it took six days," noted the respondent. "Was that six literal days, twenty-four hours around the clock, as we know days? I don't know.... I believe in what it says, that it was created in six days ... but I don't know the definition of a day...."

Bart rejected a completely literal interpretation of the Bible: "I believe that God inspired the Bible ... understanding that there are differences in interpretation of certain verses.... You and I don't understand it, but we know it's right." Phylis knows for sure that the Bible is true, yet she told me, "there are some things that may be open to interpretation to some degree, but there's no gray area, it is true." Literalness coexists with ambiguity in the congregation.

In the detailed discussions of the Bible in classes led by the pastor, one interviewee told me that she developed a nuanced interpretation of inerrancy. For instance, "day" in the Bible may mean something different from what the word means to contemporary people. Again, she went on, consider Solomon and his many wives. He should not be judged as we would our contemporaries. Marriage was something different in Solomon's time; for instance, a king would marry to create political alliances. Of course, biblical writers also described the drawbacks of polygamy. But the point was that the Bible needs to be understood contextually.

In a sermon on church growth, the pastor said that a growing church is united but not uniform:

> Growing churches are not uniform churches; they are united churches. There is a vast difference between the two. Cults are

uniform. Everybody thinks the same; everybody agrees with the other person. Growing churches are not necessarily churches where everybody is in agreement with everything. That means that people have abdicated their responsibility to do their own thinking. You know, there can be some real disagreements in areas like music, especially music. People have such incredibly varied tastes from the classical all the way to rock, all the way.

While uniformity is not the goal, growing churches are united on fundamentals.

> ... They are united in their standard of authority. Did you hear what I just said? Their standard of authority is the same. It is the Word of God. Whatever disagreements they have, they know that they have to resolve them through the Word of God, and even when their interpretations might be heard, they realize ... that this Word is the final appeal, and in humility they also realize that they might be wrong.

Growing churches "hold firmly to what they believe," yet being humble, "they respect what other people have to say."

A growing church seeks "truth in an atmosphere of love":

> ... Growing churches are biblically oriented churches. Growing churches are churches that are in love with the Word of God. They read it; they study it; they talk about it; they teach it; they promote it; they counsel it. Churches that are growing churches recognize that the truth of God's Word is paramount, no matter how difficult the subject might be. What about abortion? What about homosexuality? What about divorce? What about any one of these difficult, emotionally laden issues? What about them? We don't have to speculate. We don't have to go by our own opinions or feelings. We have the truth of God's Word. Growing churches are churches that are committed to the Word of God as the standard of authority and as the place where we find Truth, but, and this is a very important "but," it is a truth that is promoted and pursued in love. It is a truth that is spoken out of love; it is a truth that is spoken for the purpose of love.

The pastor's image of a successful church is clear. The congregation is united in believing in the authority of the Word of God. The people find the Word in the Bible, which they study, discuss, and promote. Answers about abortion, homosexuality, and divorce can be found in the Bible. Yet "growing churches are not uniform churches." Disagreements exist about such matters as music. Beyond such things, the pastor seems to imply disagreements over more serious matters are possible: Humility requires respecting the opinions of others. All discussion should occur in a loving way.

The beliefs of our respondents do reflect the pastor's image; they are committed to the truth and authority of the Bible. However, some respondents find more literal truth in the Bible than the pastor believes is justified. But what unites pastor and people is that they come to church to study the Bible, knowing that it alone is a trustworthy standard by which to judge goodness.

LEVELS OF COMMITMENT

As should now be evident, not everyone who attends activities at Truth Church is equally committed to the church. The church allows people to visit freely. Moreover, if you are a regular attendee, you may participate in church activities except formal church votes.

Within the denomination, there are four levels of expected conformity. First, pastors are expected to believe in the Westminster Creed and the Church Book of Order. However, some questioning is not only tolerated but appreciated as a sign of serious reflection on the denominational documents. For instance, pastors have questioned the Creed's requirement to keep the Sabbath holy by not even thinking about worldly matters. Again, pastors sometimes justify exceptions to the Creed's prohibition against images of God or Jesus. "Church officers" form the second level. It is assumed they will be less knowledgeable about the Creed and Book of Order.

"Members" must only believe they are sinners whom Jesus has saved; in addition, this belief must make a difference in their lives, and they must participate in some church activity. Members may not accept some beliefs, such as infant baptism, as long as they show a willingness to listen to people explaining the church's position. To become a member, you must attend a membership class on Sunday mornings for about ten weeks. Then you are interviewed by members of the board of elders for fifteen to twenty minutes. Interviewees must accept Christ as their savior and are asked about their salvation experience, that is, how they came to be saved and the difference it has made in their lives.

Finally, about the only expectation for "attenders" is that they do not disrupt the service. They can participate in all religious activities except taking communion. On communion Sunday, which is once a month, the pastor announces that anyone is welcome to participate who has publicly proclaimed in a body such as Truth Church that he or she is saved by Christ's blood. The church bulletin reads, "All are invited to join us in taking communion who have made a public profession of faith in Jesus Christ as their Lord and Savior, as Scripture requires, and who are not estranged from the church or engaging in unrepentant sinfulness."

Having varied levels of commitment explains some of Truth Church's appeal. People not ideally suited to the congregation feel comfortable becoming involved without actually becoming members. No one mentioned to me that the congregation's "strictness" regarding membership was important in making Truth Church appealing.

EVANGELISM

Many respondents knew about outreach programs and were glad that their church participated in such programs. They believed Christians should not separate from the world. Programs connected with Truth Church that were mentioned in the interviews included Dorcas Circle (a group making clothes for pregnant women avoiding abortions), Heart-to-Heart Crisis Pregnancy Center (an anti-abortion organization), prison ministry, the Salvation Army and the "Middletown" Mission (aid to the poor), annual missionary medical trips to Mexico, and a summer Bible camp in Middletown's inner city. Such programs are group activities not necessarily involving personal testifying.

But lifestyle evangelism is probably personally more important for most church members. As Phylis said about her and her husband,

"We live our life as a testimony," said Phylis, "and that in itself draws people, because you find there are so many hurting people, so many broken homes, so many divorces, so many kids that are on drugs, and families that are hurting that they are drawn to people and families that, you know, appear to be an anchor or appear to have a focus, and we've had a lot of opportunities to, you know, really spend a lot of time with people in those areas. So I think the Lord uses that . . . in our life as well as theirs."

Ruth and her husband had belonged to an old-fashioned conservative church whose evangelistic style was quite different. Ruth shared "the gospel with everybody just so that everyone would hear it while there is still time to hear it. . . ."

"Today, certain people, if you wanted to witness to them about spiritual things, would consider that a harassment . . . and say, 'Well, you are infringing upon my personal right to be a nonbeliever,' so I think that this may be one of the reasons why there is not as active a program [of witnessing at Truth Church]."

Ruth's reflection implies two things. Her old church had a greater sense of urgency; nothing mattered except salvation and spreading the Gospel. In contrast, at Truth Church people are more sensitive to people's right to privacy.

CHURCH AND POLITICS

Unlike Spirited Church, Truth Church did not publicly display the propaganda from the Christian Coalition. In discussing the success of Truth Church with me, a church leader was critical of the Christian Coalition. He does not accept the notion of a Christian nation; assuming the state does not try to control the churches, he focuses on making individuals into Christians.

The people who attended Truth Church were more outspoken on political matters than those at Spirited Church. Yet, like the latter group, opinions about the Christian Right were diverse. One interviewee, after distancing himself from the Christian Coalition, said, "But still, as a conservative Christian, I'm glad that they're out there. They are a strong political voice, and I imagine that if nothing else, they do encourage numbers of conservative Christians to get involved politically, to really think about choices before them when they step into the ballot box. . . ."

Allen tends to be politically as well as theologically conservative, yet he is on the mailing lists, for instance, of both the Christian Coalition and the American Civil Liberties Union. Allen believes, for instance, that the abortion problem relates to basic cultural issues and cannot be eliminated by legislation. He also believes we must reduce welfare, yet it must be done compassionately. Regarding the Christian Coalition, he stated that they are working for some important goals, but he is suspicious that the leaders do some things just to gain influence. Ultimately, Allen said, politics requires compromises.

Others expressed views inconsistent with a political movement to create a Christian society. Sarah emphasized her belief in the Bible and her moral conservatism, but said, "I vote my conscience, and I vote after I've made choices based on what I believe and what I think is right and wrong, and I don't care what the church says." As Bart said, "I believe as Christians we should let our views be known, but once again I'm not one to hit people over the head with it. You don't have to believe something because I do. If I'm living and it works, people can tell."

An essential aspect of Truth Church is a belief that certain moral norms are clear and require acceptance. In a sermon, the pastor "warned the congregation against accepting new or 'liberal' ideas on social issues. Abortion, homosexuality, and divorce are three specific issues the pastor said people should be strongly against because they are against the word of God."[12] Such convictions, until recently, were a widely accepted, socially established dogma. In the United States, this is no longer true. Truth Church is important as a countercultural bastion, a place where conservative morality is unquestioned. Allen noted that conservative churches are coming together; evangelicals are working even with Catholics – "because of a sense of I don't know what – circling the wagons." Certainly the people at both Spirited and Truth churches would come together around the issues of abortion, homosexuality, and divorce. Yet none of the interviewees at Truth Church said that an interest in the religious right was related to the choice of Truth Church. Some people at this church do want a government along the lines proposed by the Christian Coalition. However, libertarian viewpoints also exist within the congregation, limiting any corporate support for the religious right.

In sum, Truth Church is not like the congregation at Bob Jones University. Truth allows greater diversity of belief, accepts varied levels of commitment, does not privilege direct evangelism, and is not part of

12. This comment is from a student's report, Kevin McElmurry's "Observations at Truth Church." Phylis gave the longest list of issues: abortion, premarital sex, marrying divorced persons, smoking, and drinking. Other respondents, however, expressed moderate views on the last two issues. According to a church leader, smoking is not opposed on theological grounds, and while drunkenness is wrong, simply drinking alcoholic beverages is not.

the religious right. As the church's denominational brochure reads, "We are 'conservative,' but not old-fashioned."

When I asked the associate pastor at Truth Church about its popularity, he made the point that (like Spirited Church) Truth Church's more popular Sunday morning service was so full as to inhibit further growth. As to Truth's appeal, the pastor simply emphasized that people want to hear the good news that salvation is possible through Jesus Christ. In response to this and other questions I posed, the pastor developed some distinctive traits of Truth Church: Salvation is possible *only* through Jesus Christ, the congregational identity includes being countercultural (for instance, regarding abortion), and the church rejects both legalism and separation from the world. Appropriately, the pastor emphasized beliefs. He also differentiated Truth Church from the classical traditionalist Protestant congregation. Indeed, his analysis is quite consistent with my own. Truth Church is a modernized calvinist congregation. On the one hand, Truth Church stands for authoritative religion. On the other hand, it allows significant diversity of theological belief, personal commitment, evangelizing style, and church-state viewpoint. It is this combination that explains the appeal of Truth Church.

PROBLEMATIC ASPECTS OF CALVINISTIC CHRISTIANITY

I will discuss predestination, enthusiastic rituals, and a caring congregation.

PREDESTINATION

I learned the opinion of eleven people about predestination: Four accepted it, three accepted but with some reservation, and four rejected it.

Allen was raised in the Arminian tradition, in which people often speak of "accepting" Christ, implying that salvation resulted from their decisions. But Allen now believes that the doctrine of election is more consistent with the nature of God and of human nature: "The problem with the notion of 'I accepted Christ' (is) that somehow I elevated myself out of my sinful nature." I asked Allen how his family reacted to his conversion:

"No problem," said Allen. "In fact, they've really enjoyed coming down here and going to church with us . . . the criteria in my family is 'does the church preach the Bible?' 'Does the church operate from the point of view that the Bible is God's Word and that it is to be believed?' You know, in earlier years, earlier centuries, the Arminian-Calvinist divide was much more serious in terms of what it meant for people's lives and finding families and stuff, but there is this sense in which the conservative church in America is closing ranks."

What is really important to Allen, as for his family, is the view of scripture and not whether Truth Church is Arminian or Calvinist: "What you have is a different view of some aspects of the Scriptures, but an agreed sense that the Scriptures are true. . . ."

Although Truth Church is a part of a calvinistic denomination, some interviewees rejected the theology of Calvin. As one person said,

"I am an Arminian in theological thinking. I don't believe in predestination. When it comes to a personal relationship with Jesus Christ, I believe that the human will is involved, and that we as individuals have to choose for our own selves whether to accept the grace of God. . . ."

But his disagreement with the church's official position is not a big problem, he said, because predestination is not discussed much from the pulpit.

Another respondent did not reject predestination, but its implications are difficult for her to accept. She fears for the fate of the people she loves. Are her children predestined for heaven? Hopefully so, but the possibility that she cannot help her children gain salvation disturbs her greatly.

Raised a Baptist, Sarah found predestination a troubling notion, but she gave the issue much study. Then Sarah reached a crucial point:

" . . . you read that one statement," said Sarah, "and it just sort of pulls it all together for you, and that pivotal statement was that if God chooses those people who will go to heaven, then He also chooses those people who will go to hell. And my understanding of God and my understanding of the universe and the world is that while I don't understand it all, there is a logic to it . . . what I know about a loving God and a forgiving God, and an accepting

God no matter even though He gets angry and all that jazz, too, those two things don't work together."

Bart told me that Arminianism makes each responsible for the salvation of all, and that, he felt, is "a difficult thing to carry around." He went on to explain that he probably is neither fully Arminian nor fully Calvinistic:

> "The more Arminian you are," said Bart, "the more you feel how important it is to be preaching the gospel . . . to people. The more Calvinist you are, the more you believe you should be going out and showing your care and concern for the world and then you give yourself. For us [he and his wife], we're somewhere in the middle. . . ."

In sum, predestination was difficult to accept because it eliminates choice, because it means we cannot help our loved ones to achieve salvation, and because the doctrine is not consistent with the image of a loving God. However, predestination does relieve people of the burden of holding themselves responsible for everyone's salvation.

The issue is the lack of fit between calvinism and American culture. When I asked Beth about predestination, she said she is "on the fence." She believes there are biblical statements favoring predestination and there are other statements consistent with Arminianism; she concluded God is purposely unclear. In fact, Christianity has been on the fence; theologians have not agreed on a doctrine that simultaneously acknowledges God's power and human freedom, and some theologians perceive the dilemma as an eternal mystery. But the issue is not just the age-old one of can God's sovereignty be limited. In the American context, predestination is inconsistent with the cultural importance of libertarianism. Individuals in our study found it hard to believe that destiny ought not to be the result of individual choices.

ENTHUSIASTIC RITUAL

Some respondents actually preferred the enthusiastic style. As one person told me about a previous church he attended that had an enthusiastic praise worship, "I came to really appreciate being able to express my own self in worship. . . and that freedom doesn't exist at Truth Church." At his previous church, there was "a lot of raising of hands, clapping, a lot of agreement from the congregation with what was being said or presented, sung, from the platform. In a certain way it was more reaffirming, more encouraging actually than the experience at Truth Church." At Truth Church, said another interviewee, the ritual "is very much from the platform directed out." In a charismatic service, influence flows both ways. She enjoyed being able to express herself in worship, and "that freedom doesn't exist at Truth Church."

Several respondents who had visited Spirited Church preferred its energetic praise service because it creates a sense of being free. For them, the nonsermon part of the service was preferable at Spirited Church, but the sermon part was preferable at Truth Church. Obviously for such people, the quality of the sermons carried the day.

A CARING CHURCH

Outside the sanctuary, the pastor is a good shepherd. He calls people or sends them cards for important moments. As an interviewee said, "If he knows that you're going through a struggle or a difficulty, he'll just call to check up and see how you're doing, and see if there is anything that can be done to help out." The pastor visited Jenny once. "It was almost like I was meeting a friend instead of a pastor. That was kind of neat, too, and he's been very helpful and real friendly and everything so that's why I started [attending the church]."

When Jenny heard about the beliefs of Truth Church, she concluded they were basically what she already believed, with one exception: the belief that women cannot hold positions of authority.[13] Once she had been in a Methodist church, whose female pastor had been a dear friend, so she believes that women may hold positions of authority in the church. Jenny believes the pastor does not fully accept his church's belief about female leadership, "but it is the doctrine of the church, so, and it's nothing, I mean if that's the only thing I could disagree with, I figure this was a pretty good church for me. . . . "

13. Jenny was younger than forty and is highly educated.

As it turned out, however, the role of women is not the only subject on which Jenny is not in the church's mainstream. She is moderately prochoice:

Jenny does not believe in using abortion for birth control but believes there are cases in which abortion would be justified. At Truth Church, people are not hostile to her, as they had been earlier at a Methodist church, because of her ideas about abortion. At Truth Church, people understand that she has reasons for her belief. They have been supportive and concerned about her.

As a teenager, Jenny was involved in a conservative Southern Baptist church – "no dancing, no rock-n-roll, no card playing, girls all wore dresses." She still loves Southern gospel music. What Jenny remembers most happily were the uplifting verses she was made to memorize – "comfort verses," she called them, like the twenty-third Psalm. At my request, she recited. "The Lord is my shepherd and I shall not want; He maketh me to lie down beside green pastures; His rod and His staff comfort me; He giveth me, you know, comforteth me in the presence of my enemies." When Jenny was sick, the aforementioned Methodist female pastor consoled her with biblical verse; "I think she must have been a Baptist at heart." The pastor read from Ecclesiastes; " 'there's a time for everything, you know, a time to live, a time to die, a time to grieve, a time to enjoy.' You know, it was real helpful. . . . "

Members at Truth Church seem to have avoided being self-righteous, yet we might well wonder why Jenny attends Truth Church. The answer concerns the people at the church. Discussing a carry-in dinner at church, Jenny said,

". . . even if you don't discuss church or, you know, your beliefs or anything, it's just a warm fuzzy feeling to get together with people who like you unconditionally and who like that funny-looking ["fiesta"] pasta salad you brought in, or if they didn't, they would never tell you. They would have at least one helping of it."

The pastor and the people at Truth Church are caring. They place comforting others ahead of judging others. One consequence is the attraction to a theologically oriented church of people who are probably misfits:

> Truth Church was the first church that Ralph ever attended.[14] He came to church at the urging of a friend, a church member, at a time when he was feeling lonely and distraught about the way he was living. Initially Ralph came with the friend and his family, then as he met people, he felt more comfortable joining in various activities, including the singles group, and finally he began attending on his own. His social calendar filled up.
>
> As Ralph said, he wanted to "break out" of his lifestyle, but he needed help. The pastor, with whom Ralph had a personal meeting to discuss his problems, exemplified the "personal fortitude" he needed. His new friends supported his change. Moreover, when he discussed his past life, they accepted him and his past.
>
> Ralph will likely leave town in the near future, so I asked him what he would be looking for in a new church. He would want a "middle-of-the-road" church such as Truth Church. Ralph was referring to his experiences when he visited two other churches with yet another friend before settling in at Truth Church. A mainline church was too formal; on his one visit, no one greeted him. The other visit was to Spirited Church; the environment and the ritual were not his idea of "church"; for instance, portable chairs were used, people wore jeans, and guitars produced loud music. He perceives Truth Church as expressing a degree of formality midway between the other two churches. A combination of friendliness and formality makes Ralph comfortable. Thus in choosing a new church, "comfort-fit" would take precedence over theology.

What is significant is how little Ralph seems committed to Truth's theology. He had wanted to change his lifestyle. Ralph apparently needed firm guidance (from the pastor) and a new personal network that encourages and supports change. He was lonely and wanted a new life. The church became a source of friends, and its conservative theology appropriately emphasized breaking with the things of the world. The same traits could characterize any conservative congregation.

Ralph referred to Truth Church as a middle-of-the-road church. Jenny told me, "I really didn't think of Truth Church as a conservative church."

---

14. Ralph was younger than forty and is highly educated.

Neither one seems ideally suited to Truth Church. Jenny is theologically out of step at Truth Church, and Ralph is unconcerned about theology. They are there because this conservative church provides a warm environment. In a congregation that stresses theology, the presence of such people is as much a sign of organizational weakness as of strength.

The interest in a caring environment was a secondary theme in the stories of other people who talked about the discussion groups at Truth Church. Such groups are valued, in part, because they hold participants accountable (a frequently used word among the respondents) for living by biblical rules. In addition, the fellowship itself is important; participants wanted to make friends and be in a familylike environment. When Ruth moved to Middletown, she appreciated the social aspect of the small groups. As she said, "They do encourage a lot of Bible study in small groups, and that is just another way of bonding and reaching out, and we just felt that those things helped to meet our needs since we just really felt like we were in a foreign country." Another interviewee especially enjoyed the Men's Bible study group, where he made some good friends. As he said, "So it's good to get to know people and establish those relationships and start to make church a family rather than just a religious expression . . . the fellowship aspect along with the worship is just really important to us."

In several ways, then, Truth Church seemed inappropriate for the people with whom I talked. First, predestination clashed with libertarian sentiments. Moreover, the doctrine forces people to accept that their loved ones may be eternally damned and that they can do nothing to help them – a very distressing way to live. For instance, a mother does not want to believe she is helpless to aid her children in reaching heaven. Similarly, if people perceive God as a loving figure, they do not want to believe He has not chosen people for heaven. Second, the solemn ritual was not appreciated by those who wanted to be more personally expressive in church. Third, some people are attracted to Truth Church not because of its truth but because the pastor and people have created a caring environment.

Of the eighteen respondents, seven were members, six were not; I did not ask five people about their status. In all, ten of the interviewees fit into one or more of the aforementioned three categories; I specifically asked seven of them if they were members, and five had not yet joined Truth Church.

The problematic aspects of Truth Church are rooted in its inadequate accommodation of modernity. Both predestination and solemn rituals

are inconsistent with individualism. The church's stress on authoritativeness has meant that creating a therapeutic environment, although it
does exist, is not clearly a part of the congregation's identity; as a result,
people drawn to Truth Church by the caring people there may at some
point feel out of place.

CONCLUSION

Truth Church is part of a universe of conservative churches that is
defined most obviously by the assumptions that the Bible is true and
knowable. Sermons are biblical lessons. Bible classes, especially for the
young, emphasize learning the rules for biblical living. Congregants are
expected to immerse themselves in the life of the church and to base
their lives on the Bible.

However, Truth Church and Spirited Church are different models of contemporary conservatism. Whereas the latter illustrates the
charismatic type, as discussed in Chapter 3, Truth Church exemplifies a calvinist type (see Table 4). Whereas Spirited's theology focuses
on each person's spiritual relationship, Truth emphasizes the creation
of a Christian society. Whereas Spirited's theology implicitly encourages ultrasupernaturalism, Truth's theology can be used to legitimate
dedifferentiating church and state as well as centering society's culture
on religion. While Spirited downplays or criticizes denominational differences, Truth is committed to its denominational heritage. Truth's
theology is identified with a specific denomination and implicitly affirms the individual's need for pastoral guidance and the obligation for
worldly involvement. Although both churches require potential members to present evidence that they are committed to God, they also differ
regarding membership criteria, with Truth giving more importance to
accepting the denomination's creed.

Whereas Spirited's ritual encourages self-expression and feeling the
Spirit, Truth's ritual is conducive to self-control and creating a reverential atmosphere. Whereas Spirited's pastor is respected for being
inspired by the Spirit, Truth's minister is respected for his biblical expertise. (However, when some suggested to Truth's pastor that the sermons are too long, he responded that you "can't quench the Spirit,"
meaning that if he gets carried away, it is because he is Spirit-filled.)
While Spirited Church is pastor-led, Truth Church is a representative
democracy. While both churches accept diverse evangelizing styles,
those at Spirited Church include more personal ones, such as street

Table 4. Two Types of Modernized Traditionalist Protestantism

Trait	Charismatic Church	Calvinist Church
Theology	Enthusiasm • develop a personal spiritual relationship • extreme: ultrasupernaturalism Restorationist • one church	Calvinist • create a Christian society • extreme: theoracy Denominational • unique heritage
Ritual	Spirit-filled • self-expression • applause • exciting music • feel joy	Solemn • self-restraint • no applause • calming music • feel awe
Pastor	Spirit-directed	Word-directed scholar
Organization	Charismatic authority	Institutional authority
Evangelism	Street Servant Lifestyle	Institutional Lifestyle
Politics	Minimize the role of government	Representative democracy is God's preferred form

and servant evangelizing. Regarding politics, whereas Spirited deplores dependence on a government, Truth Church tends to focus on the legitimacy of government and trying to ensure that it is led by good Christians.

In a calvinist-type church, social change is more the point than personal change. To put it starkly, Truth Church serves better those who are worried more about social decline than personal regeneration. Only one person told the following kind of anecdote, but I think it is a revealing one. Beth and her husband had attended a Wesleyan church before coming to Truth Church.[15] At the end of each Wesleyan service, there was an altar call. People were invited to come forward to express their commitment to Jesus. This event disturbed Beth and her husband because it seemed that every Sunday the church was questioning their religiosity. They could not confidently feel they were good Christians. Altar calls do not occur at Truth Church. Those at Sunday service can feel confident they are saved Christians. As a staff member told me, the equivalent of the altar call at Truth Church is a private meeting with a staff member. The Sunday service is for

15. Beth was over forty and is highly educated.

believers to worship God. In a solemn ritual, the focus is not on the individual sinner but on God, who is being worshipped by the assembly of people.

Truth Church seems ideal for the Allens, Phylises, and Sarahs of the world: people who go to church to support a Christian counterculture. In contrast, the Ruths and Edys would seem to be types of people more easily drawn to charismatic congregations. They can feel comfortable at Truth Church, I believe, because of the prevalence of the theme "Jesus loves me" in contemporary American Protestantism. Thus Truth Church supports the image of a loving relationship with Jesus. In his sermon on a growing church, the pastor said that in such a place people do not serve out of guilt. "It is joy and is a kind of joy that comes from that relationship with Christ that makes us want to honor Him and serve Him and make His church grow, because she is His bride. He loves her, and we love her, too, because we love Jesus." But congregational members may focus on this loving relationship, relegating the search for truth to a secondary status. For Ruth and Edy, religion means their personal relationships with God. Scriptural knowledge and rules are important because they show these women how to express concretely their personal relationship with Jesus. Whereas in his sermon on church growth the pastor spoke about people "in love with the Word of God," some congregants think mainly of their love for Jesus.

As I have discussed, calvinist congregations lost their share of the religious market during early-modernity. Given the cultural importance of libertarianism, this decline is not surprising. Moreover, the American emphasis on the individual means that people would have been more likely to turn to religion for personal transformation than out of a desire to promote social change, and enthusiastic congregations are more appealing to personally troubled people than calvinist ones because, as I discussed in Chapter 2, not only do they expect profound personal change but their rituals are structured to encourage and confirm such change.

My analysis, moreover, suggests that even modernized calvinist churches such as Truth Church will be less successful than charismatic congregations. The doctrine of predestination continues to be difficult to accept for people raised in a culture influenced by libertarianism. In late-modern times, calvinist churches have an additional problem: The image of God conveyed by the doctrine of predestination does not fit late-modern culture.

A God responsible for predestination is inconsistent with a therapeutic God. Mark Coppenger, the president of a Southern Baptist seminary, argued that "moderates" in the denomination are critical of calvinism because it "is the antithesis of their notion of God as a sensitive guy" (Coppenger 1998:2). Such a "guy," "very easily, gets in touch with his inner child...does at least half the housework (even when Mom has no outside job)...," and so forth. Coppenger then asserts that the "sensitive guy" is really the "hypersensitive guy" whose opposite is not the insensitive guy but the normally sensitive guy. The calvinist God "can be wrathful, revolted by sin and sinner, and perfectly capable of damning folks to eternal torment" (p. 2).

But such a god is rapidly becoming a misfit. As I have discussed earlier, late-modernity has meant that values on the periphery of culture have entered its core. Personal relationships are to be therapeutic. People should enjoy life in this world. Correspondingly, spirituality should result in peace and happiness. People want an intimate, emotional relationship with God; they want to feel close to and loved by God. As some respondents at Truth Church told us, the god of predestination is not consistent with their belief in a loving deity.

This problem is a sign of the general situation that modernized calvinist churches are less consistent with late-modern values than charismatic ones. An emphasis on denominational creeds and solemn rituals gives people less opportunity to be themselves. Moreover, having fun seems less important at calvinist churches, judging by the emphasis on a reverential attitude during church services and the use of impersonal forms of outreach at Truth Church. Thus, contemporary calvinist churches not only continue to lag behind charismatic ones in accommodating libertarianism, they now also are behind in accommodating late-modern values as well. Because modernized calvinist congregations are less congruent than charismatic ones with libertarianism, Third Force Psychology, and the affluence ethic, I believe the calvinist churches will be less successful in late-modern society.

While Spirited and Truth churches may be studied as examples of different types of churches, both of them are distancing themselves from the Bob Jones University type. Truth Church is not a "cult"; individuals do think for themselves, and all do not think alike.[16] Some degree of religious libertarianism is evident in Truth Church. As a church leader told me, people join Truth Church because they want the truth;

16. Ruth admitted she and her husband see a little more freedom in lifestyle at Truth Church than they would prefer. But maybe a freer culture works better with today's kids, "maybe there won't be so much rebellion."

avoiding relativism is the issue, but a certain freedom of interpretation is granted to all. While denominational heritage is important, the pastor said, denominational boundaries are not meant to denigrate others or to prevent contact with them. Moreover, as I have pointed out, the church tolerates varied levels of commitment among participants, encourages diverse forms of evangelism, and does not participate in the religious right. In the next chapter, I more systematically discuss what distinguishes the conservative congregations I studied from traditionalist Protestantism.

CHAPTER FIVE

CARING CHURCH

The third conservative church we studied was a Holiness church not un-like the Church of the Nazarene discussed in Chapter 2. However, unlike the people I talked with back in the 1950s, those at Caring Church with whom Peggy discussed religion were well educated (see Table 2). One of the questions to be considered is, what does a middle-class Holiness con-gregation look like? Beyond describing our third example of conservative Protestantism, I want to emphasize in this chapter the commonalities of all three churches. Thus I conclude this chapter with a comparison of a traditionalist Protestant congregation (the Bob Jones University model) and what I call the modernized traditionalist Protestant type as illustrated by Spirited, Truth, and Caring churches.

In 1996, when our interviews took place, about four hundred people attended a Sunday service at Caring Church. Two years later, the figure was just over five hundred. What made Caring Church an attractive congregation?

THE CHURCH OF GOD MOVEMENT AND CARING CHURCH

More than the other two conservative churches, Caring Church shows the influence of the dissenting tradition. This congregation is part of the Church of God (Anderson, Indiana), a religious movement dating back to the 1880s. As a church pamphlet reads, "We do not consider ourselves to be another denomination, with a prescribed creed and an unbending organizational structure. Neither are we a sect with legalistic statements on, and enforcement of lifestyles" (Withrow and Withrow n.d.:8). The Church of God movement believes the Bible is the inspired Word of God. However, the movement does not reduce the biblical stories and teachings to a creed. Diversity is accepted. "Conformity in all matters of doctrine and practice is not the goal . . ." (p. 24). Anyone who accepts Jesus Christ is eligible to be a church member. A person need only inform a pastor that she or he is a disciple of Christ. "One maintains membership by participating in the worship services and fellowship of the congregation" (p. 10). Each congregation defines for itself its voting membership using age and length of time a person has been worshiping with the group.

The Church of God (Anderson, Indiana) is part of the Holiness movement and thus emphasizes leading a Spirit-filled life, that is, being sanctified (Ronald A. Knox's ultrasupernaturalism). This means that the Spirit purifies the mind and habits of the believer for God's use; the believer commits the self to God for His use, accepts God's calling to evangelize and serve, and leads a holy life. Doctrine is not of primary importance. The focus is on piety, on the relationship with Christ, and on how Christlike people are toward others. The back of the Sunday brochure contains a short paragraph that begins, "Welcome to a church where you can sense the presence of God." This idea was repeated in the interviews. Caring Church emphasizes the spiritual relationship.

Churches of God are not Pentecostal, so they do not encourage speaking in tongues as a sign of a Spirit-filled life. The movement does believe in divine healing. "In many congregations persons come forward following the sermon and request that the pastor anoint and pray for them" (Withrow and Withrow n.d.:27). I witnessed such a scene at Caring Church. During the anointing, the pastor emphasized the power of the prayer.

The pattern of the Sunday service approximates the ritual at Spirited Church. The "welcome" and invocation, at the beginning of the service, might be done by an associate pastor, one of whom was a woman at the time I studied the congregation. About thirty minutes of music, a scriptural reading, and the "sharing of God's message" are the major components of the service. However, prior to the sermon, a pastor leads the "Congregational Prayer," which mentions the needs of specific people. Then there is an open altar, an invitation for anyone to come forward to request prayers for themselves or others. After the sermon there are "moments of response," when the altars are again open for prayer.

The atmosphere is casual. There is no strict dress code; older men tend to be in jackets and ties, whereas younger people sometimes dress quite casually, perhaps wearing jeans. Women are not expected to dress in a gender-specific manner. Preaching by a woman would be possible at Caring Church.

A lectern is on the platform in the front of the church, but the pastor uses a lapel microphone and roams the platform. The atmosphere is relaxed, with no "air of stuffy perfectionism." As one person said, in churches with highly structured rituals and formally robed pastors, if a baby cries out, even the people get annoyed; at Caring Church the pastor is flexible and easygoing; if a baby cried, he would praise God for it.

The music is quite enjoyable. The choir leader, the choir itself, and numerous individual performers are very talented. When I visited, the program included a twenty-member choir in robes and an eight-piece band. The music is eclectic, tilting toward the contemporary – no Bach organ music. The choir is energetic; as one respondent said, "They are all white but they sound very black." A contemporary air comes through in the upbeat music, the enthusiasm of the choir, and the modest expressiveness (some hand-clapping with the music, an occasional "amen") of the congregation.

But musically no one would mistake Caring Church for Spirited Church. Ida had visited Spirited Church before choosing Caring Church.[1] Although she liked several aspects of the Spirited congregation, she found the style to be too much like entertainment. The music did not put her in a worshipful mood. Indeed, the music program at Caring does not remind one of a rock concert, as was said of Spirited's ritual. Because of the stylistically varied music program, Ida described Caring Church as "updated traditional." Caring Church may be ritually conservative within its denomination. Within the movement, "Spontaneity marks many of our services. In some congregations persons will affirm the message of the pastor or a song with an 'Amen!' Occasionally persons may respond to a well-sung song, greet special guests, or receive an important announcement with applause" (Withrow and Withrow n.d.:28). The people at Caring Church may be a little more reserved than those at a typical Church of God congregation.

As at Spirited Church, the bulletin contains the biblical references for the day and a place to take notes. Harry and Lela compared Caring's sermons with those at a Methodist church they had attended.[2] The pastor preaches from the Bible as did their old Methodist minister.

---

1. Ida was over forty.
2. Both Lela and Harry were over forty and are highly educated.

(Harry noted that unlike his old church, Caring Church does not provide Bibles in the pew racks; you are expected to bring your own Bible.)
The difference in the preaching is in the mix of Bible instruction and
personal stories. The Methodist minister tilted toward the latter, giving
the impression of using filler material, of drifting. The Caring pastor
sticks more continuously to explaining the scripture and how it relates
to how you are living. The emphasis is on Christian action.

The pastors at both Spirited and Caring churches were described as
being led by God. Though the church program says that the pastor is
going to do one sermon, and though he may actually start that sermon,
Caring's pastor may change the topic along the way because God directed
him to do so. Several people at Caring Church said they feel that God
is in the pastor's life. Each week he shares something going on in his
life. He is not just quoting the Bible, giving a talk on some theme set
by higher authorities. Listening to preachers at other churches, you may
never know anything about them personally. At Caring Church, you
experience the pastor's spiritual growth.

In sum, Caring Church is (in my terms) a dissenting, charismatic
congregation. Caring differs from Spirited Church in several ways. For
instance, church boundaries are less strong at Caring Church, which, I
shall now argue, contributes to its popularity. (I recall that all indented
material is my paraphrasing of the interviewees' comments unless the
material is in quotation marks.)

CONGREGATIONAL BOUNDARIES

Grace had switched to Caring Church from a congregation that she said
had no boundaries[3]:

> Grace had been raised in a conservative church. Upon marriage,
> she joined her husband's mainline congregation. They attended for
> several years, but Grace was never comfortable at this church be-
> cause the pastor was too liberal. The first time Grace attended Sun-
> day service at the church, she forgot her Bible. This deeply troubled
> her. The pastor's wife told her not to worry about it, since attendees
> don't need a Bible there. This attitude took Grace aback. She won-
> dered why she didn't need her Bible. The pastor did preach from the
> Bible, but the church was more this-worldly than other-worldly.

3. Grace was younger than forty.

An especially upsetting event concerned homosexuality. Many groups held their meetings at the mainline church even though they were not formally affiliated with the church. For instance, a support group for abused women met at the church. Grace became upset when a support group for homosexuals asked to meet there. The pastor supported the request. Grace understood the group to favor homosexuality, and feared the church premises would become a pickup place for homosexuals. In fact, the matter never came to a head because the support group chose to meet elsewhere.

Grace understood this event to symbolize the pastor's lack of standards. He had tolerance for everything – "nothing was really ever wrong." No lines were drawn.

The pastor even accepted Unitarian-Universalists, who believe in everything, which means they do not believe in anything. The Bible is clear that the only way to God is through Jesus Christ. You either do or do not believe in the divinity of Christ and your need for Him. You must take a stand. But the mainline pastor seemed to say that if a person can justify what he believes or does, the pastor would accept it too. There were things he considered wrong, "but he was such an accepting person that it didn't seem that there were any boundaries."

Another source of frustration for Grace was that the mainline church was more a social thing. As she used the term, "social" was opposed to spiritual. Grace was not happy that the pastor devoted so many sermons to social issues. The lack of spirituality was especially evident among the members of the congregation.

At Caring Church, if she has a problem, she can stop anyone there and ask the person to pray over it with her. They would stop whatever they were doing and pray with her, because they realized the importance of prayer. At the mainline church, she could never request such prayer support because churchgoing was more of a social get-together. She could have asked, and the congregants would have prayed with her, but Grace would have felt it was superficial. They were not prayer warriors. They might feel compassion at her plight, but they were not taught to make prayer an integral part of their lives.

Grace now prays at least daily. She knows there is prayer support in the church and she asks for it. Grace loves the prayer time during the Sunday service. People pray spontaneously, which Grace thinks evidences their sincerity.

Grace is a much happier person. She loves the people and the pastor. He is a tender, compassionate person very accepting of others, and he has standards. He is not wishy-washy. If a point is scriptural, he will affirm it even if he has to step on people's toes.

Grace made clear her need for a conservative congregation. In effect, she defined the boundaries of conservative Protestantism. Salvation can come only through Jesus Christ; a congregation must take a clear stand on this matter. A conservative church is other-worldly–oriented. The Bible is the key to everything; everyone needs a personal Bible. Sermons should be about the supernatural, not social issues; spirituality gets expressed in prayer, that is, by communicating with God. A conservative congregation must also have moral standards, such as the condemnation of homosexuality. It is unacceptable to tolerate someone's moral conviction just because it was sincerely formed. In Grace's view, Caring Church has all these traits.

Others we talked with put more emphasis on how Caring Church diverged from the traditional model. For example, Carla described her former congregation, which was also part of the Church of God movement, as more traditional because people were expected to conform to an official code.[4] At Caring Church, there is more diversity – "they're just very accepting of different people and the differences in people." In fact, the people we talked with had varied ideas about the literal truth of the Bible. They tended to accept the holy book as true, but not always literally so. For instance, Vera said that Caring Church follows a literal interpretation of the Bible, but when asked whether the congregation believes that a "day" in the creation story is the same as our "day," she emphatically said the church is not *that* literal.[5] Vera does believe that miracles really happened. She also believes in evolution, and thinks that is the belief of Caring Church as well, though if individuals rejected evolution, Vera does not believe that would bother the pastor.

Paul explained the situation this way[6]: The church's emphasis is not on doctrine; the leaders allow some diversity in biblical interpretation. For one thing, a "day" in the creation story need not be understood as meaning our day. For another thing, the pastor is a-millennial, and if you are a strict literalist you must be a millennialist because of the statement

---

4. Carla was over forty and is highly educated.
5. Vera was younger than forty and is highly educated.
6. Paul was younger than forty and is highly educated.

in Revelations 20.[7] Paul compared the church's position with an event he witnessed in a Methodist church. The Methodist preacher read a passage from the Old Testament. His commentary included his refusal to accept a God who punishes children for the sins of their fathers. He did not try to understand who God is as God had presented Himself in Scripture, wrestling with the issues raised by what God had said. Instead, Paul said, the preacher defined God by his own criteria.

This story brought to Paul's mind a recent debate in the United Methodist Church about whether to recognize same-sex marriages. If you support such unions, you have to use "pretty loose" interpretations of the Bible. The "liberal elements" inside the Methodist Church did not win acceptance of same-sex marriages. However, such infighting would not even take place in the Church of God, Paul said, because it does not include a significant number of "far-left" people. When it comes to matters that are "plain," such as that homosexuals will not inherit the kingdom of God, the church takes a literal position.

Diversity does exist about some lifestyle rules. Ida believed that Caring Church is against drinking and smoking. But as Ida's interviewer, Peggy, wrote in her analysis, "It's interesting that she stated that Caring Church was against smoking and drinking and yet other interviewees have said that what they like about Caring Church is that it is not at all judgmental and that they can feel free to enjoy an occasional drink without feeling guilty."[8]

The image of Caring Church seems a bit blurry, which suited Wilma[9]:

> Wilma had attended a mainline church. She left because the church was too conservative. She needed to be in a more tolerant church whose priorities were closer to her own. At her old church, ordaining gay ministers became a big deal. Wilma believes that as long as people are starving to death, as long as young girls are

---

7. The Church of God movement is a-millennial. They view scriptures, such as Revelation 20, that speak of last things, as figurative. "Most Church of God congregations accept a range of opinions and beliefs on 'last things'" (Withrow and Withrow n.d.:28).

8. The movement does favor abstaining from drugs and sexual immorality. "We see our bodies as 'temples of the Holy Spirit' and therefore urge abstinence from some specific behaviors such as the use of alcoholic beverages, tobacco, drugs for pleasure or psychological escape, and indulgence in sexual immorality (1 Corinthians 6:15, 19–20)" (Withrow and Withrow n.d.:24).

9. Wilma was younger than forty and is highly educated.

having babies, a church must see that there are bigger problems than whether a gay person may lead a church service.

Wilma knows Caring Church is against homosexuality, but it is not like the narrow, bigoted atmosphere at her old church. Wilma herself is a conservative person. For instance, while abortion sometimes may be the necessary thing to do, generally she is prolife and certainly is against the use of abortion as a means of birth control. Wilma's attitude is that you have to reserve *judgment* of specific people in such matters. She fears the butchery that will occur if abortion is made illegal. Perhaps fortunately, the issue has not come up at church, although a table was set up at church one Sunday where people could sign up for a prolife Walk for Life.

Importantly, she has found little at Caring Church that offends her. The pastors and people do not dwell on the negative side, on arousing guilt. Peggy asked Wilma if the people have a literal understanding of the Bible. "They take it not literally, but they take it as fact, they take it as God's word handed down. Almost, *almost* as if it were written by the inky finger of God." But they try to interpret biblical statements in the context of the time they were written.

Wilma admitted, "I am a little afraid to delve too deeply; if I knew more than I know, I might feel differently." Not much sermon time has concerned the Old Testament, which contains descriptions that bother Wilma, such as when God hardened Pharaoh's heart. Why would He do that? Nor has the pastor gone into irritating issues such as not letting women preach. If people are against this, they should be consistent and, as the Apostle Paul advised, not let women cut their hair.

Peggy Shaffer, the interviewer, wrote this comment:

Wilma is not the typical Caring Churcher. . . . And she knows it. As I was leaving she said that she was "shocked" to find herself attending such a conservative church and she was "attending with trepidation," afraid that the church would do something so conservative that she would have to respond. She hopes this doesn't happen because she likes going there.

Wilma does not want to be in a congregation that builds its identity on forbidding gay ordinations, outlawing all abortions, or limiting the religious role of women. She ended the interview with Peggy by saying she sincerely hopes that the church is not involved with the Christian Right. Wilma worries, however, that she may find out that many people she likes and respects are rightists.

As in the other congregations we studied, the people at Caring Church are not generally supporters of the religious right, although Paul (whom we met earlier) expressed an attitude that would probably find some support. Paul sees himself as part of a saving remnant. Few people go to heaven because so many have hardened hearts. It is "difficult to stand up for the truth in a dying world," and so he appreciates that the Christian Right has organized to fight the power of the very liberal media. The country has drifted dangerously to the left. But, Paul said, the "hard-lineism" and drive for power of the Christian Right make conservative Christianity appear cold, giving people a poor impression of his form of Christianity. Wilma is not likely to be turned off by such ambiguous support for the religious right.

In sum, while Caring Church has boundaries, they are not strong. Caring does not interpret the Bible literally, as does Spirited Church, and Caring does not stress denominational beliefs, as does Truth Church. Morally, while most participants probably have similarly conservative views on issues such as abortion, a person such as Wilma, who wants to refrain from judging specific people who violate the rule against abortion, can enjoy Caring Church. Such relatively weak boundaries are consistent with an emphasis on the spiritual relationship.

In a recent article, a conservative scholar, Roger E. Olson (1998), analyzed the division within conservatism (or in his terms "evangelical Christianity"). "Traditionalists" have and use specific criteria for deciding what or who is "in" and what or who is "out." They view theologies other than their own as false and feel obliged to expose them as heresy. Olson's traditionalists maintain, as he put it, "strong boundaries," by admitting of no fundamental doubts or ambiguities and by rejecting pluralism. Caring Church would not be part of the traditionalist camp. Moreover, and this is the critical point, it is because the church has blurred boundaries that it is appealing to some people.

The absence of strong boundaries is not surprising since Caring Church is part of a movement that exists as a protest against creeds and rules for membership. The people whom we interviewed at Caring Church came from a variety of religious backgrounds. One had been a Catholic, four came from mainline Protestant churches (three of them from Methodist churches), five had been going to other conservative churches, and three had been unchurched. Relatively blurred boundaries would explain this unusual diversity. Church-shoppers of varying degrees of conservatism can feel comfortable at Caring Church.

The absence of strong boundaries, then, contributes to the appeal of the congregation. However, what makes the church worthy of the participants' commitment is the communal nature of the congregation.

THE COMMUNAL ASPECT

The visitor's card, inserted into the Sunday bulletin, is the size of a postcard. In the upper-left corner is "We're Glad You're Here!" – in large deep black print. The paragraph next to this message begins as follows: "The Caring Church Family is delighted that you have joined us to worship today! We want you to consider yourself among friends who care."

The people with whom we talked described the atmosphere on Sunday morning as "welcoming" and "caring." People seem excited about newcomers. People greet newcomers, shake their hand, tell them how glad they are that the newcomers are there, and ask them to participate in things. The people go out of their way to remember names. One respondent said of her first visit, "I don't feel like I met a stranger that morning."

First-time visitors to Caring Church can expect an effective soft sell. There is no pressure. A plate of cookies will appear on the doorstep. Members of a welcoming team will call, asking if the newcomer needs anything or would like some information. A newsletter will begin to arrive from the church. The visitor may receive an invitation for dinner at the pastor's house, after which he will always call the visitor by first name. The approach works.

Ann moved to town and was looking for a church.[10] After visiting Caring Church, she received the dinner invitation from the pastor. She was reluctant to go but she went and to her surprise had a good time. Ann chose Caring Church because of the pastor. He makes you feel comfortable. The pastor is not pushy and does not preach *at* you. At other churches Ann had felt pressured. She likes to go at her own pace: "When I am ready to do something, I will do it." The pastor and the people show interest in newcomers but also seem to respect their autonomy.

---

10. Ann was younger than forty.

Here is the portrait of the pastor presented by our interviewees. What distinguishes the pastor at Caring Church is his personal openness. He listens. You can tell when another person is genuinely interested, when what you are saying is not going in one ear and out the other. He is someone to whom you can tell your troubles. He is open about himself and shares troubles he has had. The pastor speaks from experience, revealing a lot about himself and his personal history. He has suffered, and he is not above telling others what he has gone through. One respondent believed it to be significant that one day he saw the pastor cry about a tragic event.

Caring is an essential element of this church. People begin to feel it when they first visit, when they receive cookies, and when they dine with the pastor. The feeling of care comes out in the pastor's openness and in the prayerful concern of fellow members. The pastor's vulnerability allows listeners to identify with him and to believe he can empathize with them. At Caring Church, the boundary between pastor and people has been lowered.

Alex came into the congregation because of the love he found there:[11]

Alex had been unchurched for years. Shortly before his interview, he publicly rededicated himself to Christ during a Sunday service. Alex committed to Caring Church after the sudden death of his best friend. The friend had been a church member and had been gently urging Alex to join the church.

Alex said that his life has changed since he joined Caring Church. His problems do not seem so important. They are less traumatic because Alex knows he has Jesus's love and acceptance. At work, Alex may lose a power struggle – it would be devastating – but it would not be the end of the world. Such things are not that important anymore.

Alex is married. He and his wife are closer than ever since they are now together as Christians. They love each other, they love the Lord, and the Lord loves them. He and his wife have grown; neither is perfect, now they accept each other. If God can accept them, they can accept each other, weaknesses and all.

When praising Caring Church, Alex kept returning to themes of acceptance and compassion. For instance, people at church are farmers, factory workers, doctors, lawyers, and so forth, yet they all

11. Alex was over forty and is highly educated.

get along. Again, when people show an interest in Caring Church, the members do not pressure them to join; a plate of cookies appears on the doorstep, and a few calls will be made to inquire about how everyone is and to ask if the church members can do anything for them. As Alex said, the church brings you in with love.

After a few Sunday visits, Alex and his wife were invited for dinner at the pastor's house. They were uneasy, especially after seeing the imposing house. "Oh, it's going to be a long evening," said Alex, who comes from a working-class family. But in the end he and his wife hated to leave. The pastor was funny and personable. They had a relaxed evening. Since then, the pastor has addressed them by first name.

Alex compared Caring Church quite favorably to other churches he had visited over the years. People at other churches worried about money matters or tried to impress each other by the way they dressed or the cars they drove. The leaders used fear of damnation to get you to go to church. They pressured you to tithe and to follow a lot of rules, whether or not they are in the Bible. The people went to church on Sunday, then during the week they gossiped about each other or were womanizers or got drunk, and so forth.

In contrast, Caring is the "first sincere church I ever attended." The meaning of Christianity is to love people sincerely. The church's message of caring and love is the spirit of Christianity and is religiously more effective than all the Bible study classes, preaching, and revivals. These people "grab your heart" – because of that, you want to learn about Christ and the Bible. At church you can feel God's love and comfort, can feel God coming into your life. You feel the people at church care.

You are not expected to be perfect. People are tolerant. Divorced people are accepted. They do not oppose dancing. Nor do you have to spend every minute trying to save others by making them Christians. You "don't have to be a servant of the Lord every waking hour of the day; you can live your own life."

If you believe in God and live a Christian life, you will go to heaven. Alex's friend epitomized the saved person. He was a caring man who was "happiest when he could help other people." He had a drink or two, did not tithe although he helped out at church in various ways, and did not go to church every week although he went regularly. But he was always a servant.

Alex believes in the power of prayer. If you love people, you will not argue with them and try to scare them into accepting Jesus. You pray for them, you do not pressure them. People do have a choice. It is up to them to choose Christ. But it is easier if they have your prayers and love. Alex believes his friend's prayers helped him back to Christ.

The loss of his friend certainly led to Alex's joining Caring Church, but the nature of this congregation was also important. Alex juxtaposed "the spirit of Christianity," exemplified by Caring Church, to tradition-alist churches that routinely preach fear of damnation, do not embrace divorced people, equate personal life with church activities, and prac-tice legalism. Alex had problems: He had lost a dear friend, was anxious about his job, and was perhaps still learning how to accommodate a less than perfect marriage. He needed the "spirit of Christianity" that he found at Caring Church. He gained a conviction that Jesus loves him. The spirit of Christianity is caring and loving, and this spirit is visible in the lives of the people at church and in the teaching about Jesus and the spiritual relationship.

Marsha's story also illustrates how caring can be the essential aspect of the conversion story[12]:

Marsha almost did not give Caring Church a try because she heard it was a Church of God congregation, which to her meant prohibitions against dancing, the use of make-up, and who knows what else. At the time, she was attending a fundamentalist con-gregation. However, she had been raised a Methodist and had not been fully "indoctrinated" into the ways of fundamentalism. She had joined the fundamentalist church because of family pressure.

Decades later, Marsha found herself alone. Soon after, she was also rebaptized. Everything had blown up in her life. She lived alone and had nothing to do. Then, a friend asked Marsha to accompany her to Caring Church. Marsha quickly agreed. One day she read about a ladies' retreat and signed up.

It was a turning point. At first she could hardly talk with the other women. Marsha had been depressed. But on the retreat she slowly opened up. The first night, she and her roommate, strangers till then, talked intimately. Marsha revealed how distraught she

12. Marsha was over forty and is highly educated.

was. Her roommate took Marsha's hand and said, "Let's pray to-gether." Marsha had been a Christian her whole life, but something like this had never before happened. They prayed aloud for each other. So much caring was expressed in the prayers that weekend. Marsha could only marvel at the love the women showed for each other.

The women were not solemn. They had fun. It was amazing. So much laughter and emotion. Marsha had never experienced anything like it. People cried for each other. But it was "not emo-tionalism with no intelligence behind it." It was not like rituals when people are "not in their right mind." It was just that the women on retreat were being their real selves, just as now Marsha is herself.

The retreat experience continues at weekly meetings of a ladies' group. Like a family, they share their problems. Marsha is a valued member of the group. "I couldn't believe they wanted to hear what I had to say." Because her previous church emphasized Bible study, Marsha was able to impress the other women with her knowledge of the Bible. But it is the praying for each other that Marsha holds dear.

The women accept each other as they are. They make her feel loved, wanted, cared for. The women "even act like they need me." They miss her, if she is absent, because they expect Marsha to make them laugh.

She summed up the attraction of Caring Church by praising the joy that she felt there and the love that the women had for each other. However, it must be added that she lost all hesitation about switching to Caring Church when she heard the pastor's own story, which included personal suffering.

Marsha has a relative who continued to go to her old church. She cried when Marsha switched churches and still worries that Marsha will go to hell. Marsha told her, "I need this joy, and I need this love." Recently she told a friend from the old church that she was going to marry a mainline Protestant. Her friend told Marsha that she cannot pray for her because she is living in sin, suggesting even that Satan might be guiding her. Marsha called her friend closed-minded and self-righteous. Joy does not exist in her former congregation. If she did not go to her former church, the congregation "put a guilt trip on me." Now, Marsha goes to church, not out of fear, but because she loves God.

The old church seems to deny God's intervention in the world. Certainly they do not believe in healing. But beyond that, they seem afraid of the mystical. At Caring Church, they believe the Spirit works through people. Marsha has come to believe that sometimes God does inspire her to do things, such as writing letters of advice to other women at church who are having problems.

Peggy Shaffer wrote about her interview with Marsha:

> The weekend that she spent on the women's retreat ... was probably the first time she had laughed and enjoyed herself for years. I could see the excitement in her face as she talked about the fun she had. She talked of being so surprised that Christian women could have so much fun, but it was clear to me that the biggest surprise was that *she* could have so much fun – and not feel guilty about it ... !
>
> This woman obviously experienced an incredible change in self-concept ... I have seen that look of new-found self-esteem on the faces of other women – a look of wonder – I'm a person."

Marsha gave credit for this change to the women in Caring Church. The involvement Marsha felt was not at the expense of a loss of self, an outcome she associated with emotionalism. Rather, through her involvement at church, Marsha has emerged a stronger person who can enjoy life. On the retreat and in the Bible study group, women shared their problems. Marsha felt accepted as she is, felt loved, and felt valued. She now feels good about herself and enjoys life.

But the spiritual involvement is also important. God is an important and immediate part of Marsha's life. The caring in this church is both spiritual and social. People want each other to grow closer to God on a daily basis. This sentiment is expressed in the sermons and in conversations among church members. Congregational members emphasize the power of prayer and, it seems, routinely pray for each other, an act that simultaneously symbolizes that God cares for them and that they care for each other.

Caring Church has a bureaucratic side. The Church of God movement has a congregational structure; each congregation calls its pastor and establishes its own bylaws. However, no one at Caring Church said that the way the church was organized was important to them. Surprisingly, church programs also were not particularly important, except for the Bible study groups and the monthly ladies' night out. When specifically asked about programs at church, people mentioned missionary trips, Habitat for Humanity, Promise Keepers, and prolife activities.[13] It was important to the people with whom we talked that such programs existed, but few of the interviewees participated in the programs. Caring, and being cared for, spiritually and interpersonally, is what this congregation is about.

As I have pointed out, Spirited Church tends to attract people with personal problems, whereas Truth Church attracts people concerned about the state of society. The stories of Grace, Wilma, Alex, and Marsha more closely approximate those told to us by people at Spirited Church. However, there is a difference. Whereas some of those at Spirited Church veered toward ultrasupernaturalism, I sensed none of that at Caring Church. That is, at the latter church, spiritual involvement was not at the expense of this-worldly involvement; at Caring Church, spiritual involvement is entwined with social involvements. This difference is consistent with the philosophy at Caring Church to emphasize the communal aspect of the congregation.

In 1999, I asked the pastor at Caring Church how he explains his church's success. He mentioned the members' invitations to outsiders to visit the church, the drawing power of a very polished musical program, and the importance of a large children's educational program (when I was studying the congregation, there were seventy to eighty children in classes on any one Sunday). But what the pastor emphasized the most were relationships: to God, oneself, church members, and others. People come to the church because of networking, he told me, and they stay because they have made friends. Thus small groups within the congregation are crucial: It is there that interpersonal bonds are formed. In his class for new attendees, the pastor tells people they need to forge relationships with others by joining a small group. He tells them the congregation is about relationships, and they need to connect with others.

I encouraged him to talk about his role in the congregation's success. In response, the pastor discussed his sermons. He approaches the Bible as a guide to daily living in this world. His sermons, therefore, are about real-life experiences: how to relate your faith and your vocation, and

---

13. The variety of programs is appropriate for Caring Church. Habitat for Humanity was mentioned only by people at Caring Church and at our mainline Protestant church (i.e., Open Church, discussed in Chapter 6).

how to be a good spouse, parent, neighbor, citizen, and so forth. The "holiness of life" (a denominational phrase) means good living and that can be equated with good relationships. Thus he returned to the topic of the importance of social relationships.

In Chapter 3, I defined a charismatic congregation as one that has accommodated the alternative tradition, libertarianism, and late-modern values. Both Spirited and Caring churches fit this definition, yet they are different. I suggest the differences between Spirited and Caring churches reflect differences in the social class composition of the congregations. First, there is a difference in the ritual, with Spirited's being more like a rock-n-roll event. After interviewing Ida, who had visited both churches, Peggy Shaffer made this comment:

> Ida's house is immaculately clean and fussy (you'd swear no one lived in this home or had ever eaten a meal in the kitchen), and she was baking cookies when I arrived. The scene was so 1950s perfect I almost expected Wally and the Beaver to come down the stairs any minute. . . . She is a very tidy, controlled lady, and I can't imagine her getting into the spirit of a charismatic church – too emotional for her. She talked about how the biggest problem with Spirited Church was its size, but I think the charismatic stuff bothered her more than she admitted. It occurred to me also, given her lifestyle, that the social class differences between the two churches might have been a factor. This is a family for whom appearances are obviously important – nothing is left to chance. She also commented that she sees the "masses" going in and out of Spirited Church and she doesn't see how they can be getting anything out of the service in such a large church.

Peggy's analysis shows how personality and social class can affect the choice of a congregation. Peggy intuited that Ida's aversion to Spirited's Sunday service, at least in part, resulted from her desire to separate herself from the masses who in turn are associated with emotional rituals. The middle-class emphasis on rationality and self-control lingers on in people such as Ida.

Second, Spirited and Caring churches differ, I believe, in the prevalence of ultrasupernaturalism. As I discussed in Chapter 3, while the availability of counseling at Spirited Church seems to have lessened the need for withdrawal from the social, which is implied by ultrasupernaturalism, some of the people at Spirited Church did evidence signs of such withdrawal. In contrast, what distinguishes the people at Caring Church is the successful development and intertwining of spiritual and communal bonds. Prayer plays a pivotal role. True to its pietist roots, the congregation prays a lot. On the one hand, people pray to God, bonding with Him. On the other hand, people freely pray with and for each other. Spiritual and social bonds are meshed. Recall Jenny (from Chapter 4) and her love of "comfort verses": "The Lord is my shepherd and I shall not want . . . ," "there's a time to live, a time to die, a time to grieve, a time to enjoy." Caring Church effectively combines spiritual comfort with human caring.

I suggest the tendency toward ultrasupernaturalism is related to social class. Generally, the lower the class, the more severe the problems. Poverty, a sense of worldly failure, and living in patriarchal, cold families are more often lower-class realities. I argue that because better-off people do not experience such a harsh world, they less often feel the need to be as other-worldly as possible and thus can find relief in congregations such as Caring Church that entwine the spiritual and the communal. In Caring Church, I suggest, we see the future of charismatic Protestantism.

Christians looking for a new congregation would have been drawn to Caring Church because of its quality programs. It had a well-developed youth program, led by the young female youth minister, and a polished musical program, led by a full-time minister of music. The congregation was large enough that many people shared the work of maintaining its programs. While all these traits are important, they exist in many congregations. Why, then, were people attracted specifically to Caring Church? People liked the Holiness emphasis on prayer and spirituality. This religious orientation allowed Caring Church to have appealing traits: (1) relatively blurred boundaries that make it easy for diverse people to feel at home, and (2) a caring environment that is both spiritual and communal. The nurturing of caring relationships is basic to the pastor's theology as well as to his strategy for building a congregation, and this approach works.

COMMUNITY VERSUS COMMUNAL BONDS

In part, people go to all the congregations we studied because of the social relations they formed in these churches. While such bonds may be especially important at Caring Church, they were also mentioned by people at Spirited and Truth churches. Indeed, Robert Wuthnow (1994:8) suggested that today people choose congregations not on the basis of doctrine or liturgy but because of small groups within the congregation (e.g., Bible study groups, groups for a variety of addicts, women's groups), and that cutting across the range of groups is the common reward of community. According to Wuthnow, traditional Bible study groups are supposedly being replaced by groups that "are essentially fellowship groups" (p. 148). "Singing, eating, and other activities must be present to enrich the experience. Having fellowship has come to be more important than learning religious ideas" (p. 146). Wuthnow's analysis raises several questions for me: Assuming he is using "fellowship" and "community" interchangeably, exactly what does it mean to say that a congregation provides community, and is "community" the right word to use in describing the social rewards of churchgoing?

To clarify matters, I begin with an understanding of "community" rooted in classic sociology and consistent with a standard dictionary meaning (Tamney 1975:1–2). "Community" refers to an aggregate of people who think and act as one. Such an aggregate may be called a "body of people." Individuals, like bodily parts, serve the interests of the whole. The root idea is a sense of oneness with others such that personal interests become the interests of the collective. When the members of a group feel one with the group itself, or its leader as the symbol of the group, we can say that the group is a community. Do the congregations we studied appeal to people because they are communities?

Religious congregations are socially important because, as people told us, newcomers to a community make new friends there. At least in the United States, this is nothing new. Robert S. and Helon Merrell Lynd (1929:275) found that newcomers to Middletown were told, "affiliate yourself with some church if you want to get acquainted." Churches feel obligated to take in strangers – out of kindness, a desire to save them, and so forth. Today, newcomers to the area and single people still use churches this way. For example, Paul and his wife felt disconnected when they moved to Middletown. They had no friends. Now, after affiliating with Caring Church, they feel they belong, as a result especially of joining the choir and participating in a Bible study group. Because so many Americans move so often, extended families and stable neighborhoods are not common experiences in the lives of many Americans, and their absence has been compensated for by churches (cf., Warner 1990; Wuthnow 1994; and Hoge, Johnson, and Luidens 1994:204–5).

Our respondents, however, also spoke appreciatively of the quality of the fellowship found at church, usually in terms of how they were personally affected. Both Alex and Marsha made clear how important were the social aspects of congregational life. Like a wayward son, Alex returned and was met not with condemnation but love and compassion. Marsha could hardly talk about herself – what she felt, what she needed. On the retreat, her new family reached out to her with caring. Then, Marsha could express herself, feel happy, and become a stronger person. The bonds were sufficiently significant to confer forgiveness (Alex) and validate self-respect (Marsha). Such rewards came not from the fact of membership in a group nor from the pastor but from specific laypersons accepting Alex and Marsha as they were.

Debbie, whom we met in Chapter 3, had left another local church after a well-liked pastor was forced out. Debbie was feeling hurt and angry, and after leaving, she had to go through a grief process. Debbie had to learn to let go of her feelings "because it hurt so bad." "It's like – I'd never been through a divorce and hope I never have to, but I just, I mean, it was such a horrible, horrible hurt place that I couldn't stay in that hurt mode too awful long because I just hurt too bad. . . ." Debbie almost cried while talking about her old church with me. The Sunday after the pastor left, Debbie sat in church "just reading my Bible. . . . I couldn't hear what was being said out of the tears and things." Having the minister "ripped out" of her congregation hurt bad. Debbie was helped by being in a group that was discussing how to cope with grief and that was run by a staff person from Spirited Church. Participating helped her deal with grief and anger.

The stories of Alex, Marsha, and Debbie illustrate a point that was heard often from our respondents: What was important was not simply belonging to a church but the social relationships developed with fellow churchgoers. In other words, people go to church not for community but for communal bonds. The rewards come not from being a member of the congregation (from being part of a body of people), but from a certain kind of interpersonal relationship. Communal relations are personal and diffuse, that is, nothing is ruled out ahead of time as being possibly an aspect of the relationship; the commitment is to the person. In contrast, associational relations are impersonal and specific, that is, explicitly restricted to a certain purpose. People who value congregational small groups want to be with others making open-ended commitments to them as persons. This kind of commitment may be expressed in tangible ways such as giving money or offering child care. More importantly, today this commitment is expressed in therapeutic ways: conferring forgiveness, validating self-worth, or helping people come to terms with grief or other emotions. My argument, then, is that people in the types of congregations that we studied are not searching for community but for therapeutic communal bonds. The basic reward of participation stems not from feeling a part of something larger than the self but from feeling better about one's own self.[14]

The people we interviewed at Spirited and Truth churches also emphasized accountability. In the small groups, individuals confess their transgressions and seek not forgiveness, but acceptance, as well as support to change their ways. Again, however, this process is to be done in a caring way.

Rosabeth Moss Kanter wrote a well-known study of nineteenth-century communes to which she added a discussion of late-modern ones, which included the following comment:

> Today there is a renewed search for utopia and community in America – for alternative, group-oriented ways of life. But, overwhelmingly, the grand utopian visions of the past have been replaced by a concern with relations in a small group. Instead of conceptions of alternative societies, what is emerging are conceptions of alternative families. Whereas communes of the past were described in books about socialism, communes today are increasingly discussed in books about the family. Communes of the past called themselves "societies" (the Society of Believers, the Harmony Society), indicating their interest in comprehensiveness; today's groups are more frequently called "families" (the Family of the Mystic Arts, the Lyman Family) (Kanter 1972:165).

Is it accurate to say that our respondents were looking for "alternative families"? For some, or many, people in these congregations, the groups they joined are the families they never had – not because they had no families but because families are only now becoming in fact what we have come to imagine as an ideal family. Max, who attended Spirited Church, talked about his Life Group as a "family," yet he also said that it

14. I asked a pastor at Truth Church why there are gender-defined Bible study groups. There is a heritage of separating the sexes; for instance, in the early Puritan churches, men and women sat on different sides of the sanctuary. However, the pastor believes that gender homogeneity is popular because it furthers interpersonal openness. For instance, men get openly emotional in their study group, which would be harder, the pastor said, if women were there. Moreover, both men and women share with others their personal needs and problems, which would be less likely if their spouses or children were sitting there.

was the first time in his life that he had relationships in which he felt free to discuss personal spiritual matters. Kanter (1972:197) described late-modern communes as "a family of brothers and sisters without parents," who are held together not by a shared ideology but by interpersonal bonds. Similarly, the small church groups I am discussing are "fatherless" and are less a body of people than a network of individuals. The new family emphasizes openness and trust, sharing and compassion. People are moving from congregations that make them feel dead to those that help them to grow; from congregations requiring conformity to ones communicating acceptance; from congregations that stand in constant judgment to ones that reach out with compassion.

When I discussed the distinction between community and communal relationships with the pastor of Caring Church, he quizzed me about the meaning of these terms. I responded that the former connotes a body of people, while the latter implies that a congregation is an interpersonal network. In reflecting on this distinction, the pastor pointed out that covenantal theology is important to conservative Christians, which means that they think of the church as the soul of a body of people; conservatives are comfortable talking about "a people." The pastor seemed hesitant about conceiving a congregation as a network, although he did not deny that it was an emphasis on communal bonds that describes his own congregation. The network analogy spotlights individuals. A network does not rule out the possibility of strong personal identities. Bonds among members may be more important than members' ties to the corporate group, to the church. Moreover, the network might be open: Not all members may be linked to all other members, and some links may go outside the group. Traditionalist Christianity is more consistent with picturing the congregation as a body than as a network.

Two Types of Traditionalist Protestantism

In their life histories, some of the people with whom we talked had visited or been part of congregations that exemplified traditionalist Protestantism, or what I have called the Bob Jones University model. They told us what they did not like about these congregations. I will use their comments to pinpoint what our respondents disliked about the traditionalist model. Then I will specify the traits shared by our three conservative churches that differentiate them from the Bob Jones University model.

For instance, Alex contrasted a congregation that expressed the spirit of Christianity with ones that used fear of damnation to get people to church, or that had a "holier than thou" attitude, or that pressured people to follow a lot of rules not explicit in the Bible. The last is called "legalism," that is, when holiness is equated with following specific rules of conduct that all imply rejecting worldly pleasures. Such rules prohibit the use of alcohol or tobacco, swearing, gambling, attending movie theaters, and social dancing. Other rules apply specifically to women: make-up, jewelry, and revealing necklines are forbidden; dresses or skirts are preferred to slacks (Corbett 1994:202).

In Chapter 3, I summarized Irene's story. As the reader might recall, she had become dissatisfied with an independent Baptist church, had gone church-shopping, and finally selected Spirited Church. In this journey, Irene learned that she disliked a church that emphasized denominational beliefs. Her old church expected everyone to accept that only full-immersion baptism worked and that once a person was saved, she or he remained saved forever (the doctrine of eternal security). Behaviorally, the church was legalistic – for example, requiring women to dress properly on Sunday, that is, to wear appropriate dresses, a rule that Irene disliked. Moreover, Irene came to realize that she did not like the degree of separation her old pastor practiced, as he was even unwilling to work with other pastors. Irene, like others with whom we talked, joined one of the congregations in our study because it did not fit the traditionalist model.

The experiences of Allen, Ruth, and Bart – who were introduced in Chapter 4 – also help us to understand what our respondents disliked about traditionalist Protestantism.

Allen grew up in a "fundamentalist subculture." In the church of his youth, "there was an implicit . . . sense that the only really good work to do was to be a pastor or a missionary. . . ." As an accomplished professional person, Allen is now attracted by the notion that all forms of work are part of God's plan. One can be called by God to do what is considered secular work, as was Allen. He referred to the need to maintain balance in his life, as for instance between church and home. He does not want his children to feel rejected: "My parents were very, very active when I was small, and they made it clear that the church came before the family. . . . What I want to make clear to my children is that both are important, and I don't want them to feel I'm choosing." Being a professional and being a parent are ways of being religiously called. Allen does not want to be a part of a congregation that so extensively denigrates secular or worldly activities as did the church in which he was raised.

In earlier years, Ruth had belonged to a "fundamentalist" church. She continues to believe that she must separate from worldly things. But Ruth was uncomfortable with the legalism and judgmental attitude that she associated with her old church. She found it difficult to explain exactly what upset her. I asked for an example. She described another church that she and her husband had visited when they moved to Middletown:

"... you just had this feeling that because you didn't go to certain theological seminaries or schools that they went to, you were not quite spiritual; and a lot of emphasis was put on three or four major sins and dress codes and lots of things that you really wondered if they were," said Ruth, "if that was a true measuring stick of the depth of your Christian life, because then on the other hand you could see other areas that were very weak-like – such as materialism and things of that nature."

Ruth said that moderation in things rather than total abstinence from some pleasures is really the biblical message, although, she added, "you must not be a stumbling block to a weaker brother." That is, in order to keep others from being tempted, a person might practice abstinence, for instance, by not drinking any alcohol or by not going to any movies. But as Ruth continued talking, her illustrations moved away from legalism: "If you don't live trying to be Christlike in your love and your relationships, etcetera, then it's just like sounding brass and tinkling cymbals."

Bart had also become disillusioned with legalism:

"For instance, it would not be uncommon in any independent [fundamentalist] church that they would state simply that if you want to be a member of the church," said Bart, "you may not consume alcohol of any sort of any kind. ... Well, that would be legalism ... because the Bible doesn't actually specify that you can't, and it's very easy for churches to begin to develop these lists – thou shall nots of their own, you know, dress codes, things of that nature."

In Bart's way of thinking, legalism also includes avoiding anybody not of the "exact same mind." Yet Bart believes that Christians should "love and commune with other Christians."

At his previous church, Bart and others had worked hard to make the church grow. Many visited, but few joined. He realized that just being right, just having God's word preached, is not enough. You need to have compassion.

> "...you can't go out and smack people up the side of the head with your Bible and expect to change the world....I believe," said Bart, "before someone is going to listen to you, I honestly believe you need to earn the right to be heard.... Before someone listens to me, I believe the first thing is I need to listen to them, I need to become involved in their lives. Once they've found that they can trust me to listen to them, to be understanding of their problems, then I find they're more than willing to listen to me...to me there's a lot more of that at Truth Church than any place I've ever found – a desire to go out and earn that right to be heard."

For Bart, evangelism means "loving our neighbors and showing compassion." In judging a church, you weigh their doctrine against the biblical presentation of the nature of God: "There are things in the Bible that tell us about God; God is just; God is loving; God is forgiving; God is caring." Evangelism should be done through caring about, and for, other people.

These respondents would never be satisfied with a traditionalist congregation such as the one at Bob Jones University. The composite picture of the religion from which our respondents were moving away is as follows:

- Enforced acceptance of denominational doctrines
- Legalism: equating holiness with specific rules such as dress codes and abstinence from alcohol and moviegoing
- Secular activities being deemed ungodly
- A congregation of "saints," having no place for sinners
- Separatism: avoiding involvement with people of a different mind
- The use of fear to make people religious
- Judgment, rather than love, of others

Overall, what our respondents found most disturbing about traditionalist Protestantism related to the matter of strong boundaries – against other Christians, the world, the supposedly unsaved. Of course, Alex and the others did not talk about boundaries. The core of their analyses was that a Christianity of dogma, rules, and separatism should give way to a Christianity of love.[15]

MODERNIZED TRADITIONALIST PROTESTANTISM

Table 5 lists the traits shared by Spirited, Truth, and Caring congregations in the rightmost column. This list composes the modernized traditionalist type of Protestantism. I prefer the latter term to Olson's (1998) "reformed Protestantism" because my term makes clear the significance of modernization in determining the nature of the new form of conservative Protestantism. I want to emphasize that the traits are not ones that I or my fellow sociologists think are important; rather, the listed traits are those aspects of the modernized traditionalist type that our respondents found attractive. This table also contains a comparable list of traits that describe the traditionalist model so that the changes taking place in conservative Protestantism during late-modernity are clear.

The specific items in Table 5 that describe the traditionalist type share an underlying function: They establish and maintain clear boundaries, the essence of what Dean Kelley meant by a strong church. Biblical literalism – required acceptance of doctrines that are denominationally specific (i.e., doctrines that serve as identity markers for specific Christian groups) – and legalism are the foundations of theological and

15. One of our interviewees was attending Caring Church only reluctantly out of a sense of family duty. Helen had been unchurched for decades, although both she and her husband were Bible-reading Christians. Helen regrets that Caring Church is not old-time religion, but she is unique in that regard. When she visited Caring Church, her reference point was the small, one-pastor fundamentalist church of her youth. What Helen chose to emphasize is interesting: an inerrant King James Bible to be taken literally, a church service that is just about the Bible (skip the fancy music), and the need for hellfire and brimstone sermons. Helen's religion is all about a paternalistic God speaking directly to people through His written word. Among people such as Helen, a belief in an inerrant Bible is necessary; assuming that everything means exactly what it says allows the Helens of the world to study the sacred text on their own. No wonder that she and her husband could stay away from church for so long and yet feel Christian. Helen's "old-time religion" shows the influence of the dissenting tradition. Possibly she would feel more comfortable in a Bob Jones University–style congregation than she felt at Caring Church, but this would be true not because she valued or needed a strong church, but rather because she needed confidence that she was hearing the Word of God.

Table 5. Two Forms of Conservative Protestantism

Traditionalist	Modernized Traditionalist
• Interpret the Bible literally; enforce conformity with doctrinal litmus tests	• Minimize theological conformity
• Reject wordly pleasure; no drinking, dancing, moviegoing (legalism)	• Enjoy pleasures in moderation
• Dress codes • Formal • Gender-appropriate	• Informal dress; less uniform code
• Congregation of saints	• More open policy on participation
• Separatism except for direct evangelism	• Lifestyle evangelism valued
• Emphasis on judgment; use of fear	• Emphasis on therapeutic values
• Sense of community	• Communal relationships
• Support for the religious right	• Acceptance of pluralism

moral boundaries. Dress codes that reinforce traditional gender roles and that deindividualize by requiring "uniforms" reinforce the symbolic boundaries. The next three traits limit involvement with outsiders. Participants in the congregation should all be saints, while contact with others should be minimal and ideally restricted to spreading the good news of Christianity. By emphasizing judgment and approving the use of fear-based techniques of persuasion, a religion conveys that what is important is the individual's submission and not a willingness to convert, which would imply a prior resolution of inner conflict. In other words, the use of fear is less respectful of the individual. The penultimate trait in the left column of Table 5, a sense of community, expresses the consequence of all the other traits, which is the affirmation of the importance of the group relative to the individual members. Lastly, traditionalist groups today, given that they mostly eschew the truly separatist option, will support the religious right, since this religious-political movement seeks to implement the goals of expanding the control of conservative religion over other social institutions and cultural domains (e.g., popular culture).

The three conservative congregations that we studied give less importance to firm boundaries than Bob Jones University does. These congregations do not identify Christianity with following dress codes and abstaining from worldly pleasures. Rather, they consider moderation proper, and encourage individual expressiveness in dress codes, ritual participation, and evangelism. All three conservative congregations allowed people with varied levels of commitment to participate in church activities. Our respondents contrasted an emphasis on doctrinal conformity, moral legalism, and continual judging of the saintliness of others with what Alex called the spirit of Christianity. Their image of Christ connotes acceptance and compassion; successful evangelism may mean living a Christlike life by being involved with outsiders in a forgiving and caring manner; while Christians would be advised to spend their free time within a conservative subculture of friends and leisure activities, they are not to separate totally from others of a different mind or shrink from participating in worldly activities.

Regarding biblical literalness, the congregations we studied were not the same. Unlike the others, Spirited's leaders taught the literal interpretation of the Bible. However, various theological perspectives were represented among the pastors, and on a topic such as baptism, Spirited's pastor recognized diverse opinions. The important point is that a tolerance, albeit limited, of theological diversity exists in modernized traditionalist churches.

As we have seen, some people in each of the three conservative churches supported the religious right. But overall, attitudes toward the right were mixed and in no case was a person drawn to one of the three congregations out of a rightist commitment. I discussed the Christian Right with the pastor at Caring Church. There were no formal ties. Some church members endorse the Christian Right, but an equal or larger number are uncomfortable with the Christian Right. The discomfort results more from disagreement over strategies, such as sit-ins and civil disobedience, than over beliefs. But such disagreement, in turn, reflects the very important conviction, endorsed by the pastor, that morality cannot be legislated. Individuals must be free to choose to be holy.

A conservative scholar, David P. Gusbee, juxtaposed the Christendom assumption and lifestyle evangelism. Many evangelicals want "the informal or even formal establishment of Christianity as the national religion" (Gusbee 1997:13). Gusbee counseled accepting life "in a wildly pluralistic post-Christian society." Instead of trying to coerce institutions into conforming with conservative values, the "emphasis needs to be on living the story of Christian faith so compellingly and authentically, both individually and in our communities, that people of all types will be drawn to Christ." The practice of lifestyle evangelism implies the rejection of Christendom, at least as a political goal. Such an attitude is inconsistent with the religious right program but at the heart of modernized traditionalist Protestantism.

MODERNIZED TRADITIONALISM AND KELLEY'S ARGUMENT

Given the appeal of the three conservative congregations in our study, Kelley's argument cannot be accepted as a total explanation for the relative success of conservative Protestantism. Modernized traditionalist congregations have weaker boundaries, *and because of that*, people are attracted to them. Conservative Protestantism is shifting away from moral legalism. The rules being abandoned or softened are just those that were most costly to religiously conservative people. For example, among students at self-defined evangelical colleges, several activities were condemned by strong majorities in the 1950s and 1960s but only by minorities in the 1980s: social dancing, playing cards, drinking alcohol, and heavy petting (Hunter 1987:58). Significantly, people are attracted to modernized traditionalist congregations because they are not legalistic; they have appeal, in part, *because they are less costly.*

Despite such evidence, Kelley's ideas will no doubt remain influential. The recently published *Encyclopedia of Religion and Society* (Swatos 1998) contains an entry on Kelley in which the writer notes that Kelley's "best known and most widely cited book," *Why Conservative Churches Are Growing,* "has been actively debated in the social science literature for several decades" (Bromley 1998:262). The work endures, at least in part, because it has a positive symbolic significance for some people so that they claim to be using Kelley's theory even when they are not. For instance, the influential church-growth consultant, Lyle Schaller, claimed that "growing churches seek a high level of religious commitment from their members" (Schaller 1994:25). His language, as well his reference to Kelley's book, suggests that Schaller agrees with Kelley – but this is not true. In Schaller's model for success, church leaders would allow for various levels of commitment. Growing congregations, he wrote, make it easy for almost anyone to participate in church activities, contrary to Kelley's model (p. 98). Full members have to meet high standards (attend a lengthy membership class, hand in a written testimony of faith, commit to tithe, attend worship regularly, and participate in Bible study or prayer groups), but leaders allow just about anyone to participate – as in the conservative congregations we studied. Schaller also noted that limitations on who can take communion are becoming less restrictive (p. 94). He advised denominations to offer five or so different types of congregations, only one of which even roughly approximates Kelley's "strong church" (p. 61). Moreover, another aspect of Schaller's model for success is that congregations move away from "permission-withholding" (pp. 31–4). Rigid rules and a judgmental attitude are detrimental. To grow, churches should emphasize acceptance, forgiveness, and love. Schaller's model is not Kelley's. The Kelley myth about why churches grow is perpetuated even by people who in fact deny the myth – a story worth studying in its own right.

CONCLUSION

Olson (1998:40) defined the characteristics of conservative Protestantism (or, in his terms, "evangelicalism") as: (1) "It looks to the Bible as the supreme norm of truth for Christian belief and practice," (2) "It holds a supernatural worldview that is centered in a transcendent personal God who interacts with, and intervenes in, creation," (3) "It focuses on the forgiving and transforming grace of God through Jesus Christ in the experience called *conversion* as the center of authentic Christian experience," and (4) "It believes that the primary task of Christian theology is to serve the church's mission of bringing God's grace to the whole world through proclamation and service." Olson put more formally what Grace told us she wanted in a church, and which I take to be the defining characteristics of conservative Protestantism. Normal life must be understood using a supernatural framework. Sermons must be about the other world or the role of the supernatural in this world. Prayer personalizes the supernatural dimension of daily life. The Bible is the guide given by God for this-worldly activity. Morality is not dependent on human reasoning nor is sincerity relevant in judging whether someone acted morally. It follows that Christianity is the only road to salvation and that everyone who knows this has an obligation to spread the word. As Olson implied, however, these traits do not stand alone in the real world. They are embedded in more encompassing religious worldviews, which vary in the strength of the boundary created with "the world."

Traditionalist congregations create strong symbolic and social boundaries. In contrast, their modernized counterparts accept more blurred boundaries. Of course, when Americans go church-shopping, they do not consciously search for blurred boundaries. What draws them to modernized traditionalist congregations are the traits listed in the right column of Table 5. Church-shoppers may find these characteristics attractive because they accommodate individualism, self-realization, and the affluence ethic. Individualism is reflected in the greater latitude for differences in biblical interpretation as well as dress styles and forms of evangelism. The appreciation of a therapeutic environment implies a valuing of personal growth. A less negative view of worldly things is reflected in allowing for the enjoyment of worldly pleasures. Moreover, I believe the shift from a judgmental to a loving approach to both insiders and outsiders implies a greater acceptance of this world and of the people in it, flawed and all; again, ultimately all conservatives are working for the conversion of everyone to their version of Christianity, but in the short run, modernized conservatives are more likely to become, and stay, involved with sinners (the "world") in order to gain their trust and respect. These traits of modernized Protestantism result in congregations with more blurred boundaries. Of course, the implication of blurred boundaries is that the individual becomes more important vis-à-vis the group, making the image of a body of people less applicable. The people in these congregations do not interpret their attitudes as an accommodation of late-modernity, as I do; for them, their way of being religious is right because it expresses the spirit of Christianity.

One of the Nazarene women with whom I talked in the 1950s had a humble background, but at the time we met, Eileen was a clinical psychologist and a board member of a Nazarene church in New York City:

Since a child, when she was going to a Methodist church, Eileen has felt ill at ease if she adorns her body with jewelry or fancy clothes. When she sees a girl in church with earrings, Eileen says to herself that the girl is not a true Nazarene. But Eileen is trying to change. If she has a dress that would be completed by earrings, she would wear them. This is still difficult for her. The old idea was that bodily adornment showed pride. While saying this to me, Eileen realized that a person could be proud about being a good Nazarene. She ended by saying that she guesses that moderation in all things is the right way to live.

To appreciate Eileen's behavior, we need to know the meaning of such things as earrings. In the days before costume jewelry became widely available, good jewelry was both an investment and a status symbol (Lynd and Lynd 1937:10). Wearing jewelry showed pride in one's worldly status. But Eileen had dissociated jewelry and social status. She realized that the real sin was pride and that this attitude could even be expressed in carrying out religious activities. Sin, she came to understand, was more a matter of attitude than act. The ideal was moderate enjoyment, including her enjoyment of dressing attractively. Eileen, I believe, foreshadowed an emerging movement in Protestantism.

The development of a movement among conservative Protestants to reject moral legalism as a yardstick for determining authentic religiosity is described in John A. Schmalzbauer and C. Gray Wheeler's (1996) study of campus rules at conservative Protestant colleges. Until recently, "most religious colleges and almost every evangelical college maintained stringent student conduct codes restricting alcohol use, smoking, and in some cases social dancing. . . . Today only selected evangelical colleges maintain such rules" (p. 242). That is to say, until recently all conservative Protestant colleges, to an extent, resembled Bob Jones University. Why is this no longer the case? Schmalzbauer and Wheeler analyzed the criticisms of the rules made by students at conservative colleges. In some cases, the students simply affirmed the importance of freedom. In others, they argued that the Reformation critiqued the use of rules to make people holy (legalism): "Opponents of campus rules have often mobilized Luther's argument that good works should flow freely out of the Christian's faith and need not be imposed by external rules" (p. 249). Students also argued that while conservative movements "took a dim view of the material world and the human body . . . , Reformation Protestantism, and especially Lutheranism, strongly affirmed the goodness of bodily existence . . ." (p. 244–5). Such conservatives now argue that alcohol, dancing, the dramatic arts, and so forth are God's gifts to be enjoyed. Sensual pleasure is no longer in itself bad. The contemporary importance of individualism and the affluence ethic to conservative Protestants is demonstrated by such criticisms of legalism.[16]

16. A relevant event is a recent change in the Church of God (Cleveland, Tennessee), the oldest Pentecostal denomination in the United States. In 1988, majorities of laypeople and ministers, meeting in a general assembly, voted to change the church's 102-year-old denominational moral code. The revised code is more flexible on some worldly issues such as personal appearance; as the code affirms, "It is not displeasing to God for us to dress well and be well-groomed" (quoted in Niebuhr 1988:726). Members interpreted the changes as cutting ties to a rural, white, Southern culture of the past, that is, to a less modern past.

Churches I have been vaguely describing as "conservative" can now be more accurately labeled as traditionalist and modernized traditionalist. Of course, behind such a simple dichotomy lies a continuum of congregations differing in the strength of their symbolic and social boundaries. Among the congregations we have studied, Caring Church seems to approximate most closely modernized traditionalist Protestantism.

CHAPTER SIX

OPEN CHURCH

Truth and Open Churches are both Presbyterian. As someone who had checked out both churches told me, members of these congregations wear similar clothes, drive similar cars, and use a similar vocabulary. However, Open Church, unlike Truth Church, is part of the Presbyterian Church (USA), a denomination that exemplifies "modern religion." Compared to other American Protestant groups, generally, this denomination has put more emphasis on the sovereignty of God (e.g., predestination) and the centrality of the corporate church in gaining salvation. However, over the centuries, the church has come to tolerate Arminianism as well as those who emphasize the need for the personal experience of being born again. The Presbyterian Church (USA) is in the reforming tradition, which it interprets to mean that the Spirit is *continuously* reforming our understanding of Scripture, is continually bringing new insights about what it means to be a Christian. Thus, the Church's positions on slavery, women, and predestination have changed.

As pointed out in Chapter 2, the Presbyterian Church has included a declining part of the American population since the establishment of the colonies. During this century, the decline has been especially sharp since the 1960s, that is, during late-modernity. This change occurred because young, well-educated people raised in Presbyterian homes failed to commit to their parents' church and were not replaced by converts (Hoge, Johnson, and Luidens 1994:5–8).

However, not all Presbyterian (USA) congregations are doing poorly. My immediate concern is Open Church. During the 1990s, although the area's population was declining, church attendance increased. In mid-November 1996, 377 people attended the two Sunday morning services;

the figure for a year earlier was 320. After discussing the appeal of Open Church, I return to the issue of the decline of modern denominations in the chapter's concluding section.

Fourteen interviews were conducted by myself, Peggy J. Shaffer, and Susan P. Ryan; one was with a couple. The people we interviewed came from a variety of backgrounds: five from mainline Protestant churches, two from conservative churches, one person who had no religious affiliation, and six respondents from other congregations affiliated with the Presbyterian Church (USA). Five of those in the last category did not join Open Church automatically out of denominational loyalty; in three cases, the respondents had visited churches in other denominations before deciding on Open Church; a fourth person visited Truth Church before settling on Open Church; the fifth respondent spent most of his life in conservative churches before deciding to return to his Presbyterian heritage.[1] What attracted these people to Open Church? (I remind the reader that all indented material is my paraphrasing of the interviewees' comments unless the material is in quotation marks.)

NOT TRUTH CHURCH

Norris, Edward, and Tara checked out Truth Church before choosing Open Church.[2]

Norris and his family had been attending a mainline Presbyterian church before moving to Middletown. After trying out Open Church, they were not satisfied, primarily because their preteen children were not happy in the church. As a result, they tried out other churches, including Truth Church, where they attended services and classes for several months.

Despite some ambivalence, Norris and his wife decided that Truth Church was too conservative. Norris had been raised in a conservative church. As he remembers his childhood, he associates church with emphasizing sin and judgment, with a heavy negative tone. Attending Truth Church, Norris had the same feeling, and

1. Sociologists who studied Presbyterians concluded "a principled loyalty to the denomination was all but nonexistent among the Baby-Boom Presbyterians we interviewed" (Hoge, Johnson, and Luidens 1994:119).
2. Norris was over forty and is highly educated. Edward was younger than forty and is highly educated. Tara was over forty.

it made him uncomfortable. In his twenties, he left not only his conservative denomination but Christianity (a choice we shall discuss later in this chapter) because of such feelings.

Theology is important to Norris. Asked what beliefs are significant to him, he gave this list:

a. Jesus Christ is our personal savior.
b. I and all other children of God are forgiven by virtue of Christ's crucifixion.
c. The kingdom of heaven is available to believers.
d. All people are God's children.
e. Baptism is the process by which the Creator reclaims us as His children.

In discussing belief "d," Norris delayed on this point to emphasize he did not accept the idea of a chosen people that was preached at Truth Church. The doctrine of predestination is discussed at Open Church, but the pastors are open to diverse interpretations.

Norris finds acceptance of a wide spectrum of beliefs to be an attractive feature of Open Church. In fact, this is what Norris means by "liberal": acceptance of, and openness to, diverse beliefs as well as acceptance of people as fallible human beings, who will make mistakes, yet who will be forgiven and accepted by people in the congregation and by God.

After Norris listed his basic beliefs, his interviewer asked him what he thought of the Bible. Norris stated emphatically that it is God's word. But, he added, no humans have an infallible understanding of its meaning. Norris does his best to understand, and he looks to the ministers for help. But they are not "authoritative interpreters," as he believed about pastors when he was a child. Now, he said, "[I have] reclaimed some decision-making for myself."

Understandably Norris felt more comfortable at Open Church.

Edward and his wife are attracted to both the mainline and conservative Presbyterian denominations. They are aware that not all Presbyterian churches (USA) are the same. The one in Middletown is on the conservative side, which they like, because they are conservative on many matters such as sexual issues.

After visiting Truth Church, however, they found it to be too conservative. The policy regarding women in the ministry was not acceptable. On the church role of women, Edward said, "I gladly call myself a liberal on that issue."

Moreover, having visited both Truth Church and Open Church, Edward and his wife felt more comfortable with the people at the latter church. "You know, my wife and I are Christians and that's an important part of our lives, and yet at the same time I tend to be turned off when people are too overtly Christian.... The people at Open Church, they were just regular people.... They are people we could relate to just in a regular conversation without them throwing in, you know, 'God blessed me in this way,' and, 'I thanked Jesus for this,' every other sentence. They [the people at Open Church] didn't have to hit you over the head with that."

The people at Truth Church are "overly evangelical." They talk "Christianese," using evangelical buzz words: "If you are in the church and you've grown up in the church, and you've dealt with church people all your life, you get tired of people who use certain phrases. You know, they say a prayer and they're just too casual about it. They say, 'Oh Lord, we just want to thank and praise you. We just want to lift up your Holy Name and just give you all the praise and glory.' Stop saying 'just.'"

Edward is not a "fundamentalist." He is turned off by people who argue that God said it must be this way and so it must. The copy of the Bible used by people was not faxed to them by God. We do not have original texts. There are translation issues. The Bible must be understood in its context. People point to a verse and say, "'we have to do this exactly the way it says.' Well, I don't see them, you know, wearing their hair down the side like ascetic Jews, because that's in the Bible too. You know, which ones do you pick and choose? It's a tough issue. I don't know where I stand on every single issue. That's one of the reasons I think it's good to have educated pastors, educated clergy. They can be a good teacher; they can be a good guide."

Edward admires the people at Open Church. They are interesting to talk with – "high-quality people." It is not a matter of hobnobbing with the well-off people. "They are hard-working; they're educated; they have a high respect for education. They have a strong work ethic. I think that just in general those are very high-quality people...."

Each church attracts a certain kind of person. Those at Open Church are not perfect. They are too talkative at times.

"Sometimes they need to be a little more worshipful just before the service. You know, they need to be quieting their hearts. . . . " But the members of the congregation try to treat others ethically. Generally, the Presbyterian Church attracts such people because of the dedicated clergy – that is a reason they like the denomination. The pastor is professional, a "high-quality pastor" – intelligent, hard working, able to counsel people, able to make astute observations.

Open Church is very divided on contemporary issues such as the ordination of homosexuals. But Edward believes most of the people at Open Church, unlike many at some mainline churches, would accept the "deity and lordship of Jesus Christ," and that is *the* religious issue. "I really don't see any compromise on that issue, and if that makes me a conservative, please call me a fascist." Christ, not the Bible, is the point of Christianity. If a church does not accept the lordship of Christ, why go there? "I could go to an Amnesty International meeting, and they're going to be talking about . . . good will and moral ethics and that sort of thing." Edward considers it "liberal" to discuss just moral issues – to talk just about good works, but not about Jesus Christ.

I asked Edward to elaborate on the centrality of Jesus. "We need to strive to live as Christ would have us live. . . . I think Christ called us to be servants. He called us to serve other people. He called us to try to love one another." That is difficult. Some people believe there is no need to be in a church, but he believes "we do need the fellowship of other believers to keep us striving to live as Christ would have us to live, sometimes to reproach us, sometimes to encourage us." We are called to live holy lives. "Does that mean we can't drink or smoke? No." Personally, he thinks smoking damages our bodies and we should not do it. Having a drink is not a problem; drunkenness is.

After presenting Tara's story, I shall discuss the differences between Truth and Open churches.

Religion became very important to Tara several years ago after a close relative died. Her life changed. "I would say that I am probably more content now than I was before. I think that the presence of God in my life has just definitely made me more at peace with myself than I was before."

Tara would be very upset "if there wasn't that reassurance of the saving grace of Jesus, of the forgiveness of our sins, and salvation." She would be let down if preachers did not keep giving people this reassurance because "the most important thing to me is to know that I will be forgiven."

After moving to Middletown, Tara visited Truth Church. The sermon was about divorce, "and I felt like I was sitting for half an hour being hollered at for divorce. That's something I've never experienced, and I just didn't care for the style of preaching. I did not leave that church feeling good like I like to when I leave the church, and I just didn't feel comfortable." She didn't feel reassured that everything is going to be okay. "I left there feeling very wrong, very, just not at all good. When I leave church, I'm usually happier and I'm fulfilled, and I'm ready to go out and start my day, and I didn't feel that way at all when I left that church."

When Tara went to Open Church, she felt "very comfortable"; she felt "a very good spirit in that church...." They recited the prayers that she was used to – the Lord's prayer, the Apostle's Creed, and other prayers "that just kind of reaffirmed what I felt." Moreover, the people were even warmer than those at Truth Church.

The sermons at Open Church strike Tara as more positive than the one she heard at Truth Church, which "had to do with sins, and it was almost like a fire and brimstone kind of thing...." At Open Church, the pastors look at the good side of things.

TRUTH AND OPEN CHURCHES

Why are Norris, Edward, and Tara in any church? Norris and Edward emphasized their conviction that Jesus Christ is their savior or model. For them the Bible is their link to Christ, although its meaning is open to interpretation. Norris and Edward look to ministers as useful guides in understanding the Bible. Moreover, belonging to a congregation of similarly minded people is important because others encourage or reproach them and thereby help them to lead a Christlike life. Tara puts more emphasis on the emotional rewards of churchgoing. Ever since her existential crisis, Tara wants to be comforted. Her spiritual relationship reduces the potential anxiety that the reality of death arouses. Tara knows she has not been perfect, but the fact that God is loving promises a happy ending to her personal story.

Norris, Edward, and Tara are Christians and are personally religious, but Truth Church was not for them. The church was too dogmatic, the pastor too authoritative and judgmental. The meaning of the Bible is not self-evident, and everyone, even a conservative, picks and chooses what to believe. For some people, Truth Church has made an obviously bad choice in its attitude toward giving women religious authority. Moreover, the congregants at Truth Church think of themselves as forming a special in-group, a spiritual elite. They cut themselves off from quality people, from sophisticated and ethical people who accept the lordship of Jesus Christ. The use of "just," for example, implies a false humility, that is, self-righteousness. Finally, conservatives think they know the truth and they are constantly struggling against sin, their own or the society's. The result is that churchgoing is associated with negative feelings. Such is a modernist view of Truth Church.

Dean Kelley argued that denominations such as the Presbyterian Church (USA) were declining because they had lost their strictness. Such change has characterized the Presbyterian Church (USA). One hundred years ago, the Church expected members "to observe the Sabbath strictly, to abstain from using alcoholic beverages, to avoid 'worldly amusements' in general, to dress modestly . . . and not to seek a divorce unless their spouses had deserted them or committed adultery" (Hoge, Johnson, and Luidens 1994:192). By the mid-1960s, the Church was no longer enforcing any of these expectations. Moreover, new lifestyle rules did not replace the old ones. Church leaders have spoken out about peace, social justice, and environmental issues, but members are not disciplined for failing to support these causes.

Might Kelley have been right that modern religions declined in numbers because they lost their strictness? To some extent, the answer is yes. The very existence of the Presbyterian Church of America (PCA) attests to that. Yet, as we have seen, this denomination grows, in part, by attracting people from traditionalist (i.e., more conservative) congregations. In line with this fact, very few people who were raised Presbyterian and leave this denomination then join a conservative church (i.e., probably less than 10 percent) (Coalter, Mulder, and Weeks 1996:25). Moreover, the stories of Norris, Edward, and Tara demonstrate that some religious seekers are repelled by a congregation closer than Open Church to Kelley's model of a strong church.

Sociologists who studied the Presbyterian Church (USA) concluded that in Kelley's terms the Church is a weak institution. Then, they went on to say that if the Presbyterian Church became a "strong church," it would lose more members than it would gain (Hoge, Johnson, and Luidens 1994:208). Why do people prefer a weak church, or as I prefer to call such a congregation, an open church?

THE APPEAL OF AN OPEN CHURCH

The stories of Norris, Edward, and Tara portray their chosen congregation as a church that did not erect boundaries: The members are not a spiritual elite, emphasis is not placed on a sinful "world" (either an evil human nature or an evil society), and conformity is not required. Such openness, especially the acceptance of theological diversity, was a frequently mentioned quality of the church. The pastors and people are open to diverse beliefs and values, even, according to David, to people who say, "I don't know that I believe in Christ [as God]."[3] Carol believes that the Bible is divinely inspired, but that it also reflects the time and the specific people who set it down.[4] It is good that the church offers guidance in interpretation, but there must be room for different ideas, for people to present new views without fear of being condemned for being different. Church must be a place for open discussion. As Carol said, "I have always felt a need to think for myself."

It is not a simple matter that just because Americans tend to be libertarian, they like an open church. Respondents were not talking about independence but about a way of thinking. Carol, for instance, has never been comfortable with thinking in terms of everything being black or white or right or wrong. There are many gray areas.

Denise, also, was attracted by the openness:

Denise grew up in a traditionalist religious environment.[5] Her response was to deny the validity of the ascetic lifestyle rules. She went even further, concluding that she can decide the moral rules. Denise graduated from a conservative college that just recently allowed dancing on campus. "It's just, it's, you know, kind of silly." "I feel like if I lived my life in a Christian manner and, you know, followed the ten commandments as best I can, then God is not going to punish me because I had a beer or I danced or, you know, all these so-called bad things." As she said about her college days,

3. David was over forty and is highly educated.
4. Carol was over forty and is highly educated.
5. Denise was younger than forty and is highly educated.

"I think then I made up my mind not that I could do what I wanted to, but that I could do what I wanted to do within reason. Does that make sense? You know, I know what's right and wrong."

When asked what is a good Christian church, Denise responded, "A caring church. I think a place that I could feel someone would accept me for what I am, what I believe, you know, for someone that is going to believe in Jesus Christ and teach the Word and help me to further my knowledge of the Bible and the way we should live. I think just an open, a real open, honest, caring congregation is what we've [she and her husband] been looking for."

Denise compared Open Church with a conservative church she had attended. The latter felt that its congregation was a select group. In Open Church, if "you believe in Jesus Christ, you can be a member of the church." She likes the pastors because they are caring and open. Denise is on a spiritual journey. She needs support without restrictions.

Denise, like others with whom we talked, accepts religious ambiguity. Such congregants give the lack of certainty a positive connotation by linking it with empowering the individual and gaining new insights. Being religious is a journey, implying an unending quest for the truth.

While people such as Norris, Carol, and Denise value openness for intellectual reasons, others value it for interpersonal reasons. In Gail's case, her husband has not joined Open Church.[6] After marriage, Gail stayed away from church. One day, her seven-year-old came home and asked about God. At about the same time, a good friend's son, who went to Open Church, asked Gail's son to go. Gail said okay. Because Open Church has a good youth program and because her friend recommended the church, she and her children began attending. Gail said she had been waiting for her children to show an interest in church. Gail herself wanted to be involved in church.

Open Church suits Gail. The members of her family of origin have diverse religious preferences. In her family, Gail said, they do not challenge each other's beliefs. Understandably, Gail likes Open Church because it does not make her feel pressured. She had visited a "hell and damnation" church where she felt the minister was trying to push things down her throat, an unpleasant experience. As I see it, if Gail committed herself to such a congregation, she would alienate not only her siblings but her

6. Gail was younger than forty.

husband. Being in an open church is easier on people living in religiously diverse social networks.

Before marriage, Doris and Wylie attended quite different Christian churches.[7] After they were married, they stayed away from church. While living in another town, Wylie and Doris attended a conservative church. Doris had a bad experience, with some members telling her she was bound for hell if she did not join their church. As Wylie said, some "fundamentalist" churches "tend to be a little bit aggressive in terms of trying to get you to join the church or trying to get you to do what the Scripture says. . . ." But when a child was born, Doris and Wylie wanted to find a church satisfying to both in which they could raise their children. By this time, they had moved to Middletown. They joined Open Church.

Wylie finds Open Church to be more formal than that to which he is accustomed, although the music at the contemporary service is somewhat like what he heard in his old church. Wylie still misses a more conservative service: "I was brought up in a Bible-based believing church where the Scripture was taught week after week, notes and things and, you know, like it was like school." He "still craves sometimes the old way of pull out the Bible and read the Scripture and let's talk about what it was saying and why it was saying it and go back to reference points."

Doris feels all right about the decision to join Open Church. "I don't feel pressured. I feel more accepted by the Presbyterians. I feel like I have a say and what I believe is not being told to me, what I need to believe. I just think that there is room to question, and there's acceptance if you do and it's actually healthy." But the key for Doris is the content of the sermon. "Not only are they reading the Scripture but at the same time they're making it applicable to our lifestyles."

Wylie still misses a more conservative church. Doris emphasized the freedom to believe what she wants. The acceptance of diversity at Open Church allows these different people to share in the religious upbringing of their children.

Amy illustrates another type of person drawn to Open Church.[8] She does not socialize much with the people at church. "We kind of go in, and then we're out." She added, "Basically, I go because I know I should, and it's good for the children, and just in case, I don't want to be – you

7. Both Doris and Wylie were younger than forty and are highly educated.
8. Amy was younger than forty and is highly educated.

never know, so you had better try to do the right thing most of the time, or all the time." I asked Amy whether she saw herself as a religious person:

"I don't know what you mean by that" Amy responded. "Do I believe in – I try to do the right thing. I try never to lie, cheat anybody, I try to be good to everyone and not to be too self-involved that I, you know, lose sight of others and what, you know, how I, what I do affects other people and that sort of thing. In that way, if that's what you would consider being a religious person, I would say, 'yes.' Do I – am I, you know, I still have questions – you know, I'm still wondering . . . whether do I believe in God and all that, I would say, 'yes,' although I can't help but wonder."

I asked Amy whether she felt that the pastors of her church were sympathetic to people like herself. She replied, "Yes, I do." Amy went on to say that many people share her doubts, although "You like to think that, you know, it's all true, yet your scientific mind tells you that it's probably not or may not be. I'm hoping to get more secure as I get older."

Amy had been raised in a conservative church, where "alcohol and everything was strictly forbidden." She still is sometimes offended by biblical passages that seem to support conservative views on marriage and gender, and Amy is put off by churches that emphasize obedience. "I feel that it's, you know, nice to interpret things to a more nineties approach such that we can all relate to the basic principles that the Bible or whatever is trying to tell us without, you know, referring to obedience and this sort of thing."

Amy and her husband had wanted to find a program for their children. I asked her what she had been looking for in a preschool program. She wanted children to be taught the ABCs and to get along with each other. Amy had been looking for a school that combined playing and structured activities in ways appropriate for different age groups.

Amy used educational criteria. Religious indoctrination is the last thing she wants out of a church school.

Amy seems to be still in the process of shedding the conservative religion in which she was raised. At the same time, Christianity influences her life – especially her sense that there are right things to do. So Amy does not lie, goes to church, and perhaps most importantly believes she should expose her children to Christianity. But she needs an open religious environment for herself and her children, one that does not evoke the negative feelings she has toward conservative Christianity. Amy is clear about what she does not want: a congregation certain about its religious beliefs and intolerant of those who have doubts, a congregation with a traditional ascetic morality or conservative views on women. Amy is vaguely Christian and will be part of a congregation only if it can accept her the way she is.

SERMONS

The meaning of openness is conveyed, in part, by the nature of the sermons. Several respondents compared the sermons at Open Church with ones they had heard earlier in their lives in conservative churches.

As Denise said, "I felt like the Baptists' sermons were a little more Bible-oriented, where maybe the sermons [at Open Church] have been more topic-oriented or pick a Bible verse and kind of expand off of that, maybe into current life, which is fine. I like that." The Baptist pastors preached, "This is the Bible; we're going to talk about this." At Open Church, the pastors tell a lot of stories, and, "I love to hear stories...." Violet goes to church to learn, "not to have my sins revoked or whatever."[9] She learns from the Bible and from other peoples' experiences. The sermons include stories about the pastors' experiences or experiences of people they know, and, "you think, 'they're talking about me.'" Mary likes the sermons because they do not dwell on theology; the talks are "liveable," since they apply to everyday life.[10] In all, seven respondents made a point of mentioning that they like the pastor's style: relating Scripture to their daily lives and sometimes to his own. One person gave as an example of a sermon she liked one in which the pastor talked about the death of his aunt and how he had dealt with it; this discussion appealed to her because she had recently lost her father.

Not even the pastor's Sunday School classes resemble old-fashioned Bible school. David likes these classes:

"I grew up... listening and learning about the Bible to a point where I was so tired of 'Here's what God is saying in this verse.' Well, okay, what does that mean, though, in terms of how we live our lives in this world, if you will?" asked David. "The connection

9. Violet was younger than forty and is highly educated.
10. Mary was younger than forty and is highly educated.

wasn't made often enough, as far as I was concerned, or if it was made, it was made in the philosophical idealistic kind of perfectionist kind of way which isn't real. It's just not real."

One Sunday School class discussed a video by Rabbi Kushner about why bad things happen to good people. Another time a counseling psychologist talked about depression in our society. The main focus was to understand depression, although a connection was made between faith and depression. However, "It wasn't like all you have to do is believe in God, and pray every day, and then you aren't going to be depressed." The focus, David said, was on understanding what it is to be depressed and how it is being treated.

The sermons, then, convey a sense of openness in several ways. First, they are not schoollike lessons in the meaning of the Bible, and thus do not imply that there is a single meaning to be known. Second, openness is evident in the use of nonbiblical material for gaining wisdom. While the Bible and Jesus are the religious focus, inspiration and help come from nonbiblical sources; personal experiences, secular professionals, and non-Christians may be used. Third, by focusing his sermons on application, the pastor implicitly leaves room for individual decision-making, since more than one conclusion is usually possible whenever someone moves from abstract principles to concrete actions.

AN OPEN CHURCH IS NOT NECESSARILY A MORALLY
LIBERAL ONE

In March 1997, the Presbyterian Church (USA) adopted a constitutional change prohibiting the ordination of noncelibate gay and lesbian clergy, elders, and deacons (*Indianapolis Star*, 19 March 1996). Eighty-five of the 11,400 congregations in the United States had previously said they were willing to ordain gays and lesbians. Discussing the amendment, an Indiana Presbyterian pastor said, "We have a responsibility to be caring and loving people, but at the same time we have to have an objective standard of behavior" (Cebula 1997a:A27). The vote of the regional bodies (presbyteries) was ninety-seven to seventy-four in favor of the constitutional change. The Covenant Network of Presbyterians is seeking to replace the amendment with a more liberal statement, while the Presbyterian Coalition defends the amendment. Although it is true that the Church is divided on this issue, the overall vote means that the Church has taken a conservative stand regarding homosexual clergy and church officers.

In a sermon concerning miracles, given at the time of the meeting of the general assembly in 1997 that passed the resolution on homosexuality, the pastor at Open Church talked about social outcasts – first mentioning lepers, then people with AIDS. Later he discussed homosexuals and the decision of the general assembly not to allow them to enter the ministry. The pastor hoped that members of the congregation would reach out to homosexuals. He talked about the need for love and a caring attitude. The pastor then returned to the matter of miracles.

Such a sermon was suitable, given that the congregation is very divided on this issue. Norris does not believe that homosexuality is a sin; he believes that homosexuals are born "wired that way," and that their sexual preference is not a free choice. Sam believes that the homosexual lifestyle is wrong, but that homosexuals need to be welcomed in the church, as long as they are barred from positions that would allow them to influence his children.[11] As Edward said regarding homosexuals in the ministry, "I think that if you poll people [at church] . . . you would get five different people with five different answers on that, and I think the general attitude right now is where we're trying to look more at what unites us." Within the denomination, as within Open Church, diverse opinions regarding homosexuality will continue to be held and tolerated.

This case study of Open Church makes clear that being a modern religion does not exclude acceptance of at least some conservative ethical positions. Open's members accept the authority of Scripture and the value of a congregation that encourages individuals to reach their own understanding of the meaning of the Bible. What defines their church is not specific moral positions, but its openness – such is a modern congregation.

THE APPEAL OF OPENNESS

In sum, the key to understanding the success of this Presbyterian congregation is its openness. At Open Church, if you believe in Jesus Christ, you can take communion. Not only are nonconformists not publicly

---

11. Sam was over forty and is highly educated.

condemned or shunned, but the congregation positively welcomes diversity. Support for an open church has diverse sources, one of which I have mentioned often, the libertarian legacy: People do not want to be told what to believe. Among educated people, this conviction is strengthened by the confidence that one has the ability and knowledge to grapple with serious questions. For this reason, I believe, five of the fourteen interviewees expressed appreciation for the relatively democratic structure of the congregation. Support for openness also occurs when people do not believe that religious matters or biblical statements have obvious answers or interpretations, when they accept ambiguity and want to be encouraged and aided in their own thinking through of such matters. For such people, religious ambiguity allows for individual empowerment and expansion of our collective spiritual wisdom.

The second type of supporter lives within a religiously pluralistic personal environment and accepts pluralism as a fact. Family or friends agree to disagree. Such people need a congregation that will accept their personal tolerance. Third, support comes from people more aware of what they have left than of who they are. The United States has been a religiously conservative country. Many people today are shaped by their rejection of a religious heritage identified in their minds by such things as obedience and discrimination against women. Yet they also remain religious and want their children to learn about Christianity. Such people need an open congregation.

Fourth, support comes from people who do not believe in a literal interpretation of the Bible, who believe that wisdom can come from nonbiblical sources, and who want to be in an environment that uses diverse sources for discussing sermon questions. For them, churchgoing is not a matter of only learning about the Bible, but of learning how to live.

As this analysis implies, a church that is open appeals to people likely to have less intense levels of commitment: those married to nonbelievers (Gail), people not very interested in religion who yet want to go to a church (Amy), and married couples who need a common ground (Doris and Wylie). For example, while Gail's husband did not try to stop her and their children going to church, and had even driven them to religious events on occasion, he had asked that Gail not bring the religious stuff home, thereby restricting the extent to which Gail could be committed to her church. David commented that a lot of people at Open Church "aren't involved in the church in any way I can see." Church is packed only at Easter and Christmas. David found church programs to be inadequately supported. "The feel that I have . . . is that well, church is not a focal point for many families. . . ." Undoubtedly an open church will have members with quite varied levels of commitment – but, while this may disappoint some participants, the tolerance of marginal membership is part of an open church's appeal.[12]

As Nancy Tatom Ammerman (1997) has emphasized, most people do not live totally committed to any organization, nor is such commitment necessary for an organization's survival. "It is perfectly possible to have a thriving low-commitment religious organization . . ." (p. 206). Moreover, people's religiosity may not be totally channeled through a self-identified religious organization, and this may even be desirable at least from the point of view of society. In fact, some congregations expect their members to express their religious seriousness by getting involved in movements outside the churches (p. 206). Logically, a person serious about religion might even eschew congregational involvement. Such thoughts underline the need to go well beyond Kelley in discussing what it means to be religiously serious.

But Open Church has boundaries. In conversation with me, the pastoral staff repeatedly affirmed the centrality and authority of the Bible in their work. While they accept ambiguity in the meaning of the Bible, learning about and from the Bible is the purpose of sermons, of Christian education – of the church. Unlike traditionalist churches, Open Church does not push a literal interpretation of the Bible nor does Open's pastor have or aspire to establish the expectation that congregants will accept his understanding of the Bible. There is no sense that a person's salvation is tied to conformity with or even to membership in the congregation. However, the Bible is the focus of the services. Jesus remains the model. Regardless of the ambiguous nature of the Bible or our limited knowledge of the real Jesus, it is *the* book and He is *the* model.

Some church growth experts advise modern denominations to give more emphasis to their Christian character. A recent book about revitalizing the Presbyterian Church (USA), and modern Christianity generally, cited as the biggest problem the failure to make the Bible central to the church's mission. As the authors wrote, "One of the most important vital signs of a renewed Protestant witness will be our reliance

---

12. Based on interviews with churchgoing Protestants, Christian Smith (1998:58) concluded, "More than evangelicals, mainliners and liberals spoke of church participation as something they worked around other priorities in their schedules rather than as a baseline commitment to their lives."

on Scripture as the authority for our lives: the recognition that through those pages comes a truth that will set us free from ourselves and for others" (Coalter, Mulder, and Weeks 1996:11). The pastoral staff at Open Church has done this, and it seems a useful approach. The danger with this strategy is that it can lead to restricting congregational openness. Consider this continuum of religious organizations: Bob Jones University, Spirited Church, Caring Church, Open Church. The extremes vary greatly, but for adjacent cases the differences are less striking. If the Open Churches move to strengthen their symbolic boundaries, while the Caring Churches are weakening theirs, it is not clear why the former type would emerge as more popular.

As I wrote in Chapter 1, a "modern religion" values living in a society whose civic code is rooted in individualism. Moreover, such a religion accepts differentiation from the state as well as the fragmenting of culture. Modern congregations fit people who accept individualism and church-state separation, and who look to the Bible *and* other sources for inspiration. But what really draws people into a congregation such as Open Church is that its internal culture is rooted in individualism – that is, it is an open congregation. In part, such a congregation is attractive because it fits the modern rejection of authoritarian organization. In part, an open congregation is attractive because it can harbor people experiencing the late-modern acceptance of inescapable doubt – which can result from intellectual sources or from living in a personal pluralistic world. However, as will be discussed in the next section, accommodating late-modernity also requires ritual change in denominations such as the Presbyterian Church (USA).

RITUAL: TRADITIONAL AND CONTEMPORARY

Open Church recently tried to broaden its appeal by diversifying its Sunday services. After people decide to visit Open Church, they are faced with another significant choice: whether to attend the "traditional" service or the "contemporary" one.

The building complex is composed of two connected buildings: One is the church, the other contains offices, meeting rooms, and classrooms. The mostly brick church is large, has a traditional steeple, and a Greek-column front. The sanctuary is brick and wood, with some marble columns. A large, empty cross hangs from the ceiling over the chancel. Toward the back of the chancel is a marble communion table; behind it is a carved wooden lattice that partially hides the choir during the traditional service. On the left is a lectern used by the associate pastor, on the right a pulpit used by the pastor. Carved wood seats line the side walls of the chancel.

As the traditional service begins, an organ, located in a loft at the rear of the sanctuary, begins to play. The associate pastor and the pastor, wearing the robes of their offices, walk down the center aisle dividing the thirty rows of wooden pews. Racks on the back of the benches contain Bibles, hymnals, and the sign-in pads. The people are older than in the other churches I visited. Dress varies; many men are in coat and ties. The last six rows of benches are roped off. The rest of the church is about half full.

The pastor welcomes the congregation. The congregants are asked to sign the registration pads. The bulletin reads, "Take note of the names of persons sitting near you so that you can greet them after the service." The nineteen-member choir, wearing formal robes, enters in a procession. The congregation is standing. A traditional hymn is played by the organist and sung by the choir and some congregants. There follow collective prayers, other hymns, and the offertory, during which time congregants alternately sit and stand. A reading from the Scripture is followed by the sermon. Everyone then stands to sing a hymn and to hear the closing prayers. As congregants leave, the organ is playing, and the pastor is greeting those leaving by the main door.

This "traditional service" is preceded on Sunday mornings by a "contemporary service" that begins at nine o'clock. For fifteen minutes before the hour, the "informal praise and worship" period occurs when people sing contemporary Christian hymns, the words being printed in a handout inside the bulletin. The music is from a keyboardist, a flutist, and two guitarists. Three women and two men, mikes in hand, lead the singing. The singers stand immediately in front of the communion table. The audience quickly grows from about twenty to well over one hundred people. The associate pastor invites the congregation to stand and sing the first, lively song. The congregants sit for the next two songs. The audience ranges in age from children to the elderly, but overall is younger than the congregants at the traditional service. The soft-rock-like music varies in tempo, but is the kind that makes you want to move with it, as do some of the young singers. The audience remains largely unmoved, although some congregants sing along.

On the hour, the pastor, without his robes, enters from a door at the back of the chancel and goes to the pulpit. Announcements are made.

The congregation stands for the first of another three contemporary Christian songs. Using the bulletin insert, people follow along and some also sing along. The singers then join the congregation, while the congregants briefly greet each other. The dress tends to the informal; men with coat and tie are a distinct minority. The offertory is followed by the sermon. The singers return to the chancel platform for a final song. The congregants stand. The pastor closes with a prayer. As people leave the hour-long service, the music resumes and some congregants mingle. The pastor greets those leaving by the main door.

The contemporary service also includes the "corporate prayer"; the pastor steps down from the platform and walks up and down the middle aisle, asking for petitions – for instance, someone asks for prayers for holiday travelers. Finally, the pastor incorporates all petitions into a single prayer. He then returns to the front of the sanctuary.

As the pastor told the congregation at the early service one Sunday, joy did not exist during services at Open Church until the contemporary service had been instituted. He repeated this comment at the eleven o'clock service, adding that he likes traditional music. Slightly fewer people attend the contemporary service.

Respondents tended to prefer one or the other of these services. For example, Edward likes both country-western music, reflecting his rural roots, and classical music, reflecting his current life. He prefers the traditional service, consistent with his developing a taste for "classy" music. David also chose the traditional service because it makes him feel "like I am worshipping God." He found more contemporary services to be "kind of a social experience as opposed to a worship experience." David appreciated the views of a minister at a former church who, when someone sang a solo in the service, "didn't like it when people applauded because that's not what singing is in a worship experience. That's a performance."

In contrast, Denise likes the early service because it is relaxed: "It's a little more homey." Doris also likes the contemporary option, especially the music:

"It's very easy to get caught up in it," says Doris. "You can almost feel it spiritually with everybody, because it's very moving. I mean, there are times when I'll just cry. It's so pretty, for it really touches a part of me or it's – you can see people getting into it. Their bodies are moving, and they're just having a really good time."

As Tara said, "there's many of us women that will be sitting there just the tears rolling down our eyes. . . ." The music draws out people's emotions. Tara admitted she likes that good old rock-n-roll.

The pastor at Open Church told me that its ritual experiment has been a success. Some people prefer the contemporary service, and its availability is aiding Open's growth. The pastor believes that "seekers" come to the contemporary service, because they have no experience with solemn rituals and feel more relaxed at the less formal service. The dual offering symbolizes something basic about Open Church: Diversity is of its nature.

However, the existence of both a traditional and a contemporary service points to a possible problem. Tim and Kathy Carson (1997) discussed the process of designing a contemporary service at their own modern congregation. They advised "that events must be intentionally scheduled to compensate for the regular lack of whole church experience" (p. 15). Their church holds "four 'festival' Sunday mornings each year . . . entitled 'Come Home' Sundays." The Church does this because congregations that expand their acceptance of diverse practices run the risk of dissolving into cohabiting subgroups sharing little more than a common roof. Open Church does occasionally have blended rituals to reinforce the sense that the congregation is a single community. The pastoral staff emphasized that there is an ongoing discussion about the usefulness of holding blended rituals versus that of offering alternative rituals, such as is usually done at Open Church. Given the evidence in this study that solemn and charismatic rituals have their own unique rewards, I believe a steady diet of blended rituals would not be successful. Whether periodic blended rituals can overcome the centrifugal forces generated by diverse rituals is an interesting question for future research.

Even continuing to have separate but equal services poses a problem. Open Church looks and feels like a traditional church. The pastor and the people prefer the more solemn Sunday service. Mainline churches in Indianapolis were featured in a story about new rituals that were introduced to help the churches grow. For example, at a Presbyterian church, an unrobed minister with a wireless microphone "walks along the center aisle as if he is working the room at a night club. A drum kit and guitar amplifiers hold center stage in the sanctuary. Spirit Heart, the house band, is ready to perform music by Curtis Mayfield, the Wynans, and Sounds of Blackness" (Cebula 1997b:E1). Appropriately, Open Church's contemporary ritual is more restrained. It is a question whether the contemporary ritual can be successful in a broadly solemn environment.

The issue of applause at the contemporary service illustrates the problem:

> Violet questions the policy on applause at church services. "We were told – about a year ago – that you don't clap in church, even at the contemporary service. Supposedly the minister said, 'People who perform in church are doing it for God. They're not doing it for your pleasure, and so you don't reward them with clapping.'"
>
> This policy seemed inappropriate: "... in the contemporary service other things are so personalized. You know, ... if you miss the communion tray and if you want to go get it yourself, or if you couldn't find your money when the offering came by and you wanted to put it in later ... you just get up in the middle of the service and you do it. And then to be told not to clap, I mean, all other behavior is just kind of accepted, and then to be told not to clap, I thought was odd."
>
> In her previous church, if the spirit moved you, you clapped. Until told to stop, people at Open Church had applauded.

In fact, Open Church has no policy about applause. Although musical performances usually are not applauded, speakers and performers occasionally have received applause during church services. However, Violet's perception of the situation is significant: The contemporary service does not feel right to someone who has experienced charismatic services elsewhere.

The traditional service approximates a solemn ritual, just as the contemporary one approximates the charismatic type. The popularity of the charismatic ritual at Spirited Church, the lack of enthusiasm for Truth's solemn ritual on the part of some whom we interviewed, and the instant success of the contemporary service at Open Church evidence, I believe, the declining appeal of solemnity to middle-class Americans. Historically, as I discussed in Chapter 2, the middle class had rejected religious enthusiasm under the influence of the Enlightenment's elevation of human reason. Solemnity fits a cultural emphasis on rationality; calming music and a reverential attitude to a powerful other distances us from our own emotions, indeed from our own selves. Now in late-modernity the middle class is being drawn toward the kind of balanced ritual that I call charismatic. Such rituals encourage letting go of reason and directly experiencing God or the presence of others' or one's own emotions. Moreover, congregants can act on these experiences and emotions, such as by clapping. As Violet said, the contemporary service is "personalized." Also, the informal atmosphere allows people to be themselves. For example, children are more able to act like children. In the wake of the 1960s counterculture, solemnity is in decline.

With the introduction of contemporary rituals, merely modern congregations such as Open Church are now accommodating late-modernity. As Wade Clark Roof (1998:222) wrote, "many mainstream Protestant churches have so accommodated modernity by emphasizing creed and doctrine that they have lost the depth and experiential dimensions – emotion, feelings, soul." In my terms, such churches are "merely modern." Undoubtedly, by accommodating late-modernity, such churches will broaden their appeal. The question raised by Open Church is whether the same congregation should offer both solemn and charismatic rituals, or whether within denominations such as the Presbyterian Church (USA) congregations should develop identities as either solemn or charismatic. Of course, the first option is not practical for small congregations, and the second one is not practical in areas with a small number of denominational members.

COMMUNAL BONDS

In the last chapter, I discussed how congregations in the United States are like modern families. This is not true just of conservative congregations. Like those in the other congregations we studied, people at Open Church like the interpersonal relationships formed there. For some, it is enough that they exchange pleasantries with others at church on Sunday mornings. Others want more and find an intimacy in small groups, where the sharing of personal stories and the responses to them are the heart of the matter. Like others, Denise and her husband enjoyed the Bible study group. I asked Denise to describe a meeting:

"We have a book," said Denise, "but . . . the first thirty minutes, we socialize, we have a snack, then we get into our lesson for an hour and a half. . . . We get on all these tangents, and, you know, I think there's twelve, thirteen people in the group. You know, I really feel like we're connected with those people because we get into, 'Oh, so and so has a job offer. Are they going to take it? Well,

this person is unhappy, you know, this is going on in this relationship. This one's single,'...we're learning a little bit more about
those people that we wouldn't learn sitting next to them in a Sunday School or in a service, so that's helping us to become better
friends."

Such groups create intimacy among subsets of church members.

For two of the people with whom we talked – Violet and Nancy – the
connection between a congregation and a sense of family was of central
importance.

Violet had grown up in a mainline church in a small town.
Only one hundred people belonged to the church, including her
parents, grandparents, and everybody in her family. She switched
churches in the last town she and her husband lived in, trying to
find a church that had a sense of being a family. "I'm not concerned
about . . . whether . . . [a church is] Presbyterian or First Christian
or Baptist or whatever." Open Church appeals to her because her
husband, who has a fundamentalist background, and her kids like
it. It fits her family.

Violet and her family attended the contemporary Sunday service, which was new at the time. "The whole family liked that. We
finally decided, 'Yeah, this is for us. We're going to join.'" When
asked what was so appealing about the service, Violet said, "The
kids liked it. . . ." The family had gone at times to the traditional
service. The kids found the songs to be boring. Moreover, the
eleven o'clock service is more formal. At the earlier service, the
kids can wear shorts and tennis shoes, women may wear shorts,
and men, jeans. "I feel like if my kids peep a word during the
service at eleven o'clock, that they're an outcast, whereas at the
nine o'clock service, everybody's kids are talking, and, you know,
wanting a piece of gum, needing to go the bathroom, you know,
it just fits a family with young children much better." Violet also
likes the music because it is more like gospel music, "not real-stiff
high-brow music." She also likes the friendliness of the people and
the time during the Sunday service devoted to welcoming those
seated around you.

In explaining the family's decision to join a Presbyterian church,
Violet told her mother, "the kids like it; we have friends that go
there, coworkers that go there. We feel very comfortable there."

Violet referred to two kinds of family: She wanted the congregation to be a family, and Violet wanted a shared involvement in Open Church to strengthen the bonds among the members of her own family. I begin my analysis of Violet's comments by focusing on the first issue. Violet seems to have been raised in a church that almost literally was her extended family. At the time, the congregation may have felt like a body of people, like a community. Violet still has a lingering desire for such a church as shown in the importance to her both of the friendliness at the contemporary service and of the presence of friends and coworkers in the congregation. Yet Violet is similar to Gail as well as Doris and Wylie in that all of them were looking for a congregation in which members of families with diverse religious backgrounds could feel comfortable. Thus, when Violet first came to Middletown, she and her husband visited a number of conservative congregations, including Spirited Church, but she liked the fact that "Presbyterians seem to leave it to the individual to develop some of their own values and ways of worshipping." In her present stage of life, Violet needs a congregation that accepts diversity, which is to say not one that is a monolithic body of people.

Given that Violet talked about wanting to be in a church that had a sense of being a family, it might be thought that Violet would prefer small congregations. However, this was not true. While Violet was church-shopping in Middletown, some places she "went to were real small, and it was – as we walked in the door, they wanted to know what committees we wanted to serve on. Some people might like that instant involvement, but I wanted to kind of sit back and observe and figure out what I wanted, and Open Church allowed me to do that." Regarding small, demanding congregations, Violet said, "On the way home from such a church, I would say something like, 'they think I'm bringing the snacks for the next meal, and I don't even want to join, you know, they were just too overbearing. . . .'" Such comments suggest that Violet does not really want to be part of a body of people, that she does not want to be absorbed into the group.

However, Violet does want to feel close to the members of her family and considers church a valued means for achieving this goal. Indeed, uppermost in her mind is that a congregation must help to bind together Violet, her husband, and her children. She does not care about the denominational affiliation of a church but whether it would unify her family. Violet is quite sensitive to how the members of her family, especially her children, react to a congregation. In this regard, the contemporary service is quite appealing because the music bores her kids less and because the casual atmosphere better suits children accustomed to acting on their needs immediately. Solemn rituals do not fit young people no longer raised to be seen but not heard.

In sum, while Violet has a nostalgia for the old-fashioned kind of church community she experienced as a child, she needs an open church that allows people to be different. Open Church appeals to Violet because she has a network of friends there and because going there has helped bring her own family together.

Nancy also emphasized the link between church and family unity:[13]

When Nancy and her family moved to Middletown, they visited several Methodist churches, since their previous church was part of that denomination. They went for about six months to first one, then another such church. Nancy was never satisfied. She and her husband felt "alienated" (a matter to which I shall return). A major problem was that her children did not like these churches. If the children are not happy with the church, every Sunday is a struggle. Then a friend, whose children were friends of Nancy's children, suggested she try Open Church. It was Palm Sunday, when a donkey is paraded down the center aisle of the sanctuary. Nancy's family went and the people there "just sucked us in." Nancy found some of her friends were there. Her children were quickly involved in activities such as the youth choir and Sunday School. Although a "soccer mom," Nancy is now involved with two church groups.

She attended Open Church for about a year before the family decided to join. Having done so, Nancy now feels a deep loyalty to the congregation. As she told her interviewer, choosing a church is like getting married: Neither should be lightly selected or once chosen, abandoned. Understandably Nancy does not like the Methodist practice of regularly moving pastors around, "as if changing underwear." She deliberately chooses a minister and a people, then stays loyal to them. Of the two, the latter seems the more important to her; as she said about the appeal of churches, it "goes back to people." For Nancy, "church is a family."

As the interview went on, Nancy reexamined the sense of alienation she felt visiting churches when her family moved to Middletown. She wondered if these churches had not attracted her

13. Nancy was over forty and is highly educated.

because she had been so deeply involved in her previous church. She speculated that it is hard to move into a new church family, that the wounds resulting from leaving the former church had to heal before she could fully accept what the new churches were willing to give her family. As she described how much she missed her old friends, Nancy cried.

She believes that a congregation "takes a big city and makes it a small town." In today's society, you may not know even your neighbors. People need to get together with similar people. Kids need a supportive group. It is the church that brings a "family" together.

Nancy believes that theologically Methodism and Presbyterianism are similar. There is a Presbyterian stereotype: "not rooted in the Word, more social." This does not fit Open Church. The pastors preach from the Bible; the Word takes precedence over denominational statements. When asked whether she accepts the Bible literally, Nancy responded that the Bible does contain parables, but it is mostly true; Nancy described her attitude as "literal with some interpretations." Later in the interview, Nancy praised the sermons because the pastor referred to the Bible and what Jesus did, and then applied the biblical material to life today, making the Bible relevant to Nancy's life.

Nancy's story resembles Violet's. Nancy wanted the congregation to be a family and she wanted church life to strengthen her nuclear family. Like Violet, Nancy does not seem to assign much importance to theology. Moreover, Nancy seemed vague about her own views on the Bible. All this is understandable, however, because for Nancy a congregation is its people.

Nancy wants a congregation to turn a big city into a small town. By that, she seems to mean that church should be a place for making close friends. Leaving her old church was, in my terms, like becoming a widow. She so missed her old friends that when Nancy first came to Middletown, she could not replace them. The visit to Open Church coincided with the end of her mourning, when she was "sucked" into a new family. She found friends were there, and she joined several church groups.

Nancy also wants church to bring her family together. It is especially important that her children like the church service and its programs because it is painful to have to pressure children to go to church every Sunday. Open Church unifies her own family because she and her children have found interesting things to do at church. (Nancy did not discuss her husband's involvement.)

Both Violet and Nancy want churchgoing to strengthen family ties. What struck me is the influence of the children on the affiliation process. Their children had to like a church if Nancy and Violet were going to attend its services. According to a recent newspaper article, more teens than ever "are taking the lead in finding a faith that fits," with their parents following after them. Such teens "give high marks to congregations with worship, mission, and outreach geared to their age groups" (Religion News Service 1999:G5). The prevalence of "teen power" implies that many American adults expect congregations to reinforce family life by involving all the members of their families so that each attends voluntarily.

Another implication concerns the nature of the modern family. In Chapter 5, I described the new American family as symbolically "fatherless," meaning the family was less a patriarchal institution and more a network of individuals, each of whom is to be respected, and among whom relationships are to be based on openness and compassion. The "teen power" just discussed implies this new model of the family; the decision to join a church is not made, or at least ratified, by a powerful father; rather, a congregation should appeal to every member of the family, so that each one goes voluntarily. More specifically, child-rearing is not a matter of teaching obedience but of gaining cooperation. The family is not a body of people but an intimate network of individuals.

The stories told by Violet and Nancy illustrate the continuing practice of talking about congregations as families without acknowledging the changed meaning of such imagery. In late-modern society, both congregations and families are less bodies of people than they are networks of personal bonds. These stories also reinforce a by-now familiar point: Congregations are successful because they involve people in communal relationships. As with Nancy and Violet, one consequence is the presence of members little interested in theology. But this situation is less problematic at an open church where diversity is the hallmark.

MEANING AND STRICTNESS

Kelley argued that people want to give meaning to their lives and that they will choose a meaning associated with a strict church. Violet's story is relevant to this argument. However, before I finish telling her story, I want to present another part of Norris's life.

As discussed earlier, Norris left Christianity because of his negative experience in a conservative denomination. He became a spiritual seeker. At the time, the Beatles created a popular interest in Indian religion, and Transcendental Meditation was at its height. Norris checked out various Eastern religions, but he remained "unchurched" for over a decade.

One day, Norris was at the hospital happily watching his wife give birth to a son. Soon it became apparent something was wrong; the doctor could not stop his wife's bleeding. Norris felt as though he were walking between the valley of life and the valley of death. (Norris's use of biblical imagery shows the lingering influence of his Christian upbringing.) Before him were his newborn baby and his hemorrhaging wife. He felt alone. God was not with him. "[I] recognized at that moment that I desperately needed God in my life." Norris's wife was saved. His "spiritual reawakening" motivated him and his wife to visit churches. They joined a Presbyterian church, although, because they lived elsewhere when these events occurred, not the one in Middletown.

Violet's daughter became seriously ill soon after her family moved to Middletown:

"I don't think it impacted my decision to get involved with that church [Open Church] in particular," said Violet, "but it probably did cause me to go ahead and join a church. I mean, it – whatever church I would have been going to at the time I probably would have joined, because it was then I started thinking of all these things of, you know, what if she hasn't been baptized yet, what would happen to her, or, you know, it just started a whole thinking that I'd never been prepared to consider."

Her daughter recovered. Because Violet happened to be going to Open Church, the family joined the church.

Violet's and Norris's stories illustrate how the possible death of loved ones may raise profound issues that come under the heading of "meaning." When this happened to Violet and Norris, they did not go searching for a strict church. Instead, they joined churches where they could be comfortable because the churches were consistent with the values they already held. This is also what Tara did when a close relative died. Since I told her story earlier in the chapter, there is no need to repeat it. Significantly, Tara rejected Truth Church, which is closer to Kelley's strong church than is Open Church. Tara wanted to be reassured that everything was going to be all right; she wanted to leave Sunday service happy. At Open Church, she felt very comfortable.

David's story is also relevant. We met him earlier as someone who preferred the traditional service. David grew up hearing that if you are not born again, if you do not accept Jesus Christ as Lord and savior, you were going to hell. But for him there are too many good people who do not meet this born-again criterion to accept such a conservative perspective. Moreover, David likes the "open interpretation" of the Bible at Open Church. The Bible accepts slavery and condones killing homosexuals, but David does not believe God wants such practices. The Bible is not literally the mind of God. Finally, and relevant to our present topic, David cannot accept a traditionalist view of God. A close relative died when she was young. Why did she have to die? "Did God have anything to do with that? I don't think so." David perceives a world in which bad things happen that cannot be directly connected to God. God is somewhat detached from the world. David could not feel comfortable in a conservative church, in part because of the insistence on the active role of God in daily life.

Norris, Violet, Tara, and David experienced the possible or actual loss of a loved one, experiences that made them think about the meaning of life. Their response was not to search for a strict church. Rather, they joined a congregation that fits the religious and ethical beliefs they had come to at the time of the trauma or as a result of the trauma. They needed an open church. All of them turned to the supernatural, but not in a conservative context. Encounters with death result in reflection on the meaning of life. But in such circumstances, people do not change their values in order to feel comfortable in a strict church. Rather, they take more seriously a kind of religion already compatible with the values they have come to accept over the course of their lives.

CONCLUSION

Based on their study of Presbyterians, sociologists concluded that Baby Boomers in such a church want five things:

- Maintenance of a family tradition
- Religious education for their children
- Small open and supportive groups
- A place to meet new people
- Spiritually nourishing worship (Hoge, Johnson, and Luidens 1994:204–5)

The first four points are important but they apply both to traditionalist and modern congregations. They do not explain the unique appeal of a modern congregation. The last item on the list is the intriguing one. The sociologists' brief elaboration on this point contains rather vague phrases such as "inspiration from the Bible" and "uplifting and empowering worship." Their analysis does not tell us what makes an Open Church appealing.

An essential aspect of Open Church's attractiveness is that it is *not* a conservative church: Neither pastor nor creed is authoritative, and the congregation is not a spiritual elite distancing itself from people who have different theological views. There is a list of basic beliefs for which the church stands, but each person is *expected* to make up her or his own mind. Biblical study is combined with the use of non-Christian religious sources and the expertise of people whose wisdom may be secular in nature. (Appropriately, while I was visiting Open Church, the pastor mentioned a new program "Open Church on the Go." Everyone was invited to go watch the Australian film *Shine* that afternoon, and then to go out for a pizza.[14]) Among the congregations that we studied, Open Church is distinctive with its breadth of internal diversity, as evidenced in the range of positions on an issue such as homosexuality and in the use of both traditional and contemporary services. Of all the congregations we studied, Open Church least approximates a body of people. The shared acceptance of, possibly even the celebration of, weak boundaries *is* the boundary for a modern congregation. For both intellectual and social reasons, as previously discussed, some people prefer such a congregation.

When I asked the pastor at Open Church how he explained his congregation's success, he mentioned the worship service, mission opportunities, and a good physical location in Middletown that makes the church visible to a large potential pool of members. Regarding the ritual, he mentioned the quality of the preaching and music, as well as the fact that people have a choice between traditional and contemporary music. While I would give relatively little weight to mission opportunities, overall I accept the pastor's assessment as far as it goes. What he left out of his analysis is the importance of openness, although he had earlier told me of a family who recently joined his church because the pastor at their previous conservative church was too authoritarian. This

14. This film is about the troubled life of Australian pianist David Helfgott. The film was described as inspirational because it showed the healing power of a woman's love, and it demonstrated that no matter how bad life gets, one should never cease to believe in a redeemable human spirit.

omission, I believe, occurred because he perceived his church in compe-tition (my word) with other mainline congregations, who are also open. While this understanding is generally true, I believe the pastor underes-timated the importance of openness; without this quality, people from other modern congregations would not join his church; moreover, it is because of this quality that some religious people leave the conservative universe of congregations for Open Church.

While the most important difference between modern congregations and all traditionalist ones, including the modernized ones, is the pref-erence in the former type to be a "weak" group, I believe differences in their attitudes toward "the world" are also important. Illustrative of the difference between a modernized traditionalist congregation and a modern one are the divergent approaches to outreach programs. For example, both Presbyterian congregations in our study sponsor outreach work in Mexico. In a conversation with me, Open's pastor praised the work carried out by his church members as an effort to bring about a more just world. In contrast, evangelizing seems a more important part of the work in Mexico supported by Truth Church. Neither modern nor traditionalist congregations are uncritical of "the world." However, modern ones do not link the transformation of the world with expanding the social control of their churches.

For our respondents at Open Church, then, it was the weakness of the congregational boundary that was the most important aspect of their church. However, we have also learned that they accept the use of secular cultural resources for inspiration. Moreover, members do not seem as concerned about evangelism as people at other congregations in our study. I suggest, then, that modern congregations are attractive primarily because they are open and secondarily because they are more accepting of "the world": Secular culture need not become religious, and everyone need not join their churches.

As I pointed out at the beginning of this chapter, modern congrega-tions generally seem not to be doing well. Based on my study of Open Church, I suggest that modern congregations face three problems unique to late-modernity. First, some churches undoubtedly remain "merely modern," that is, they have not accommodated people who have ac-cepted religious doubts as a permanent condition or developed charis-matic versions of their rituals.

A second problem for modern groups is that some reasons for rejecting traditionalist Protestantism could lead to participation in a late-modern religion just as easily as to participation in a modern one. Living with ambiguity and doubt, as well as having to accommodate diverse religions within one's personal network, is in fact part of what it means to be a late-modern-religious person. As I mentioned at the beginning of this chapter, many young and well-educated people raised Presbyterians are no longer in that church; nearly half of the Presbyterian confirmands in one study had eventually left not only Presbyterianism but all churches (Hoge, Johnson, and Luidens 1994), and some of these people may exemplify the late-modern religious type. What keeps modern people from taking this route is their commitment – whether strong or weak – to the specialness of Christianity.

Yet public support for such specialness seems on the decline in the United States. Perhaps the most dramatic finding about religion in the numerous studies of Middletown concerns the preeminence of Christianity. In 1924 and 1977, roughly comparable populations of high school students in Middletown were asked whether or not they agreed with this statement: "Christianity is the one true religion and all people should be converted to it." In 1924, 94 percent agreed; in 1977, only 41 percent concurred (Caplow, Bahr, and Chadwick 1983:94). Similarly, a growing proportion of Americans believe that "all religious faiths teach equally valid truths"; in 1994 the figure was 40 percent (Barna 1996:14). Such changing attitudes would seem to pave the way for late-modern religion.

In such a context, traditional religious symbols lose their protected status. In his religious column in the New York Times, Peter Steinfels (1998) argued that current events require a discussion of how respectable people respond "to what would have once been considered insulting renderings of sacred figures, symbols, or rituals especially Christian and Roman Catholic ones" (p. A13). The immediate reason for Steinfels's concern was an art exhibit with paintings, for example, of Jesus hanging from a cross of penises and of pages of the Bible defaced with satanic remarks. Steinfels acknowledged that while sometimes "insulting rendering" of sacred images are "trivializing uses of religion for commercial ends," sometimes "there are deliberately shocking uses of religious imagery that, even in their hostility, are aimed at religious ends." Both uses suggest that Christianity is losing its special status in American culture.

The appeal of modern Protestantism was related to its accommodation of the modernization process, but new developments suggest that continued accommodation is unlikely. Signs are appearing that Christianity is losing sacredness, its specialness, in popular culture. Late-modern religions beckon to members whose doubts have come to include questioning the superiority of Christianity.

The third problem is the strain caused by the diversity of opinions in modern congregations on moral issues such as homosexuality. The temptation for those with conservative views to leave modern congregations probably increases as modernized traditionalist churches multiply. As conservative Christianity accommodates modernity, the difference between, for example, a Caring Church and an Open Church declines, making it easier for people with conservative ethics yet modern sensibilities to leave modern religion. Despite such problems, modern congregations fill a niche. They attract people who want an open church and who believe in the specialness of Christianity.

CHAPTER SEVEN

CONCLUSION

In this chapter, I present my full explanation for the appeal of tradition-alist Protestantism in late-modern America. Then I discuss the impli-cation of my analysis for modernization theory. To begin with, however, I consider the relevance of our research for the "new paradigm" in the sociology of religion.

THE NEW PARADIGM FOR EXPLAINING THE POPULARITY OF AMERICAN CHURCHES

Among Western countries, the United States has an unusually high per-centage of its citizens who attend church (Lipset 1996:61). Since Alexis de Tocqueville's analysis (1954), which was written in the nineteenth century, the American involvement in churches has been linked to the absence of a state church. The resulting religious pluralism has meant that churches "can no longer take for granted the allegiance of their client populations"; thus religions must be "marketed," and churches must produce results desired by potential followers (or at least seem to do so) (Berger 1967:138). Because an open market has resulted in a good fit between American churches and the religious needs of the people, many Americans have been involved in churches.

This argument was further developed by Wade Clark Roof and William McKinney (1987). As they pointed out, until roughly the late-modern period, religious identity was related to race, ethnicity (e.g., Irish Catholics), and regionalism (e.g., the Southern Baptist Convention). Because such traits were impossible to change, or improbable of chang-ing, they are called *ascriptive*, in contrast to *achieved* characteristics such as years of education. When religious identities are strongly linked to ascriptive traits, religious change is less likely. Because of social changes such as new opportunities for college education, new affluence, and greater ethnic intermarriage, people have become more cosmopolitan and the importance of ethnic and regional loyalties has declined. Moreover, late-modern culture, as argued in Chapter 1, places more emphasis on each individual's self-development and gives less importance to group memberships. The effect of all these developments has been to weaken the connection between personal identity and ascribed statuses, thus making personal changes, including religious ones, more likely (pp. 63–71). For instance, if being a Southerner became less personally significant to people living in Atlanta, Georgia, then being affiliated with the Southern Baptist Convention because it is a major carrier of Southern culture would also become less important, making religious change more likely for such people.

In late-modern America, "an individual is in a position of 'shopping around' in a consumer market of religious alternatives and can 'pick and choose' among aspects of beliefs and tradition" (pp. 67). In 1998 a national sample of Americans was asked, "As an adult, have you ever shopped around for a church or synagogue – that is, gone to different churches or synagogues or other places of worship in order to compare and decide which one you wanted to attend regularly?" Thirty-nine percent said "yes." About half of these people said that the last time they church-shopped was when they had moved (National Opinion Research Center 1999).

These analyses have been brought together in the "new paradigm for the sociological study of religion in the United States" (Warner 1993). Much that we heard in our interviews is consistent with this paradigm. Respondents felt free to leave congregations that no longer satisfied them, although at times this was an emotionally difficult process. In addition, some of the respondents truly did shop around, especially if they had just moved to Middletown. However, people shopped within segments of the market. For instance, none of the people with whom we talked had tried out a Catholic congregation. For them, the market was limited to Protestantism. Moreover, the relevant suppliers in that market, as far as our respondents were concerned, were those attended by people with whom they had personal relationships.

What is missing from the new paradigm is an analysis of the demand side. An open market with numerous suppliers does not automatically result in high sales volume. Suppliers must be providing what people want. In this book, I have used modernization theory to understand what kind of religious products Americans want as they enter the twenty-first century. Before summing up what I believe has been learned from our research about the kind of religion that attracts contemporary people, however, I want to present some findings from our study that suggest an additional reason for the popularity of American churches that is not explicit in the new paradigm.

VOLATILE PROTESTANTISM

When I returned to the congregations in 1998 and 1999 to talk with the pastors, at least two of them were in the midst of reading books about how American churches need to change in order to stay current. Among the pastors, there is a desire to grow and a constant effort to learn how to reach their potential participants.

A growth mentality can produce volatility in three ways. First, growth may mean changing from a small to a large congregation and this implies a change in the rewards of churchgoing. In our study, some respondents pointed out that in a large church, newcomers can pass unnoticed and that warm relationships are not possible with most of the people encountered at a Sunday service. For example, Truth Church seemed less friendly than the smaller charismatic church that one respondent had previously attended. "[I]f you came to visit, people realized that there was a visitor there, and they would make an effort to approach you and welcome you, really make you feel welcome, to let you know that they were glad that you were there and invite you to come back, and they would want to find out about you and that kind of thing." In this respondent's experience, such a greeting does not usually happen at Truth Church, although he and his wife routinely introduce themselves to people they do not know. He asked me if anyone tried to talk with me when I visited Truth Church. No one had, at the time. "That shouldn't happen ... I see that as a problem." If people do want their church to be a warm and welcoming place, they may leave growing congregations.

Second, growth may trigger internal conflict over control of the congregation. At Spirited Church, members who were present when the current pastor took office felt invaded by so many newcomers; worship used to be like a family reunion. As a church historian wrote, "It was difficult for gifted excited new members to be patient in finding a place to use their gifts in ministry. Old leaders viewed the newcomers with suspicion." When a larger building was purchased to be the new church, some old members left the congregation.

Third, growth may result in a changed mission that may not be acceptable to everyone. In 1999 Caring Church split into two congregations. In exploring how to increase the number of participants, church leaders decided that a new, more visible location would be very helpful. They found a desirable parcel of land. The purchase was put to a vote. The motion to move was one vote shy of the two-thirds majority needed; four hundred people voted. Subsequently the pastor and four hundred people formed a new congregation that will build on the new property. About two hundred people have remained in the old church. From the pastor's point of view, the conflict reflected alternative visions: One group wanted the congregation to focus on serving the needs of the people in the congregation living in the small town where the old church is located; others wanted to reach out to the six-county area from which the congregation was drawing participants. As the pastor put it, some wanted a community church, some a regional church.

Caring's pastor was optimistic about the future: "People like to be part of a new thing." After Spirited Church split up, it grew rapidly and, "in growing churches, there is a sense that this is 'the place to be' " (Hadaway and Roozen 1993:129). Spirited Church became a magnet for those in Middletown who see themselves in stagnant or dying churches. The new Caring Church may have a similar experience.

The splitting up of congregations may aid church growth. In effect, new congregations are formed:

Viewed this way, the formation of breakaway congregations acts as a promulgation of the faith, and an improvement in the performance of the larger church. Thus, it is possible that the formation of breakaway congregations acts as a backhanded way of church planting. . . . While there may be better ways to plant new congregations, it seems that an intense conflict creates an emotional energy that is helpful in forming a congregation in a way that well-reasoned church-planting strategies cannot match (Starke and Dyck 1996:172).

I believe it is quite probable that in two years the combined attendance at the two congregations will be larger than the attendance was at Caring Church.

Conceivably the volatile nature of American Protestantism helps to explain why so many Americans are in churches and – given the fact that until recently growth was a greater concern among conservative Protestants – why this religious family has done relatively well in the United States. I return now to the issue of what kind of religion Americans want.

EXPLAINING THE POPULARITY OF CONSERVATIVE PROTESTANT CONGREGATIONS

How, then, do we explain the appeal of traditionalist religion in a late-modern society? Traditionalist religion is an attempt to approximate the premodern condition when religious rules and values were meant to preserve a sacred group, when religion was not a differentiated and limited institution, and when culture was centered on religion. A traditionalist religion struggles to reverse the growing acceptance of individualism, structural differentiation, and cultural fragmentation. However, a traditionalist group does not try to undo structural differentiation, for this would require the group as such to dissolve into an undifferentiated, all-purpose institution. Rather, a traditionalist group works to create a society in which the group's ideology would be the controlling force in all social institutions and cultural expressions, although because of the decline in support for such a society, traditionalists perceive themselves as under attack by an elite representing modernity. After summing up my argument about Dean Kelley's theory, I will consider the usefulness of modernization theory for understanding the current appeal of traditionalist Protestantism.

Kelley's explanation for the success of traditionalist Protestantism starts with the assumption that everyone wants to give meaning to his or her life. However, people (at least those outside premodern societies) are faced with alternative explanations. How do they choose? According to Kelley, they will prefer one that seems serious – that is, one that embodies costliness. But as the stories in Chapter 6 illustrate, when people need meaning, they do not automatically seek out a costly religion, but commit to one that is consistent with their ongoing values and beliefs. Thus the foundation of Kelley's theory is wrong.

Kelley also argued that strong churches would attract people because such an organization connotes the serious intent of its members. While we cannot deny that some people may be drawn to strong congregations, the importance of the dissenting tradition makes such churches unattractive to many Americans. Moreover, enthusiasm has always influenced American Protestantism, and this makes Kelley's concept of a strong church an especially inappropriate tool for understanding congregational success. Because of the primacy of the spiritual relationship, religious organizations are less important to enthusiasts. Indeed, in old-fashioned Pentecostal services, the group almost disintegrates. Anne Parsons noticed this in an Italian-American Pentecostal service: "Prayer-period was so individualistic that one's first impression was of a babel of sounds, each voice uttering its own pattern of lament, vehemence, or supplication with no attempt to harmonize with the whole" (Parsons 1965:190). American Protestants have emphasized "soul liberty," have severely criticized Catholicism for being authoritarian, and have frequently given greater importance to the voice within (to the Spirit) than to church officials. Given this heritage, the strong church model cannot explain the success of conservative Protestantism in the United States.

Undeniably, many Protestant churches have, until recently, practiced legalism, which was what Kelley meant when he described American churches as having strict rules. But was legalism important to people because the rules were costly, as argued by Kelley? Steve Bruce made this observation about the early British Methodists: "Their good living and religious conversion were immensely important to the Methodists because they created a clear barrier between themselves and the undeserving poor below. And they had the additional virtue of justifying criticism of the upper classes" (Bruce 1996:119). Similarly, the way of life of American conservative Protestants defined them as a spiritual elite over and against both the worldly elite and their fellow sufferers. In addition, compliance with ascetic rules helped troubled people gain a degree of self-control that allowed them to meet their family and work responsibilities under painful conditions.[1] Costliness itself was not why people joined the popular churches of early-modernity. What was important about the rules was not the costs of compliance; rather, the rules were significant because of their symbolic value in constructing a spiritually

---

1. Benton Johnson (1961) argued that Holiness and Pentecostal churches socialized their members into ascetic Protestantism, which could have encouraged work habits conducive to economic success. Conceivably, then, the lower class perceived members of conservative churches as economically successful and for that reason joined the churches. I am not aware of any evidence for such a process.

elite community and because they helped troubled people gain control of their lives.

Moreover, during late-modernity, legalism is becoming an obstacle to church growth. The emergence of modernized traditionalist Protestantism signals the declining importance of what Kelley meant by strict lifestyles rules. Such Protestants see legalism as an unjustified limit on their freedom; being a good Christian means loving others, and the legalistic rules seem unrelated to love. In addition, pleasure is no longer in itself bad, or at least always religiously suspect. The affluence ethic is gaining acceptance, making rules embodying asceticism less justifiable.

Kelley's framework can be criticized, then, because (a) a desire for meaning in one's life does not result in people necessarily desiring a costly religion, (b) American Protestants are unlikely to join a congregation that is a "strong church" because of the influence of libertarianism and enthusiasm, and (c) legalistic, ascetic norms were important during early-modernity, but not because they were costly, and now such norms are losing their importance among religious conservatives. While some people may prefer Kelley's ideal church, given the importance of individualism, self-actualization, a therapeutic environment, and the affluence ethic to contemporary Americans, Kelley's theory cannot be the only, or even the main, explanation of congregational success in the late-modern United States.

My explanation for the relative success of conservative Protestantism in the contemporary United States uses modernization theory. This form of Christianity has done well by evolving a new variant without totally replacing the old one. Today, conservatives can choose between classic and modernized traditionalism, or to put it more realistically, can choose from along a continuum of congregations from a Bob Jones University type to a Caring Church type. By accommodating late-modern culture, traditionalist Protestantism has been able to retain or attract religiously conservative Protestants who benefited from the affluence of post–World War II America. In the following section, I bring together my ideas about why the new form of conservatism Protestantism appeals to people.

MODERNIZED TRADITIONALISM

Spirited, Truth, and Caring congregations have been successful because they do not exemplify traditionalist Protestantism. Rather, each of them illustrates the new form of conservative Protestantism that has emerged during late-modernity which I have called modernized traditionalism. Scholars studying American Protestantism have been aware of such a change using labels such as "post-fundamentalism" (Noll 1994) and "contemporary evangelicals" (Shibley 1998) to describe the new form of Protestant conservatism. I prefer the label "modernized traditionalist" to emphasize both the roots of this religion in the premodern world and the connection between the emergence of this new form and the modernization process. As described in Chapters 3 through 5, the conservative congregations we studied have adjusted, albeit to different degrees, to the current stage of the modernization process.

ACCOMMODATING LATE-MODERNITY

The specific conditions that the new form of traditionalism accommodates are those I have identified with the 1960s counterculture: the affluence ethic and the popular interest in self-actualization (Third Force Psychology). In discussing the decline of legalism, I made the point that, in part, this change reflects the growing importance of an ethic affirming the new affluence of many conservative Protestants. Moreover, religious practices are to be fun; participants should enjoy the ritual and evangelizing should be done in a fun way. These details reflect a basic change: The rejection of the world – in the form of pleasure and fun – is no longer an essential aspect of conservative religiosity.

Neal Gabler (1998) has described how American society is being transformed into an entertainment, which is to say that life must be fun (p. 20). This transformation has affected religion. As he wrote, "Evangelical Protestantism, which had begun as a kind of spiritual entertainment in the nineteenth century, only refined its techniques in the twentieth ..." (p. 120). Middletown churches have always blended religion and entertainment in their rituals. They did so in 1924 and they do so today:

> On April 19, 1924, the local newspaper [in Middletown] listed the churches' complete Easter programs, including the names of soloists and musical ensembles. For instance, the program at Grace Episcopal listed Miss Dunn singing "Lord Have Mercy upon Us" by Gounod, and on the same day at First Baptist Mrs. Olin Bell played "Spring Song" by Mendelssohn on the organ.
> ... [In 1980] the First United Presbyterian church held a "clown worship service, conducted in mime with musical background."

But the most unusual addition to a Middletown church service in
1980 was surely the following: "Dr. Wendal Hasen, internationally
known bird trainer, will present a special program at 10:30 A.M.
Sunday in the First Church of the Nazarene. Tropical and exotic
birds gathered from around the world will be featured." The ad-
vertisement for this event promised "Unbelievable Feats! Flying
backwards! Sword Swallowing! Plus Much more!" (Tamney 1983:
139–40).

Notice that not only were religious rituals presented as entertainment,
but this was true for modern and conservative congregations. What
denominational differences did exist seem to have reflected class-related
differences in what was considered fun.

At least for American Protestants, entertaining rituals are an old story.
Recall the joke that Spirited Church's pastor told during Sunday service,
and how much the people with whom we talked about the church appreciated his sense of humor. Similarly, using the music people enjoy to
draw them to church is an old tactic. Recently, a Kenyan Pentecostal
Christian told an interviewer, "Before we were saved we used to dance
in night clubs; now we dance for Jesus. This is a sanctified rumba, so
don't feel inhibited" (Brouwer, Gifford, and Rose 1996:157). As Liston
Pope found in Gaston County, churchgoing can be fun.

Yet, like Gabler, I believe something new is appearing. It is not that
congregational popularity is related to providing entertainment. What is
new, I suggest, is that contemporary people are ceasing to identify religion
so totally with sacrifice and believe it is right for being religious to be
enjoyable. The affluence ethic is undermining the ascetic Protestant
ethic. Affluent people want to enjoy the world and are in search of
rules that will allow them to do so in a manner consistent with their
spirituality. Even religious practices, in this new view, should be judged
using the provision of beauty and pleasure as norms. People have always
managed to have fun; now its provision is a normative expectation.

Similarly, we can see in this new form of religiosity some accommodation of the self-realization ethos. Individuals are allowed to choose
their own level of congregational commitment and style of evangelism. Greater informality, exemplified in minimal dress codes, allows
for greater expression of uniqueness and implies the importance of the
individual.

I believe the significance of such changes is not sufficiently appreciated. Consider dress codes. Like other forms of legalism, these codes

have become less important. Rules about how to dress are a way of affirming the importance of the group over the individual (cf. Kniss 1997). Dress codes embody a group's values; in religious groups, this usually has meant that dress should convey both a lack of interest in worldly values, such as wealth or beauty, and the implications of patriarchy. Thus religious people might not wear jewelry and might require women to dress in a stereotypically feminine fashion. But the specific values may vary. The basic point about dress codes is the conformity: Individual preferences are relinquished. It was just this fact that was the basis for our respondents criticizing dress codes. The late-modern rejection of the use of such codes to suppress individuality was epitomized by the stunning popularity of jeans beginning in the 1960s.

Originally prototypical working-men's clothes, jeans were taken over by political activists in the 1930s, bikers in the 1950s, and New Left activists and hippies in the 1960s. Jeans were an anti-establishment symbol: an implicit rejection of consumerism and the elite. They were also a clothing worn by men and women, and thus a critique of gender stereotypes. Eventually jeans were worn by all social groups – even all nationalities. In his famous *The Greening of America*, Charles Reich wrote that in a world of jean-wearers, "There are no distinctions of wealth or status, no elitism; people confront one another shorn of these distinctions" (quoted in Davis 1992:68). Of course, if you went to a party in the 1960s and everyone was wearing jeans, this "uniform" expressed a commitment to a shared value, but that value was individualism, and so the "uniform" affirmed the importance of the individual rather than the group. In due course, the fashion industry asserted itself; designer jeans and eroticized jeans have reintroduced class and gender distinctions. Yet, the jean fashion revolution remains a statement about the importance of the individual person (Davis 1992:68–72). This underlying message is communicated by the variety of clothing styles, possibly including jeans, that people exhibit at the Sunday service in Middletown churches.

The self-realization ethos is especially evident in the importance of therapeutic values and relationships. The modernized conservative congregation is not so much a community, in the sense of a body of people, as it is a network of people linked by communal ties that are meant to have therapeutic rewards. Such bonds create trust and convey acceptance so as to encourage openness, which is necessary for personal well-being and spiritual growth. By baring one's soul, a person may obtain a sense of self-forgiveness, or a conviction about one's worth, or compassionate understanding of one's suffering, or better self-understanding. In all such cases, the person is self-empowered.

It is no small matter for religious conservatives to accept the value of therapy. "I know it sounds unscriptural to say that some individuals need more than the church can offer," wrote a conservative scholar (Carlson 1998: 30), "but if my car needs the transmission replaced, do I expect the church to do it"?

> What the emotionally wounded need is for the body of Christ to be a place of love, acceptance, encouragement, forgiveness, and compassion. They need a place where Christ is lifted high and God's Word is never compromised but also where there is openness to use all available methods of healing that are not contrary to His Word (p. 35).

The pastors at the churches we studied accept the idea that psychological problems are not just spiritual in nature and that spiritual growth depends on a prior coming to terms with serious psychological issues. For this purpose, the pastors believe, a therapeutic environment is a useful tool. Therapeutic values imply acceptance of self-development and therefore of a loving rather than strictly judgmental God, pastor, and laity.

While all the congregations made use of professional therapists, a sign of the influence of Third Force Psychology, I would emphasize the importance of this change for the enthusiastic tradition. I believe, as was suggested by the material presented in Chapter 3, that the availability of counseling allows enthusiastic Christians to temper their commitment to ultrasupernaturalism. Gaining increased strength from therapy, they are more likely not to replace human relationships with the spiritual one. Like the people in Caring Church, such modernized enthusiasts can balance social and spiritual involvement. Thus, I suggest that therapy, professional or lay, has allowed the personally troubled people who have been the natural constituency for classic enthusiast congregations to find peace in charismatic ones.

The Pilgrim's Progress was widely popular from the seventeenth through the nineteenth centuries in English-speaking lands. Today it is rarely read. John Bunyan, the author, was a puritan Baptist, and his story is based on a biblical view of life. It is about a man, Christian, who leaves his family to seek salvation:

> For the essence of Protestantism, certainly as it was illustrated by one of its own number, John Bunyan in his *The Pilgrim's Progress*, is that of a lonely individualism. The Calvinist believed that one member alone of a family might be predestined to eternal salvation while the rest predestined to damnation; or the reverse might be the case. *The Pilgrim's Progress* sets forth the essential type: It is the allegorical story of an individual named "Christian" traveling on his lonely journey through life, away from the City of Destruction to the Holy City of the elect, determined not to be distracted by the things of this world. This Pilgrim has been described as the epitome of Puritan self-consciousness, a lonely figure with a Bible in his hand within which, he believes, he has the pledge of his eternal salvation. This is the essential story as Bunyan first wrote it, even though he added subsequently a happier ending, a second part, in which the Pilgrim's wife and children were persuaded that it was for them also to leave the City of Destruction and journey to the Holy City (Ling 1991:70).

"Christian" exemplifies a religious libertarianism, and so I prefer "lonely libertarianism" to Ling's "lonely individualism."

"Christian" embodies ascetic Protestantism. As a twentieth-century monk wrote about his heritage, "The Christian life is conceived of as above all, a life of detachment and of desire; detachment from the world and from sin, and an intense desire for God" (Leclercq 1974:36). Of course, Protestants added to this formula the work ethic as the means of expressing the desire for God. Robert S. and Helen Merrell Lynd described the resulting lifestyle as epitomizing the masochistic tendency in American culture:

> If the denial of life in the pursuit of "success" through "hard work" is one of the commonest current manifestations of this tendency, the Christian religion is its philosophical core. It has given certain words such as "pleasure," "idleness," "impulse," "sex," and "the human body" disreputable fringes of connotation ... (Lynd and Lynd 1937:298–9).

The Lynds, discussing the lifestyle of businessmen, referred to the spectacle of people "best able to live rich, many-sided lives, spending themselves unremittingly in work, denying themselves leisure and bending fine energies to the endless acquisition of the *means* of living a life they so often take insufficient leisure to live . . ." (p. 244). Such was life, pre-affluence ethic.

Contemporary American society is no place for Bunyan's "Christian." His asceticism is considered fanatical, his loneliness is pitied. The "denial of life" is no longer required; pleasure, sex, the body, and leisure are no longer perceived simply as sources of temptation. At the same time, the spirit of Christianity in the new religious conservatism centers on love. Evangelism is pursued not by judging others but by showing compassion for them. The self-righteousness and aggressiveness of Christian Right leaders seems un-Christlike. God is caring, so relationships with others in the congregation and with those of dissimilar mind should express the true measuring stick of Christian religiosity, the depth of one's love.

Modernized traditionalist congregations, then, are accommodating late-modern developments. However, so are modern congregations, as illustrated by Open Church (see also Tamney 1992b). The resilience of traditionalist religion, therefore, cannot be totally explained by its accommodation of late-modern secular culture. I have been emphasizing how conservatives have accommodated late-modern society. Now, I will discuss how they remain distinctive.

COMPENSATING FOR LATE-MODERNITY

In Chapter 1, I suggested that traditionalist religion is resilient because it compensates for problems identified with late-modernity. First, people influenced by ideas about self-actualization yet committed to traditional gender roles might be attracted by the "neotraditional" familial norms of traditionalist congregations. Second, given a loss of faith in reason, people who need to believe that their decisions are legitimate might be drawn to traditionalist congregations by their shared conviction of having the truth. Third, given anxieties related to new technologies and new economic conditions, people might prefer a politicized religion that defines social problems as basically moral issues and thus correctable by moral reform. The last argument I will consider in the next section of this chapter.

As to the first argument, we did not meet women who were primarily attracted to conservative churches because of "neotraditional" norms regarding the familial duties of husbands and wives. Undoubtedly, given the evidence in the references cited in Chapter 1, such norms are an important feature of modernized traditionalist congregations. However, in our sample, we heard more conservative ideas from the women who chose to emphasize gender roles. What some women like about their congregations is their consistency with patriarchy; thus two women appreciated the emphasis on male leadership at Truth Church.

Given the changes taking place within conservative Protestantism, it should not be a surprise to learn that books published by conservative Protestants vary in their support for patriarchy (Bartkowski 1997). Some advice books on family life have linked women's "liberation" to their acceptance of patriarchy. For instance, an author of a best seller advised women who accept male dominance that they "can enjoy the freedom of knowing that, along with the right to make the final decisions, your husband carries the responsibility for the consequences of his decisions" (p. 398). This was the argument that Janet (at Truth Church) gave in defense of compliance with patriarchy; being dependent, she told me, "frees" women from mundane cares and concerns. The development of such a rationale for patriarchy does help people to remain traditional and yet also to believe they are reaping benefits supposedly available only to modern people. The presence of these norms no doubt contributes to the success of modernized traditionalist congregations.

In our study, the neotraditional norms that were important concerned not gender but divorce. Several of the women with whom we spoke had been divorced, which left them feeling either rejected in their conservative churches or down on themselves because of their guilt about divorcing. These women needed to find acceptance and forgiveness in conservative churches. Modernized traditionalist congregations are important partly because they accept divorced people while condemning divorce – a combination that suits people feeling guilty about their own divorces. That is to say, some people, perhaps raised to believe in the sinfulness of divorce, feel the need to end their marriages but cannot grant themselves approval for such action; they can find peace only when their particular acts have been legitimated by clergy sharing their overall religious viewpoint.

The pastor of Spirited Church mentioned in passing one Sunday that if married people are having problems, they should work on trying to solve them; divorce is just "relational abortion." Yet some of his church leaders, including the one running a study group for divorced people, are divorced. Thus divorce is bad, but divorced people can find a home at Spirited Church. Such congregations uphold the sanctity of marriage while offering both consolation and acceptance to the divorced.

In this sense, it certainly seems true that modernized traditionalist congregations are successful partly because they aid people both affected by
late-modern ideas about family life and also committed to traditional
familial ideals.[2]

I turn now to the second argument, regarding legitimacy.

SEEKING LEGITIMACY

As I discussed in Chapter 1, late-modern culture includes a fundamental
critique of reason as a means of determining what is true, beautiful,
or good. Given that modern people already doubted whether norms
could be legitimated (i.e., declared unquestionably right) by supernatural
pronouncements, the loss of faith in reason meant having to lead lives
that were at best only tentatively justified. I suggested that some people
might find this intolerable and might be drawn to conservative religion.

The people in the congregations we studied certainly do not accept
the late-modern institutionalization of doubt (Giddens 1991). For them,
the Bible is the word of God and therefore the final source of guidance
for how to live. Bart (who goes to Truth Church) will only be in a
congregation that uses the Bible as authoritative. Bart went on to say, "if
you don't have something to mount from, if you don't have a guidebook,
you're in trouble, you're in real trouble." The crucial point for Bart is
being with others who believe the Bible is God's knowable message to us:

" . . . the Bible is inherently accurate within our ability to understand it, comprehend it," said Bart. "If God were to tell us, tell
you, let me tell you how He did it, we couldn't understand it. He's
reduced it to something we can deal with. That does not make it

2. W. Bradford Wilcox (1998: 807) found evidence in a national study of Americans
for a distinctive neotraditional parenting style among conservative Protestants:

> This style is traditional in that it maintains the classical Protestant em-
> phasis on the sinfulness of human nature and the attendant need for strict
> framing rules to address child misbehavior. However, it may be viewed
> as innovative in that it harnesses theological and psychological values to
> framing rules that dictate a warm, expressive style of parenting for most
> parent-child interaction.

The complexity of modernized traditionalism seems especially evident in regard to husband-wife power sharing, attitudes about divorce, and child-rearing
practices.

wrong; it does not mean we're not going to have differences on certain verses, and I realize that probably sounds like some great compromise, but, no, I believe that God inspired the Bible and anyone who does not believe that is not going to be someone that is going to draw me to them as a church. Again, understanding that there are differences in interpretation of certain verses, but to understand that's okay, I'll agree. You and I don't understand it, but we know it's right. The fact that we don't understand it does not take away from that. . . ."

People such as Bart want to be in a congregation that affirms the truth of the Bible and to listen to a pastor whose confident preaching affirms this message. Yet we must also heed Bart's statement: "You and I don't understand it, but we know it's right." The late-modern doubt about our capacity to know the truth seems in evidence. However, it remains the case that what distinguishes all traditionalist congregations from modern ones is the shared conviction that the Bible need be your only guide in deciding how to live, which implies that despite ambiguities and interpretative disagreements there is a sufficient, knowable biblical message.

For whom is such a religion appealing? First, some people have a personality that values structure and order, without which they become anxious; they want to hear preaching that is not ambiguous, hesitant, or uncertain. Such a personality type is likely to gravitate to more author-itarian organizations and thus is most likely to be found in the classic traditionalist congregations, but such a person could be satisfied with any conservative congregation.

Second, others believe that social problems result from selfishness and that any rules requiring sacrifice must be transcendent to be ef-fective. Allen exemplifies this mindset. As he sees it, the choice is between accepting the Bible as true or giving humans the power to decide what is moral. The latter option is unacceptable for people like Allen. Philosophically the Allens cannot believe that people can de-sign and create a good society. Giving people the power to determine what is good, in their opinion, leads to rampant selfishness and a cul-ture of convenience. The sociologist Émile Durkheim (1973b) set forth a similar viewpoint in *Moral Education*. His basic point was that limits to our desires cannot be self-imposed. As Durkheim wrote, "Someone who was, or believed himself to be, without limits, either in fact or by right, could not dream of limiting himself without being inconsistent; it would do violence to his nature" (p. 45). Without socially imposed limits that are accepted as legitimate, our inclinations "become tyrannical, and their first slave is precisely the person who experiences them"; mastering one's natural desires is a precondition "of all liberty worthy of the name" (pp. 44–5). The Allens believe that goodness can come only from self-sacrifice and that left to themselves individuals will not comply with demands for self-sacrifice. Fearing the consequences of unlimited freedom, the Allens defer to pastoral leadership and biblical directives.

Sarah exemplifies a third mindset. She is committed to a conservative sexual morality and wants her daughter to be similarly committed. Sarah needs to be part of a group that solidly supports her moral choices, because society as a whole does not. The Sarahs of the world are self-confident, yet their personal identities include traditional ascetic moral rules, especially as they prescribe female sexuality, and the Sarahs know that American society no longer assumes the rightness of such rules. They are willing to concede ambiguity about the biblical necessity of such rules, because it is beside the point anyway. The Sarahs are committed to traditional morality, or aspects of it, and want to be part of a congregation that unequivocally affirms such a morality.

The Allens and the Sarahs are not driven by immediate personal problems. The issue for them is the need for authoritative social rules. Thus, solemn rituals are appropriate because they symbolize the glory of God and are not organized to witness to personal transformation; also, a church in which membership requires acceptance of the group's creed is appropriate.

People such as Lois (at Spirited Church) exemplify a fourth reason that people need an authoritative congregation: Her life revolves around her spiritual relationship, and she is comfortable in an environment that not only affirms the importance of one's personal relationship with God but concretizes it as when God seems to be speaking through her pastor. Such a motivation is not limited to people in enthusiastic and charismatic churches. Ruth (at Truth Church), like the Nazarene women discussed in Chapter 2, wants the love she feels in the spiritual relationship with Jesus, and she needs to be in a congregation that confirms the reality of this lover. What is crucial is to have spiritual experiences confirmed by pastor and congregation. Such confirmation is undoubtedly more common in enthusiastic and charismatic congregations. Thus, the pastor of Spirited Church routinely speaks of being moved by the Spirit, just as the pastor at Caring Church frequently illustrates the power of prayer with personal stories.

The reader may have noted that although the heading of this section of the book refers to "legitimacy," I have been writing about "authoritativeness." Indeed, I do not believe the Allens, the Sarahs, and the Loises have gained a sense of legitimacy from their religious involvement. Neither Allen nor Sarah was confident that the Bible is clear. They admitted uncertainty. They understand the criticism being made of all claims to truth. Indeed, it is because of the late-modern cultural environment that they feel the need to be in a congregation that collectively affirms the truth of the Bible. But their doubts have not been eliminated. Both Allen and especially Sarah are so self-conscious about the arbitrary nature of their decisions to obey church norms that the idea of legitimacy seems inappropriate. Perhaps I can say they live as if their life choices are legitimate – and perhaps that is sufficient for them.[3] A concern for legitimacy never bothered Lois, as she takes the legitimacy of biblical rules for granted; what Lois needs is a congregation that affirms the reality of God's presence in this world.

In Chapter 1, I reported that although people overall did not like Kelley's "strong church," they did find authoritative pastors to be appealing. Indeed, even modernized traditionalists, such as we studied, like pastors who are authoritative. At Truth Church, people appreciate the pastor's biblical expertise. At Spirited Church, the pastor is admired because he is Spirit-led, because he has the kind of religious experiences that people in the pews value. Both pastors are authoritative, but in different ways – the expertise of one confirming the availability of trustworthy guides to the meaning of the Bible, the experiences of the other confirming the validity of this-worldly mystical religion. More broadly, people are drawn to conservative congregations because they want environments that affirm the truth of the Bible, even if its nature is ambiguous, or that provide evidence in the lives of pastor and people of God's this-worldly personal involvement with ordinary humans.

Authoritarian congregations require obedience and kick out deviants. This does not describe the congregations we studied. Pastors at

---

3. Christian Smith (1998:102–3) discussed Peter Berger's thesis that when people consciously choose a religion this weakens the plausibility of that religion. He refers to several studies that describe people who deliberately chose a religion and who seemed strongly committed to it. Smith concluded, "There is little reason to believe, therefore, that the modern necessity of having to choose one's own religion makes that religion any less real, powerful, or meaningful to modern believers" (p. 104). But Allen and Sarah suggest that modernity affects plausibility even among religious conservatives committed to their faith.

modernized traditionalist churches must conduct themselves so that they fit into a therapeutic environment that minimizes judgment, encourages openness, and seeks to develop individual members. Ideally these pastors would be more like wise friends than father figures. The distinction between *authoritarian* and *authoritative* is crucial for understanding the difference between classic and modernized forms of traditionalist religion.

In sum, I would explain the appeal of conservative Protestantism, in part, by its maintenance of authoritative congregations. In modernized traditionalist religion, people value authoritativeness because (1) some people have personalities that predispose them to prefer orderly groups with clearly defined roles; (2) some believe that tolerance of individual interpretation implies opening the floodgate of selfishness that would destroy society; (3) some identify with values rejected by the society and need to be in a group that unquestioningly affirms these values; and (4) some need to be with a group that confirms the reality of personal religious experiences. These reasons for the appeal of authoritativeness can also be understood in terms of the calvinist and charismatic types of Protestantism. Authoritative rules are important to calvinists because such people need lawlike propositions to use in redesigning the world. Charismatics need rules either because they are ultrasupernaturalists who believe they have surrendered their selves to God, yet need to know what it means to act Godlike, or because they want to return God's felt love and need to know what would please Him.

Even in modernized traditionalism, the group in some ways overshadows the individual. Religiously conservative people who divorce want to be with others who legitimate both their familial ideals emphasizing self-sacrifice and their decision to dissolve their marriages. The Allens admit personal doubts, so they must surrender autonomy to evade the relativism lurking beneath their doubts. For them, such behavior is rational, because to act otherwise is to encourage selfishness, which they believe will give rise to barbarity. The Sarahs also have doubts. They need a group that as a whole seems to be without any doubts. Finally, the Loises in late-modern society need the reassurance that comes from being in groups that affirm their lover's presence and thus justify their personal sacrifices out of their love for God.

Basic to traditionalism is limiting the importance of the individual. Appropriately, traditionalist Christian counseling is not the same as secular counseling. The goal of the former is not simply to help people feel good or cope with life. Rather, the goal, according to the cofounder of a national network of clinics for conservative Christians, is to help people get *"out of* themselves and to move beyond their problems so they can go on to heal others" (Maudlin 1998:32). A conservative counselor gave a relevant example: "The Christian therapist would seek to encourage the development of interdependence, this in contrast to the autonomy and independence valued in many therapeutic approaches" (Benner 1988:273).

Thus, modernized traditionalist congregations have appeal in part because they affirm the importance of the group, although not to the point of being "strong churches." Still, modernized traditionalism does value authoritative organizations that confirm the truth of biblical norms and religious experiences.

AGAINST MODERNITY: A RELIGIOUS COUNTERCULTURE AND THE RELIGIOUS RIGHT

Smith (1998) studied a national sample of people that would have included individuals similar to those with whom we talked. He found that churchgoers who describe themselves as "evangelicals," and to a lesser extent those who say they are "fundamentalists," are much more likely than other churchgoing Protestants to say that the values of Christians *should* be very different from the rest of American society (p. 128). Being different in itself seems important.

Traditionalist Protestantism – whether classical or modernized – needs boundaries. It must have an identity to defend against the enveloping hostile environment. The chosen norms must not be pleasing to everyone. Indeed, a sure sign that a rule is biblical is when its pronouncement upsets some people. The truth must be painful. God's will cannot change with the times, because such a change would indicate that God is following human wishes and not setting His own standards. Formerly the "world" was equated with violations of ascetic morality, and for some traditionalists it still is. But generally the battle lines have been drawn using abortion, homosexuality, and gender roles as markers.

Taylor University, located near Middletown, exemplifies the kind of school described by John A. Schmalzbauer and C. Gray Wheeler (1996) in their study of legalism at conservative Christian colleges, which I discussed in Chapter 5. In Taylor's catalogue for 1998, the author distinguishes biblical and university behavioral expectations. The discussion of the former emphasizes love. For example, the catalogue states, "Within our community, the greatest expression of fellowship and the highest principle for relationships is love" (p. 26). Attitudes to be avoided include greed and pride. Subsequently the author lists behaviors expressly prohibited in Scripture, such as theft, gossip, profanity, sexual promiscuity ("including adultery, homosexual behavior, premarital sex"), drunkenness, and immodest dress (p. 26).

The section on "university expectations" contains this explanation: "These standards are not set forth as absolutes or as an index of Christian spirituality but rather as expectations of this community." For instance, members are to refrain from using tobacco or alcoholic beverages. Such rules are given a social explanation, as in this example: "Because a significant number of evangelical Christians view social dancing as a morally questionable activity, social dancing is not permitted on or away from campus" (p. 28).

The section following the behavioral expectations is the "Sanctity of Life Statement," a short paragraph that concludes that "human life must be respected and protected from its inception to its completion" (p. 28).

The university's catalogue expresses the views of modernized traditionalist Protestantism. Because some conservatives continue to define the world in terms of the old legalistic rules, Taylor enforces such rules. The truly biblical norms fall into two categories: those that are widely supported (e.g., norms against greed, pride, and theft) and those more clearly identified with conservative religion (e.g., norms about legalized abortion, homosexuality, and premarital sex). It is the latter set that is most vocally defended by conservative Protestants.

The turn to abortion and homosexuality as conservative markers implies that the traditionalists define the moral problem less as the need for them to control their own nature and more as a social need for a legitimate basis for social order. The vast majority of Americans spend all or most of their lives never being tempted to have an abortion or to perform homosexual acts. However, passing laws against such actions has great symbolic significance for conservative Protestants: Such laws would reestablish the United States as a Christian society. Writing in the conservative *Christianity Today*, David Gusbee commented on "the continuing elevation of the issue of homosexuality on the moral agenda of Southern Baptists and evangelicals." He went on to say, "We are fixated on the one moral issue most remote from the daily experience of our membership..." (Gusbee 1997:13). Gusbee then linked the elevation of homosexuality to "'the Christendom assumption,' the implicit belief that American society ought to be Christian. . . ."

Given the commitment to traditional norms about abortion and homosexuality in the conservative congregations we studied, one might have thought that the people in those congregations would be supporters of the religious right, which keeps alive the Christendom ideal. However, in the three conservative churches, we found quite diverse opinions about the right. Some reject the very idea of a Christian society, believing that no human institution could ever be the perfect embodiment of God's will. Some reject the use of coercion in religious matters, believing that salvation can come only when individuals willingly comply with God's laws. Moreover, as Taylor University's catalogue illustrates, for some conservatives love is the premier value and this conflicts with a rightist mentality. Bart struggled with the complexity of having strong religious convictions and at the same time being a compassionate person. "How do you come out against something that is so, that you believe to be inherently wrong and not offend the people to where they will run away from you? Very, very, very difficult thing, and once again if you don't go forth with love and compassion, how can you possibly help reach these people?" Love is the fundamental requirement. The influence of libertarianism and the emphasis on caring are inconsistent with the militant authoritarian approach taken by rightist groups such as the Christian Coalition.

Spirited Church did offer some support to the Christian Right. Appropriately for a conservative congregation, Spirited's pastor wants to create a Christian society. He wants churches to play a more significant civic role. As in the case of the Life Chain, he uses peaceful protests and he works with a variety of other church leaders to improve Middletown. But, I was told by a member of the pastoral staff at Spirited Church that a Christian Right speaker would probably never be invited to the church. Congregational members as such, he said, would not picket abortion clinics. Spirited does not want to control others nor does it want to change people by directly pressuring them. The congregation seeks change, but by being involved with others in a loving way. They want to share their biblical wisdom and Christlike love.

Yet objections to the Christian Right do not automatically lead to a condemnation of the right. Conservatives believe that society needs political leaders who fight for God's rules. Moreover, some might believe that although having "Christian" laws might not in itself save people, such laws might create a social environment more conducive to people making the right moral decisions. The agenda of the Christian Right consists of the issues that define the religious counterculture of late-modernity. If people are drawn to religion as a way to create the good society, sympathy, if not support, for the Christian Right would be expected.

In Chapter 1, I suggested that new technological developments and the social problems linked to the emergence of a global economy might reveal the weakness of the state, with the consequence that people might support a religious group arguing for the moral reform of society as the way to relieve new anxieties. Listening to the taped interviews, I heard nothing about technological developments or the new economy. It seems to me that the rules about abortion and homosexuality are important as symbols of conservative Protestantism. The struggles around these issues are about the truth of the Bible and not the solving of social problems.

Protestant traditionalists of all kinds retain at least a lingering desire to create a Christian society because such an accomplishment would signal the triumph, and therefore the truth, of their religion. In turn, this desire assumes a frame of mind using the distinction between "Christians" and "the world." Such traditionalists must resolve the tension between these entities by achieving Christendom. While all traditionalists share such a viewpoint, modernized people in this camp are more ambiguous about goals and more hesitant in their actions. The continuing influence of libertarianism and the new emphasis on therapeutic values, especially love, severely limit support for the religious right among religiously conservative people.[4]

IN SUM: MODERNIZED TRADITIONALIST PROTESTANTISM

In contrast to modernists, traditionalists unquestionably affirm the authenticity of the Bible, seek to use the Bible as the only important foundation for their life, and proclaim the superiority of their own religion. The rightness of a person's morality is not determined by the sincerity of the individual's search for goodness but by whether it conforms to the Bible. Their ideal is a society in which individuals voluntarily base their lives on the Bible and in which all aspects of social life are consistent with the Bible.

4. Smith (1998: 216) found a similar ambivalence among people who called themselves "evangelicals."

However, the modernized version of traditionalism does not closely approximate the theoretical type of traditionalist religion. The group is less dominant, or to put it another way, the symbolic and social boundaries are more blurred. The individual has more choices. Self-realization is an approved goal. Greater involvement with those not of the same mind is encouraged. The puritanical ideal of morality identified with legalism is no longer shared or enforced among modernized traditionalists. They are numbered among the many conservatives who do not belong to the Christian Coalition because they do not want to use the state to enforce moral norms chosen only because of their religious justification. These changes, I have argued, have resulted from the accommodating of late-modernity.

In Chapter 2, I described Protestantism in terms of five traits. Three of them made Protestantism relatively modern compared to Catholicism: the emphasis on the individual spiritual relationship, spiritual equality, and a this-worldly orientation. Two traits of medieval Catholicism were initially retained by Protestantism: asceticism and the Christendom ideal. Modernized traditionalists are those in the traditionalist camp who have in practice abandoned these two remnants of medieval Christianity.

In Chapter 2, I also noted that modernization theory could not predict the pessimism about society that came to characterize conservative Protestantism during the nineteenth century. I believe such pessimism is declining and that a more positive view of the world is spreading among conservative Protestants. Of course, catastrophes such as economic depressions and wars cannot be assumed to have been eliminated. Periodic pessimism, therefore, may always occur, at least in the foreseeable future. My suggestion is that a faith in progress will always reemerge and will set the dominant tone for the future.

However, what distinguishes modernized traditionalism, in comparison with all other forms of religion, is that it not only accommodates late-modernity, but also compensates for and struggles against late-modernity – all at the same time.[5] Modernized traditionalism

5. Smith (1998) presented a "subcultural identity theory" for the "strength" ("adherence to beliefs, salience of faith, robustness of faith, group participation, commitment to missions, and retention and recruitment of members") of evangelicalism (p. 21). As I understand the argument, the strength of evangelicalism results from being simultaneously against the world but not separated from it. However, Smith never tested this theory. I disagree with Smith's analysis overall

compensates for modernity by supporting neotraditional familial norms and by establishing authoritative congregations. Modernized traditionalism struggles against late-modernity by supporting laws consistent with traditional ideas about issues such as abortion and homosexuality.

I suggest that the relative success of modernized traditionalist Protestantism results from accommodating, compensating for, and struggling against late-modern society. Of course, the art of church growth is in finding the right mix of these elements for a particular audience. Generally the difficulties experienced by calvinist-type congregations, which were discussed in Chapter 4, stem from inadequately accommodating late-modernity. However, it would be difficult to achieve some ideal balance, which suggests a propensity for modernized traditionalist congregations to lack long-term stability. What is the implication of my analysis of conservative Protestantism for modernization theory?

MODERNIZATION THEORY REVISITED

In Chapter 1, I identify the modernization process with technological development, societal expansion, individuation and individualism, structural differentiation, and cultural fragmentation. Western modernization is the ever- growing commitment to individualism and the ever-deepening awareness of its implications for how all of society should be organized. Moreover, Western modernity has become identified with a growing dependence on using reason for deciding almost anything and with a belief in progress. The late-modern stage has included the growing significance of the self-realization ethos and the affluence ethic. Now, I shall argue that religious developments reveal yet another aspect of late-modernity.

In Chapter 1, I emphasized Karen Horney's role in creating the self-realization ethos. However, another aspect of her intellectual work also seems relevant for understanding our time. Horney, following Nietzsche, distinguished Apollonian activity – the "active molding and mastering of life" – and Dionysian activity – "finding satisfaction by losing the self in something greater, by dissolving the individuality" (1937:270–1). The Greek god Dionysius is associated with the ecstatic means of abandoning

because I believe that an important feature of the emerging form of conservative Protestantism is a relative blurring of boundaries. At the same time, I agree with Smith to the extent that we both perceive conflicting elements at the core of the new religious conservatism.

the self: rhythmic music, rousing dances, intoxicating drinks, sexual abandon. Dionysian experiences are universal: "There are few persons who do not know the satisfaction of losing themselves in some great feeling, whether it be love, nature, music, enthusiasm for a cause, or sexual abandon" (p. 272). Horney (1937) used historical and crosscultural material to make the point that all people seem to desire to lose the self at times. Americans, Horney believed, were culturally influenced to pursue the opposite kind of experience: the sense of our uniqueness. Americans have a strong sense of self and find satisfaction in developing potentialities and mastering the world (p. 273). But Horney concluded, "both the preservation and development of individuality and the sacrifice of individuality are legitimate goals in the solution of human problems" (p. 274).

Her point is to seek balance, to live so as to preserve one's individuality and something beyond one's self. To explain what this means, I briefly discuss two illustrations. I will also relate these illustrations to the appeal of charismatic Protestantism – the form of Protestantism that has experienced the greatest growth in the late-modern United States. The analyses that follow are speculations, but it is important to try to discern the broad meaning of the discussion of conservative Protestantism for the modernization process.

ROCK-N-ROLL

A major cultural development during late-modernity has been the musical genre rock-n-roll. Two ways of understanding the wide array of music that is loosely identified as rock-n-roll are contained in Greil Marcus's (1997) *Mystery Train* and Robert Palmer's (1995) *Rock & Roll: An Unruly History*. These authors concentrate on the more artistic expressions of this music, most examples of which are escapist songs whose lyrics little relate to people's problems.

In *Mystery Train*, Marcus (1997) portrays rock-n-roll as an authentic expression of American culture. It is a protest on behalf of libertarianism: The music expresses "an impulse to freedom, an escape from restraints and authority that sometimes seems like the only real American story there is" (p. 15). The genre's roots are in the music of marginalized groups in American society: blues (African Americans) and country (rural folk). The restraints that are protested against have more to do with Puritanism than tyranny. Elvis Presley played music with such a strong beat, it demanded some expressiveness from the listeners, or rather the dancers; people could not simply listen to the music. Rock-n-roll freed the body. People let themselves go, spontaneously moving with the music. The music was felt, then expressed. Girls no longer had to follow the lead of boys, because people danced as individuals, not couples or groups. It was dancing without rules.

Palmer (1995) acknowledges the diverse influences on rock-n-roll but emphasizes its roots in African sacred music and black gospel music. (Detractors did refer to the music as "jungle rhythms.") He analyzes the eruption of rock-n-roll in America using the Greek schema that the world contains two spiritual forces: the Apollonian one that encourages rationality, and the Dionysian one that favors ecstasy, intoxication, and sexuality. The key is the sound, especially the beat: It makes you want to rock. Its young, educated, and affluent audience was attracted by the musical sensuousness. "In traditional Africa, as in rock-n-roll, people don't just sit and stare at a musical performance, they get into it. They shout. They get down" (p. 56). As is generally true of African music, rock-n-roll is a communal event. Dancers would lose themselves in the music, and would do so collectively at concerts or in discos. As Palmer wrote, "The patriarchal white-bread America of the 1950s was faux-Apollonian to a fault" (p. 149).

Thus, varied music called rock-n-roll can be understood as an expression of libertarianism (Marcus 1997) and Dionysian desires (Palmer 1995). The music, as experienced in the late-modern United States, can produce both a sense of freedom from previously established restraints and a sense of communion with others who are similarly captivated by the music. In this way, rock-n-roll illustrates the contemporary appeal of balancing individuality and unity.

Given the extent to which people born after the Second World War identify with rock-n-roll, it must be important to understanding the current American religious situation that it has been the charismatic congregations that have led in accommodating rock-n-roll music. Solemn rituals, characteristic of calvinism, cannot incorporate a music so emotional and so personally expressive. At Bob Jones University, "Rock music is banned because . . . as Jones III explains, 'the very beat of it is sensual. It makes animals out of the hearers, to appeal to their passions'" (Dalhouse 1996:143). But although the kind of contemporary Christian music played at some charismatic congregations, such as Spirited Church, employs Christian lyrics, stylistically the music uses rock, heavy metal, and rhythm and blues, and thus a beat that traditionalists have called demonic (Howard and Streck 1996:38). For good reason, suggestions to use contemporary music are a major source of conflict within Protestant churches (Schaller 1994:14). But when enthusiastic congregations made the transition to being charismatic, they used the contemporary music as part of balanced rituals that could appeal to late-modern people desiring to be both Apollonian and Dionysian.

THE NEW AGE MOVEMENT

The New Age movement is another prominent, relevant feature of late-modernity. In popular culture the "New Age" label is usually attached to manifestations of the alternative tradition. Stories appear about "channelers," that is, people who become vocal channels for spiritual masters. Objects with magical power are available in New Age stores; for instance, crystals are said to aid healing because of their capacity to amplify energy. Indeed, the label "New Age" may refer to all spiritual phenomena not clearly identified with the Judeo-Christian established tradition. Beneath all the public confusion lies the alternative tradition in its many guises. As such, however, the age is nothing new.

The real news is that the alternative tradition is being modernized. Like Third Force Psychology, New Age religion emphasizes that the spiritual is within us, hidden by the effects of socialization; truth comes from personal experience, not from the "voices of authority associated with established orders" (Heelas 1996:22). New Agers are quite involved in self-exploration as a means to self-empowerment (Ferguson 1980:86–7). As Paul Heelas wrote, "Given that the New Age is, above *all* else, about the self and its sacralization, its development must surely have a great deal to do with the fact that western society has become obsessed with what the person has to offer; the *value*, the *depth*, the *potential*" (p. 160). The New Age adds to Third Force Psychology the priority of developing the spiritual within us (p. 115–7), which means being concerned with what is beyond the individual person.

My argument is that what makes the age truly new is combining individualism with the alternative tradition. Western culture has portrayed humans as responsible for the improvement, if not perfection, of the world. It is supposedly our destiny to build a paradise. New Agers, however, see themselves less as responsible for the world and more as needing to be responsive to the environment. Personal growth is now understood as becoming healthy, which ultimately requires living in harmony with nature. In the New Age, less emphasis is placed on creating a self and more attention is given to learning what our bodies and minds require to be healthy. Within the movement, there are frequent references to wholeness and oneness. However, I believe a more precise formulation of this interest is that New Age people recognize the importance of interconnectedness, an image that allows for both union and individuality.[6]

The appearance of the New Age corresponds with the development of charismatic Protestantism. As previously discussed, enthusiasm is a blend of the alternative tradition and Christianity. In turn, charismatic religion is a form of enthusiasm that has accommodated late-modern values, including the self-realization ethos. The change from the alternative tradition to the New Age parallels the change from enthusiasm to charismatic religion: The New Age and charismatic religion are modernized versions of their predecessors inasmuch as these new versions have accommodated the late-modern value of self-actualization.[7] The success of rock-n-roll, New Age religion, and charismatic Protestantism suggests the cultural importance of what these three developments express: the late-modern longing for a balanced life.

Thus, the relative success of traditionalist Protestantism is due to the development of a religious variant capable of attracting people seeking a balanced lifestyle. Modernized traditionalism accommodates the self-realization ethos and the affluence ethic, while also affirming limits on the individual in the form of neotraditional familial norms, authoritative congregations, and rules about such matters as abortion and homosexuality. But it is especially modernized enthusiasm that has accommodated the spirit of the time. It has coopted the distinctive music of late-modernity, a genre that is antipuritanical and that combines libertarian and communal elements. Late-modern people seek to balance Apollonian and Dionysian tendencies. They strive to use reason and to be in touch with their feelings, to value individuals, and to preserve their environment. Among the religious types that we have studied, this cultural shift seems most compatible with charismatic Protestantism.

6. Elsewhere (Tamney 1992b: 98–102), I have analyzed two widely read New Age books on modern physics to justify that "connectedness" is a more apt concept than "wholeness" to express the New Age movement.
7. New Age religion is consistent with what I have described in Chapter 1 as late-modern religion. For instance, "A consistent refrain in New Age sources is that people have finally managed to free themselves from the tyranny of religious power structures . . . " (Hanegraaff 1999:153). Tentatively I would describe New Age religion as a blend of late-modern religion and the alternative tradition.

The implication of this analysis is that Western modernization has entered a new phase. The dominance of individualism is giving way to an ideal of balancing individual realization and the maintenance of an order, be it conceived as natural or supernatural. Develop yourself, but do not impose yourself. Think of yourself, but be part of a therapeutic environment. Enjoy life, but do not destroy it. Finding pleasure is good as long as we also conserve what is necessary for healthy living. Organization success, be it religious or otherwise, depends on accommodating this newly emerging aspect of late-modernity: the ideal of being both an Apollo and a Dionysius.

Such an analysis has meaning for modernization theory. I have written that technological development and societal expansion have resulted in structural differentiation, cultural fragmentation, and individuation. If these consequences were carried to their logical conclusions, society would cease to exist. Institutions would be uncoordinated, people would lack shared values or meanings, individuals would live without thinking about their relationships with others. Thus, we can expect countermovements to limit all three consequences. I have just discussed reactions to individuation. At least in the United States, the sense of individuality has resulted, among some people, in the glorification of independence (the loner figure) and of power (superman). Late-modernity involves the debunking of these mythological models. The process of modernization must involve movement and countermovement in the development of structural differentiation, cultural fragmentation, and individuation.

CONCLUSION

The relationship between modernization and religion occurs as a series of interactive processes resulting in an ever-enlarging array of religious responses to social change. Today, sociologists assume that people in a society such as the United States want different forms of religion (Warner 1993; Stark and Bainbridge 1996:146). I have used modernization theory to describe and explain the diverse religious needs of people living in a late-modern society. Our work portrays the contemporary religious condition as the interplay of diverse segments: traditionalist, modernized traditionalist, modern religion, and late-modern religion. Although I have emphasized the recent emergence of the modernized traditionalist type in this book, I expect all of the types to appeal to some people into the foreseeable future. The religious typology developed in this work can be used crossculturally, given that it is less Christianity-bound than previous typologies and grounded in modernization theory.[8]

American Protestant traditionalism, I suggest, has been able to compete well in the current religious marketplace because it has bifurcated into classic and modernized versions. However, traditionalist religion also has problems. Late-modern culture is decentered. Among other things, this means that writers such as Salman Rushdie will continue to appear and to offer alternative spiritual visions. Moreover, all forms of traditionalism conflict with the modern civic culture, albeit to varying degrees. The tendency for traditionalists to deemphasize the individual, to be uneasy about diversity, and to maintain an air of religious certitude and superiority runs counter to basic aspects of the modernization process. A traditionalist triumph is unlikely.

At the same time, even classic traditionalism will endure into the foreseeable future. A liberal professor at Tehran University was interviewed sometime in the 1990s about the *Satanic Verses* episode:

> "Criticizing the Rushdie *fatwa* remains one of our taboos," he said. "We all believe the *fatwa* was a terrible mistake, but no one can say it publicly. That's because Khomeini is so identified with it. He is worshiped by Iran's masses and, though we can talk more about Khomeini's mistakes than we once did, these feelings on the part of the people are not subsiding.
>
> "To the masses, the *fatwa* still represents the courage and Islamic integrity of the revolution. It symbolizes defiance of the West and imperialism. It is almost the revolution itself.
>
> "If the government tried to reverse it, there would be demagogues mobilizing crowds in the streets. Like it or not, we have to live with it" (quoted in Viorst 1998:200).

As long as social change does not benefit everyone in a manner perceived as just, some people will need symbols of defiance against the elite, who today are also perceived as the embodiment of modernity. Religion, or

8. Similar developments are taking place outside Protestantism. Heilman and Cohen (1989) describe modern Orthodox Jewry as, relative to original Orthodoxy, less isolated, more accommodating of secular culture, allowing more personal autonomy and granting more power to women. The distinction between classic and modernized fundamentalisms is used in analyzing Islam (Piscatori 1991).

other movements that express the pride of the poor and powerless, will continue to attract followers in a world that does not justly serve all its citizens.

In the twenty-first century, the creation of new religious forms will continue. The divide between late-modern and some modern groups will continue to blur, as will the differences between other modern groups and modernized traditionalist ones. In turn, the blurring processes will evoke calls for alternative, purer forms of religion. I leave the reader with the image of an ever-increasingly diverse world. Religious options will multiply. One is tempted to write about innumerable personalized religions. Such matters are in need of study and understanding.

The Interview Script

I would like to start with when you first heard about (*church*) and discuss what happened from the time you heard about your church until you joined it.

So, to begin with, how did you learn about (*church*)?
(The interviewer aids storytelling with prompts: "What happened then?," "Tell me more about _____.")

SUBSIDIARY QUESTIONS TO BE ASKED IF NECESSARY:

About past:

• Were you raised in a particular church or religion?
(*IF NECESSARY*) Which denomination is that?

About key individuals:

• What did you like about this person?
• Did you see any similarities between yourself and (*other*)?
• Was (*other*) a convert to (*church*)? What did (she, he) tell you about the church? How did you react to what (he, she) said?

Reaction of significant others:

• How did your family and friends react to your decision to join (*church*)?
• How did you explain your decision to them?

Consequences:

- Were you different after joining (*church*)?
- Was your life different?
- Did other people treat you differently?

Alternative church:

- At the time you joined (*present church*) were you looking into any other church?
- Why did you join (*present church*)?

ASK EVERYONE:

Former church:

- Had you attended a church before joining (*church*)?
  (*IF NECESSARY*) Which denomination is that?
  Church: _____
  Denomination: _____
- How long had you been in this church?
- What are the differences between (*new church*) and (*old church*) regarding the following:
  - church services?
  - church programs?
  - the people?
  - the leaders?
  - the way the church is run?
  - beliefs or teachings?

IF NO COMPARISON POSSIBLE: What has meant the most to you about the following aspects of your church? For instance:

- church services?
- church programs?
- the people?
- the leaders?
- the way the church is run?
- beliefs or teachings?

Political involvement:

- Is your church involved in community work?
- How do you feel about such involvement?
- Did the recent political involvement of religious conservatives (e.g., the Christian Right) influence your decision to attend (*present church*)?

Finally, a few simple questions:

1. How many years of schooling have you had? _____
   (If more than 12): What is the highest degree you received?
   a. Associate degree
   b. Bachelor's degree
   c. Master's degree
   d. Doctorate
   e. none
2. When were you born? _____ (*year*)
3. If I find that I need a little more information, may I just phone you?
   (*IF YES*) What is your number? _____

Interviewer Records

Gender	Race
a. female	a. White
b. male	b. other

Why Liberal Intellectuals Misjudged Conservative Religion: A Personal Story

A reviewer of a draft manuscript of this book asked, "Why is the continuing appeal of these [conservative Protestant] groups problematic in the first place?" The reviewer then wrote,

> Well, obviously because a great many people (let's call them "liberal intellectuals") expect that these conservative Protestant groups should decline. But why? What is the basis of this expectation? And doesn't this expectation (given that these groups are in fact not in decline) say more about the mindset of liberal intellectuals than anything else? Shouldn't the nature of that mindset be investigated in a book like this?

Such questions could justify a separate book. What follows, then, is a brief beginning of an answer, and one that is somewhat autobiographical.

I came of age in the post–World War II Catholic church. In my last year of primary school, I had a different nun each semester. In the beginning of the school year, the sister scared me; at one point, I even cried, although she was doing nothing to me personally. I think we saw her as very strict; she did use mild forms of physical punishment. The second semester, a younger nun taught us; I remember her as a warm, kind teacher. I do not believe either sister was a mean person, yet their manner of relating to me expressed different values and evoked quite different responses. Although at the time these events probably had no great meaning to me, I easily recall them now, some fifty years later. I believe this story came to be a metaphor of Catholicism and my relationship to it.

In my high school years, right after World War II, I was aware that some young Jesuits teaching religion were trying to change our image of Catholicism. One of them kept asking us one day, "What is at the bottom of a birdcage?" Met with silence, it was finally the priest who said publicly, "Shit!" We were not able to say the word in a religious context, a sign of a legalistic understanding of holiness.

At the Jesuit college I attended, the theology curriculum was thoroughly revised while I was there, and as part of the process, I and other students were called for interviews and asked for our opinions about the theology program. This was new!

I hope these stories make clear that I grew up thinking not about Catholicism, but about both an old-fashioned (bad) Catholicism and the new (good) Catholicism. I never waivered in my preference for the latter form, and so I was predisposed to believe that time favored the new Catholicism. I still believe that.

However, my understanding of society and social change has not remained the same. I have a better understanding of how seemingly old-fashioned ideas and practices can have great symbolic importance to people. The struggle over homosexuality, for instance, evokes meanings often hard to specify but undoubtedly myriad in form and deeply important to all sides. For some people, adherence to traditional norms may even symbolize rebelliousness against a ruling elite – a feeling that evokes sympathy from an old rebel such as myself.

Moreover, I have altered the way I think about change. In my early career, social development was all about one-way processes with clear outcomes (e.g., education increases doubting, which leads to a decline in religious affiliation). As Philip Hammond (1985:1) wrote,

A linear image dominates Western thought about society. Even cyclical views are cast in spiral form, thus helping to maintain the notion that social life is systematically "coming from" somewhere and "going" elsewhere. Social science, born in nineteenth-century evolutionism, matured with this perspective almost exclusively, indeed contributing to it many of the master terms used in contemporary discourse about social change: *industrialization, modernization, rationalization, bureaucratization,* and *urbanization,* to name but a few. All imply one-directional processes.

Now, I think dialectically. As societies modernize, religions change to accommodate the new environment, making the initial effect of modernization less enduring. For instance, it seems probable to me that atheism peaked when Christianity was perceived as thoroughly reactionary – about one hundred years ago. Moreover, it is not easy to predict what this process of continual interactions between secular change and religious change will eventually create. Such thoughts led to the study behind this book.

So, I make no prediction about the eventual fate of conservative Protestantism, in part because this form of religion is not what it used to be. The kind of religion "liberal intellectuals" wrote about, such as the old-fashioned Catholicism of my youth, is, I believe, on the wane. This has invalidated the old "liberal" mindset and requires a new understanding of the relationship between modernization and religion.

BIBLIOGRAPHY

Afzal-Khan, Fawzia. 1993. *Cultural Imperialisms and the Indo-English Novel.* University Park, PA: Pennsylvania State University Press.

Ahsan, M. M., and A. R. Kidwai. 1991. *Sacrilege Versus Civility: Muslim Perspectives on The Satanic Verses Affair.* Leicester, UK: Islamic Foundation.

Allitt, Patrick. 1994. The Bitter Victory: Catholic Conservative Intellectuals in America, 1988–1993. *South Atlantic Quarterly* 93:631–58.

Ammerman, Nancy Tatom. 1987. *Bible Believers.* New Brunswick, NJ: Rutgers University Press.

———. 1990. *Baptist Battles.* New Brunswick, NJ, and London: Rutgers University Press.

———. 1997. Organized Religion in a Voluntaristic Society. *Sociology of Religion* 58:203–15.

Anderson, Walter Truett. 1990. *Reality Isn't What It Used to Be.* New York: HarperSan Franscisco.

Appignanesi, Lisa, and Sara Maitland, eds. 1989. *The Rushdie File.* London: Fourth Estate.

Aran, Gideon. 1991. Jewish Zionist Fundamentalism: The Block of the Faithful in Israel (Gush Emunim). In *Fundamentalisms Observed*, edited by Martin E. Marty and R. Scott Appleby, 265–344. Chicago: University of Chicago Press.

Asad, Talal. 1993. *Genealogies of Religion.* Baltimore, MD, and London: Johns Hopkins University Press.

Associated Press. 1989. Islamic Gathering Opposes Khomeini. *Indianapolis Star* (17 March):A2.

———. 1993. Reverend Condones Killing Gays. *Ball State Daily News,* 23 August, 3.

Bainbridge, William Sims. 1997. *The Sociology of Religious Movements.* New York: Routledge.

Balmer, Randall. 1993. *Mine Eyes Have Seen the Glory.* Expanded ed. New York: Oxford University Press.

Barna, George. 1996. *Index of Leading Spiritual Indicators.* Dallas, TX: Word Publishing.

Barnes, Julian. 1994. Staying Alive. *New Yorker*, 21 February, 99–105.

Bartkowski, John P. 1997. Debating Patriarchy: Discursive Disputes over Spousal Authority Among Evangelical Family Commentators. *Journal for the Scientific Study of Religion* 36:393–410.

Bedford, Carmel. 1993. Fiction, Fact, and the *Fatwa*. In *The Rushdie Letters*, edited by Steve MacDonogh, 125–83. Lincoln, NE: University of Nebraska Press.

Benner, David G. 1988. Christian Counseling and Psychotherapy. In *Psychology and Religion*, edited by David G. Benner, pp. 264–75. Grand Rapids, MI: Baker Publishing House.

Berger, Peter L. 1967. *The Sacred Canopy*. New York: Doubleday Anchor Books.

Berman, Marshall. 1992. Why Modernism Still Matters. In *Modernity and Identity*, edited by Scott Lash and Jonathan Friedman, 33–58. Oxford, UK: Blackwell.

Blanchard, Dallas A., and Terry J. Prewitt. 1993. *Religious Violence and Abortion*. Gainsville, FL: University of Florida Press.

Bloom, Harold. 1993. *The American Religion*. New York: Simon and Schuster Touchstone Book.

_____. 1995. *The Western Canon*. New York: Riverhead Books.

Brennan, Timothy. 1989. *Salman Rushdie and the Third World*. London: Macmillan.

Bromley, David G. 1998. Dean M. Kelley (1926–1997). In *Encyclopedia of Religion and Society*, edited by William H. Swatos, Jr., 262. Walnut Creek, CA: Altamira Press.

Brouwer, Steve, Paul Gifford, and Susan D. Rose. 1996. *Exporting the American Gospel: Global Christian Fundamentalism*. New York and London: Routledge.

Bruce, Steve. 1995. *Religion in Modern Britain*. Oxford, UK: Oxford University Press.

_____. 1996. *Religion in the Modern World*. Oxford, UK, and New York: Oxford University Press.

Buehrens, John. 1996. Reflections. *World* (July–August):2.

Butler, Jon. 1990. *Awash in a Sea of Faith*. Cambridge, MA: Harvard University Press.

Cantor, Norman F. 1994. *The Civilization of the Middle Ages*. New York: Harper Perennial.

Caplow, Theodore, Howard M. Bahr, and Bruce A. Chadwick. 1983. *All Faithful People*. Minneapolis, MN: University of Minnesota Press.

Carlson, Dwight L. 1998. Exposing the Myth That Christians Should Not Have Emotional Problems. *Christianity Today*, 9 February, 29–35.

Carson, Tim, and Kathy Carson. 1997. *So You're Thinking About Contemporary Worship*. St. Louis, MO: Chalice Press.

Cebula, Judith. 1997a. Presbyterian Amendment on Celibacy Not Law Yet. *Indianapolis Star*, 20 March, 27.

_____. 1997b. Soul Search. *Indianapolis Star*, 31 May, E1, E5.

_____. 1998. Methodists Learning to Recognize Gay Love. *Indianapolis Star*, 21 March, B4.

Clifford, James. 1988. *The Predicament of Culture*. Cambridge, MA: Harvard University Press.

Coalter, Milton J., John M. Mulder, and Louis B. Weeks. 1996. *Vital Signs: The Promise of Mainstream Protestantism*. Grand Rapids, MI: Wm. B. Eerdmans.

Collinson, Patrick. 1990. The Late Medieval Church and Its Reformation (1400–1600). In *The Oxford Illustrated History of Christianity*, edited by John McManner, 233–66. Oxford, UK: Oxford University Press.

Condran, John G., and Joseph B. Tamney. 1985. Religious "Nones": 1957 to 1982. *Sociological Analysis* 46:415–24.

Conkin, Paul K. 1997. *American Originals*. Chapel Hill, NC, and London: University of North Carolina Press.

Coppenger, Mark. 1998. God as a Sensitive Guy. *Heartland* (Spring):2–3.

Corbett, Julia Mitchell. 1994. *Religion in America*, 2nd ed. Englewood Cliffs, NJ: Prentice Hall.

Corn, Kevin. 1998. Methodism. In *Encyclopedia of Religion and Society*, edited by William H. Swatos, Jr., 296–9. Walnut Creek, CA: Altamira Press.

Coser, Rose Laub. 1991. *In Defense of Modernity*. Stanford, CA: Stanford University Press.

Coser, Rose Laub, and Lewis A. Coser. 1979. Jonestown as Perverse Utopia. *Dissent* 26:158–63.

Curry, Melvin D. 1992. *Jehovah's Witnesses*. New York and London: Garland Publishing.

Dalhouse, Mark Taylor. 1996. *An Island in the Lake of Fire*. Athens, GA, and London: University of Georgia Press.

D'Antonio, Michael. 1992. *Fall from Grace*. New Brunswick, NJ: Rutgers University Press.

Davis, Fred. 1992. *Fashion, Culture, and Identity*. Chicago and London: University of Chicago Press.

Demerath III, N. J. 1965. *Social Class in American Protestantism*. Chicago: Rand McNally and Company.

Dempsey, Ian. 1997. The Battle of the Book Continued. *Toronto Globe and Mail*, 8 August, A14.

Dumenil, Lynn. 1995. *Modern Temper*. New York: Hill and Wang.

Durkheim, Émile. 1973a. Individualism and the Intellectuals. In *Émile Durkheim on Morality and Society*, edited by Robert N. Bellah, 43–57. Chicago: University of Chicago Press.

———. [1925] 1973b. *Moral Education*. New York: Free Press.

Eagleton, Terry. 1983. *Literary Theory*. Minneapolis, MN: University of Minnesota Press.

Edmundson, Mark. 1989. Prophet of a New Post-Modernism. *Harper's*, December, 62–71.

Eisenstadt, S. N. 1964. Social Change, Differentiation, and Evolution. *American Sociological Review* 29:375–85.

———. 1986. Introduction: The Axial Age Breakthroughs – Their Characteristics and Origins. In *The Origins and Diversity of Axial Age Civilizations*, edited by S. N. Eisenstadt, 1–28. Albany, NY: State University of New York Press.

Ellwood, Jr., Robert S. 1973a. *Religious and Spiritual Groups in Modern America*. Englewood Cliffs, NJ: Prentice Hall.

———. 1973b. *One Way: The Jesus Movement and Its Meaning*. Englewood Cliffs, NJ: Prentice Hall.

Embree, Ainslie T. 1994. The Function of the Rashtriya Swayamsevak Sangh: To Define the Hindu Nation. In *Accounting for Fundamentalisms*, edited by Martin E. Marty and R. Scott Appleby, 617–52. Chicago: University of Chicago Press.

Evans, Kathy. 1996. Censorship Tightens on Iran's Writers. *Manchester Guardian Weekly*, 29 September, 4.

Fallding, Harold. 1974. *The Sociology of Religion*. Toronto: McGraw-Hill Ryerson.

Ferguson, Marilyn. 1980. *The Aquarian Conspiracy*. Los Angeles: J. P. Tarcher.

Finke, Roger, and Rodney Stark. 1992. *The Churching of America 1776–1990*. New Brunswick, NJ: Rutgers University Press.

Foot, Michael. 1989. Historical Rushdie. In *The Rushdie File*, edited by Lisa Appignanesi and Sara Maitland, 242–5. London: Fourth Estate.

Frye, Northrup. 1976. *The Secular Scripture*. Cambridge, MA: Harvard University Press.

Fuentes, Carlos. 1989. Words Apart. In *The Rushdie File*, edited by Lisa Appignanesi and Sara Maitland, 245–9. London: Fourth Estate.

Gabler, Neal. 1998. *Life the Movie*. New York: Alfred A. Knopf.

Giddens, Anthony. 1990. *The Consequences of Modernity*. Stanford, CA: Stanford University Press.

———. 1991. *Modernity and Self-Identity*. Stanford, CA: Stanford University Press.

Gledhill, Ruth. 1991. Catholic Bishops Attack Asylum Bill. *London Times*, 5 November, 23.

Goffman, Erving. 1961. *Asylums: Essays on the Social Situation of Mental Patients and Other Inmates*. New York: Doubleday.

Goshko, John M. 1998. Iran Renounces Bounty on Novelist Rushdie. *Indianapolis Star*, 25 September, A1–2.

Greeley, Andrew M. 1989. *Religious Change in America*. Cambridge, MA: Harvard University Press.

Gress, David. 1998. *From Plato to NATO*. New York: Free Press.

Gusbee, David P. 1997. The Speck in Mickey's Eye. *Christianity Today*, 11 August, 13.

Habermas, Jürgen. 1981. Modernity and Postmodernity. *New German Critique* 22 (winter): 3–14.

Hadaway, C. Kirk, and David A. Roozen. 1993. The Growth and Decline of Congregations. In *Church and Denominational Growth*, edited by David A Roozen and C. Kirk Hadaway, 127–34. Nashville, TN: Abingdon Press.

Hadden, Jeffrey K. 1970. *The Gathering Storm in the Churches*. Garden City, NY: Anchor Books.

Hall, Thomas Cuming. 1930. *The Religious Background of American Culture*. Boston: Little, Brown.

Hammond, Philip E. 1985. Introduction. In *The Sacred in a Secular Age*, edited by Philip E. Hammond, 1–6. Berkeley, CA: University of California Press.

Hanegraaff, Wouter J. 1999. New Age Spiritualities as Secular Religion: A Historian's Perspective. *Social Compass* 46:145–60.

Harder, Keith. 1985. All Things in Common. In *Christianity in Today's World*, edited by Robin Keeley, 114–22. Grand Rapids, MI: Wm. B. Eerdmans.

Harrell, Jr., David Edwin. 1995. Christian Primitivism and Modernization in the Stone-Campbell Movement. In *The Primitive Church in the Modern World*, edited by Richard T. Hughes, 109–20. Urbana, IL, and Chicago: University of Illinois Press.

Hatch, Nathan O. 1989. *The Democratization of American Christianity*. New Haven, CT: Yale University Press.

Heelas, Paul. 1996. *The New Age Movement*. London: Blackwell.

Heilbroner, Robert. 1995. *Visions of the Future*. New York: Oxford University Press.

Heilman, Samuel C., and Steven M. Cohen. 1989. *Cosmopolitans and Parochials: Modern Orthodox Jews in America*. Chicago: University of Chicago Press.

Heyrman, Christine Leigh. 1997. *Southern Cross*. New York: Alfred A. Knopf.

Hill, Christopher. 1975. *The World Turned Upside Down*. Middlesex, UK: Penguin.

Hiro, Dilip. 1989. *Holy War*. New York: Routledge.

Hoge, Dean R., Benton Johnson, and Donald A. Luidens. 1994. *Vanishing Boundaries*. Louisville, KY: Westminster/John Knox Press.

Hollingshead, A. B. 1949. *Elmtown's Youth*. New York: John Wiley and Sons.

Horne, Laura. 1997. Building Straw Houses on a Firm Foundation. *Christianity Today*, 3 February, 56.

Horney, Karen. 1937. *The Neurotic Personality of Our Time*. New York and London: W. W. Norton.

———. 1950. *Neurosis and Human Growth*. New York: W. W. Norton.

Howard, Jay R., and John M. Streck. 1996. The Splintered Art World of Contemporary Christian Music. *Popular Music* 15:37–53.

Hudnut-Beumler, James. 1994. *Looking for God in the Suburbs*. New Brunswick, NJ: Rutgers University Press.

Hunter, James Davison. 1987. *Evangelicalism: The Coming Generation*. Chicago: University of Chicago Press.

Iannaccone, Laurence R. 1994. Why Strict Churches Are Strong. *American Journal of Sociology* 99:1180–211.

Ignatieff, Michael. 1989. The Value of Toleration. In *The Rushdie File*, edited by Lisa Appignanesi and Sara Maitland, 249–52. London: Fourth Estate.

Inglehart, Ronald. 1990. *Culture Shift in Advanced Industrial Society*. Princeton, NJ: Princeton University Press.

Inskeep, Kenneth W. 1993. A Short History of Church Growth Research. In *Church and Denominational Growth*, edited by David A. Roozen and C. Kirk Hadaway, 135–48. Nashville, TN: Abington Press.

Islamic Society of North America. 1989. Statement of Position on 'The Satanic Verses.' *Nur-The Light* 7 (March–April):12–3.

Jencks, Charles. 1989. *What Is Post-Modernism?*, 3rd ed. London: Academy Editions.

Johnson, Angella. 1990. Rushdie Makes Peace Overtures. *Manchester Guardian*, 27 November, 5.

Johnson, Benton. 1961. Do Holiness Sects Socialize in Dominant Values? *Social Forces* 39:309–16.

Johnson, Stephen D. 1986. The Christian Right in Middletown. In *The Political Role of Religion in the United States*, edited by Stephen D. Johnson and Joseph B. Tamney, 181–98. Boulder, CO: Westview Press.

Johnson, Stephen D., and Joseph B. Tamney. 1986. The Clergy and Public Issues in Middletown. In *The Political Role of Religion in the United States*, edited by Stephen D. Johnson and Joseph B. Tamney, 45–70. Boulder, CO: Westview Press.

Juergensmeyer, Mark. 1993. *The New Cold War?* Berkeley, CA: University of California Press.

Kaminer, Wendy. 1996. The Last Taboo. *New Republic*, 14 October, 24–32.

Kanter, Rosabeth Moss. 1972. *Commitment and Community*. Cambridge, MA: Harvard University Press.

Kelley, Dean M. 1977. *Why Conservative Churches Are Growing*. New York: Harper and Row.

———. 1978. Why Conservative Churches Are Still Growing. *Journal for the Scientific Study of Religion* 17:165–72.

———. 1979. Is Religion a Dependent Variable? In *Understanding Church Growth and Decline, 1950–1978*, edited by Dean R. Hoge and David A. Roozen, 334–43. New York: Pilgrim Press.

Keppel, Giles. 1994. *The Revenge of God*. University Park, PA: Pennsylvania State University Press.

Kniss, Fred. 1997. *Disquiet in the Land*. New Brunswick, NJ: Rutgers University Press.

Knox, Ronald A. 1994. *Enthusiasm*. Notre Dame, IN: University of Notre Dame Press.

Kosmin, Barry H., and Seymour P. Lachman. 1993. *One Nation Under God*. New York: Crown Trade Paperbacks.

Kroll-Smith, J. Stephen. 1982. Tobacco and Belief: Baptist Ideology and the Yeoman Planter in 18th Century Virginia. *Southern Studies* 21:353–68.

Lechner, Frank J. 1993. Global Fundamentalism. In *A Future for Religion?*, edited by W. H. Swatos, Jr., 19–36. Newbury Park, CA: Sage.

Leclercq, Jean, O. S. B. 1974. *The Love of Learning and the Desire for God*. Revised ed. New York: Fordham University Press.

Lee, Simon. 1990. "Satanic Verses" Sacred Novels. *The Guardian* (17 November):27.

Levy, Leonard W. 1993. *Blasphemy*. New York: Alfred A. Knopf.

Ling, Trevor O. 1991. The Weberian Thesis and Interpretive Positions. In *The Triadic Chord*, edited by Tu Wei-ming, 57–85. Singapore: The Institute of East Asian Philosophies.

Lipset, Seymour Martin. 1996. *American Exceptionalism*. New York: W. W. Norton.

Lynd, Robert S., and Helen Merrell Lynd. 1929. *Middletown*. New York: Harcourt, Brace, and World.

———. 1937. *Middletown in Transition*. New York: Harcourt, Brace, and World.

Macionis, John J. 1997. *Sociology*, 6th ed. Upper Saddle River, NJ: Prentice Hall.

Manor, James. 1994. Organizational Weakness and the Rise of Sinhalese Buddhist Extremism. In *Accounting for Fundamentalisms*, edited by Martin E. Marty and R. Scott Appleby, 770–84. Chicago: University of Chicago Press.

Marcus, Greil. 1990. *Lipstick Traces*. Cambridge, MA: Harvard University Press Paperback.

———. 1997. *Mystery Train*, 4th ed. New York: Plume.

Marsden, George M. 1980. *Fundamentalism and American Culture*. New York: Oxford University Paperback.

———. 1991. *Understanding Fundamentalism and Evangelicalism*. Grand Rapids, MI: Wm. B. Eerdmans.

Martin, David. 1978. *A General Theory of Secularization*. New York: Harper and Row.

Marty, Martin E. 1990. North America. In *The Oxford Illustrated History of Christianity*, edited by John McManners, 384–419. Oxford, UK: Oxford University Press.

Marty, Martin E., and R. Scott Appleby. 1991. Conclusion: An Interim Report on a Hypothetical Family. In *Fundamentalisms Observed*, edited by Martin E. Marty and R. Scott Appleby, 814–42. Chicago: University of Chicago Press.

Marzorati, Gerald. 1989. Salman Rushdie: Fiction's Embattled Infidel. *New York Times Magazine*, 29 January, 24FF.

Maslow, Abraham H. 1968. *Toward a Psychology of Being*, 2nd ed. New York: Van Nostrand.

———. 1971. *The Farther Reaches of Human Nature*. New York: Viking Press.

Maudlin, Michael G. 1998. I'm Not OK, You're Not OK. *Christianity Today*, 9 February, 31–2.

McGregor, J. F. 1984. The Baptists: Fount of All Heresy. In *Radical Religion in the English Revolution*, edited by J. F. McGregor and B. Reay, 23–63. Oxford, UK: Oxford University Press.

McLeod, Hugh. 1996. *Piety and Poverty*. New York and London: Holmes and Meier.

McLuhan, Marshall. 1964. *Understanding Media*. New York: McGraw-Hill.

Mensching, Gustav. 1973. Folk and Universal Religion. In *Readings on the Sociology of Religion*, edited by Thomas F. O'Dea and Janet K. O'Dea, 83–91. Englewood Cliffs, NJ: Prentice Hall.

Milani, Mohsen M. 1994. *The Making of Iran's Islamic Revolution*, 2nd ed. Boulder, CO: Westview Press.

Miller, Donald E. 1997. *Reinventing American Protestantism*. Berkeley, CA: University of California Press.

Miller, Kevin Dale. 1995. Putting an End to Christian Psychology. *Christianity Today*, 14 August, 16–7.

Mojtabai, A. G. 1989. Magical Mystery Pilgrimage. *New York Times Book Review* (29 January):3, 37.

Mottahedeh, Roy P. 1998. What to Make of Iran's Overture? *New York Times*, 9 January, A19.

Myerhoff, Barbara G. 1975. Organization and Ecstasy: Deliberate and Accidental Communities Among Huichol Indians and American Youth. In *Symbol and Politics in Communal Ideology*, edited by Sally Falk Moore and Barbara G. Myerhoff, 33–67. Ithaca, NY: Cornell University Press.

Naïm, Mouna. 1994. Censors Strike Back in Iran. *Manchester Guardian Weekly*, 27 November, 16.

National Opinion Research Center. 1999. *General Social Survey Codebook 1998*. Storrs, CT: Roper Center for Public Opinion Research.

Neitz, Mary Jo. 1993. Inequality and Difference: Feminist Research in the Sociology of Religion. In *A Future for Religion*, edited by William H. Swatos, Jr., 165–84. Newbury Park, CA: Sage.

New York Times. 1989. Words for Salman Rushdie. *New York Times Book Review* (12 March):1.

———. 1991. Polish Copy of Rushdie Book on Sale Without Translator. *New York Times* (28 July):Y8.

Niebuhr, Gustav. 1988. Church of God Revises Moral Code. *Christian Century* 105:725–6.

Niebuhr, H. Richard. [1929] 1957. *The Social Sources of Denominationalism*. New York: Meridian Books.

Noll, Mark A. 1992. *A History of Christianity in the United States and Canada*. Grand Rapids, MI: Wm. B. Eerdmans.

———. 1994. *The Scandal of the Evangelical Mind*. Grand Rapids, MI: Wm. B. Eerdmans.

O'Dea, Thomas F. 1966. *The Sociology of Religion*. Englewood Cliffs, NJ: Prentice Hall.

Olson, Roger E. 1998. The Future of Evangelical Theology. *Christianity Today*, 9 February, 40–8.

Palmer, Robert. 1995. *Rock & Roll: An Unruly History*. New York: Harmony Books.

Parekh, Bhikhu. 1990. The Rushdie Affair and the British Press. In *The Salman Rushdie Controversy in Interreligious Perspective*, edited by Dan Cohn-Sherbok, 71–96. Lewiston: Edwin Mellen Press.

Paris, Bernard J. 1994. *Karen Horney*. New Haven, CT, and London: Yale University Press.

Parsons, Anne. 1965. The Protestant Immigrants: A Study of an Ethnic Central City Church. *Journal for the Scientific Study of Religion* 4:183–97.

Peel, J. D. Y. 1993. An Africanist Revisits *Magic and the Millennium*. In *Secularization, Rationalism, and Sectarianism*, edited by Eileen Barker, James A. Beckford, and Karel Dobbelaere, 81–100. Oxford, UK: Clarendon Press.

Penton, M. James. 1997. *Apocalypse Delayed*, 2nd ed. Toronto, Buffalo, and London: University of Toronto Press.

Perrin, Robin D., Paul Kennedy, and Donald E. Miller. 1997. Examining the Sources of Conservative Church Growth: Where Are the New Evangelical Movements Getting Their Numbers? *Journal for the Scientific Study of Religion* 36:71–80.

Perry, H. Francis. 1899. The Workingman's Alienation from the Church. *American Journal of Sociology* 4:621–9.

Piscatori, James. 1990. The Rushdie Affair and the Politics of Ambiguity. *International Affairs* 64 (October)(4):767–89.

———. 1991. Religion and Realpolitik: Islamic Responses to the Gulf War. In *Islamic Fundamentalism and the Gulf Crisis*, edited by James Piscatori, 1–27. Chicago: Fundamentalist Project.

Poloma, Margaret M. 1989. *The Assemblies of God at the Crossroads*. Knoxville, TN: University of Tennessee Press.

Pope, Liston. 1942. *Millhands and Preachers*. New Haven, CT: Yale University Press.

Rashid, Ahmed. 1994. In God's Name. *Far Eastern Economic Review*, 26 May, 20.

Religion News Service. 1999. Teens Are Finding Faith That Suits Them. *Indianapolis Star*, 24 April, G5.

Riesèbrodt, Martin. 1993. *Pious Passion: The Emergence of Modern Fundamentalism in the United States and Iran*. Berkeley, CA: University of California Press.

Roof, Wade Clark. 1998. Modernity, the Religious, and the Spiritual. *The Annals* 558 (July):211–24.

Roof, Wade Clark, and William McKinney. 1987. *American Mainline Religion*. New Brunswick, NJ: Rutgers University Press.

Roozen, David A. 1980. Church Dropouts: Changing Patterns of Disengagement and Re-entry. *Review of Religious Research* 21:427–50.

Rushdie, Salman. 1989. *The Satanic Verses*. New York: Viking.

———. 1990a. In Good Faith. *Newsweek* (12 February):52–7.

———. 1990b. Is Nothing Sacred? *Granta* 31 (spring):97–111.

———. 1991a. *Imaginary Homelands*. London: Granta Books.

———. 1991b. Lessons, Harsh and Difficult, from 1,000 Days "Trapped Inside a Metaphor." *New York Times* (12 December):A16.

———. 1999. Rethinking the War on American Culture. *New York Times*, 5 March, A25.

Ruthven, Malise. 1990. *A Satanic Affair*. London: Chatto and Windus.

Sadri, Ahmad. 1994. Adjusting to the World According to Salman Rushdie. In *The Subversive Imagination*, edited by Carol Becker, 168–84. New York: Routledge.

Schaller, Lyle E. 1994. *21 Bridges to the 21st Century*. Nashville, TN: Abingdon Press.

Schlesinger, Jr., Arthur. 1995. The Opening of the American Mind. In *The Truth About Truth*, edited by Walter Truett Anderson, 224–31. New York: A Jeremy P. Tarcher/Putnam Book.

Schmalzbauer, John A., and C. Gray Wheeler. 1996. Between Fundamentalism and Secularization: Secularizing and Sacralizing Currents in the Evangelical Debate on Campus Lifestyle Codes. *Sociology of Religion* 57:241–58.

Shahabuddin, Syed. 1989. You Did This with Satanic Forethought, Mr. Rushdie. In *The Rushdie File*, edited by Lisa Appignanesi and Sara Maitland, 45–9. London: Fourth Estate.

Shibley, Mark. 1996. *Resurgent Evangelicalism in the United States*. Columbia, SC: University of South Carolina Press.

———. 1998. Contemporary Evangelicals: Born-Again and World Affirming. *The Annals* 558 (July):67–87.

Sjogren, Steve. 1993. *Conspiracy of Kindness*. Ann Arbor, MI: Vine Books.

Skerkat, Darren E., and John Wilson. 1995. Preferences, Constraints, and Choices in Religious Markets: In Examination of Religious Switching and Apostasy. *Social Forces* 73:993–1026.

Smith, Christian. 1998. *American Evangelicalism*. Chicago and London: University of Chicago Press.

Spickard, James V. 1998. Rethinking Religious Social Action: What Is "Rational" About Rational Choice Theory? *Sociology of Religion* 59:99–115.

Stark, Rodney, and William S. Bainbridge. 1980. Networks of Faith: Interpersonal Bonds and Recruitment into Cults and Sects. *American Journal of Sociology* 85:1376–96.

———. 1996. *A Theory of Religion*. New Brunswick, NJ: Rutgers University Press.

Starke, Frederick A., and Bruno Dyck. 1996. Upheavals in Congregations: The Causes and Outcomes of Splits. *Review of Religious Research* 38:159–74.

Staudenmeier, Jr., William J. 1998. Alcohol-Related Windows on Simmel's Social World. In *Illuminating Social Life*, edited by Peter Kivisto, 7–35. Thousand Oaks, CA: Pine Forge Press.

Steeman, Theodore M. 1975. Church, Sect, Mysticism, Denomination: Periodical Aspects of Troeltsch's Types. *Sociological Analysis* 36:181–204.

Steiner, Wendy. 1995. *The Scandal of Pleasure*. Chicago: University of Chicago Press.

Steinfels, Peter. 1998. Beliefs. *New York Times*, 16 May, A13.

Swatos, Jr., William H., ed. 1998. *Encyclopedia of Religion and Society*. Walnut Creek, CA: Altamira Press.

Sztompka, Piotr. 1993. *The Sociology of Social Change*. Oxford, UK: Blackwell.

Tamney, Joseph B. 1962. *An Exploratory Study of Religious Conversion*. Ph.D. diss. Cornell University.

———. 1965. The Prediction of Religious Change. *Sociological Analysis* 26:72–81.

———. 1966. A Study of Spiritual Involvement. *Sociological Analysis* 27:146–56.

———. 1970. The Social Psychology of Conversion. In *Catholics USA – Perspectives on Social Change*, edited by William Liu and Nathaniel Pallone, 390–418. New York: John Wiley and Sons.

———. 1975. *Solidarity in a Slum*. New York: John Wiley and Sons.

———. 1983. Middletown's Rituals, 1924–80. In *All Faithful People*, edited by Theodore Caplow, Howard M. Bahr, and Bruce A. Chadwick, 128–45. Minneapolis, MN: University of Minnesota Press.

———. 1992a. *American Society in the Buddhist Mirror*. New York: Garland.

———. 1992b. *The Resilience of Christianity in the Modern World*. Albany, NY: State University of New York Press.

———. 1994. Conservative Government and Support for the Religious Institution: Religious Education in English Schools. *British Journal of Sociology* 45:195–210.

———. 1996. *The Struggle over Singapore's Soul*. Berlin: Walter de Gruyter.

Tamney, Joseph B., Ronald Burton, and Stephen D. Johnson. 1989. Fundamentalism and Economic Restructuring. In *Religion and Political Behavior in the United States*, edited by Ted G. Jelen, 67–82. New York: Praeger.

Tamney, Joseph B., and Stephen D. Johnson. 1997. A Research Note on the Free-Rider Issue. *Journal for the Scientific Study of Religion* 36:104–8.

———. 1998. The Popularity of Strict Churches. *Review of Religious Research* 39: 209–23.

Tamney, Joseph B., Jennifer Mertens, Stephen D. Johnson, Ronald Burton, and Rita Caccamo. 1992. Personal Experience, Ideology, and Support for Feminism. *Sociological Focus* 25:203–17.

Tamney, Joseph B., Shawn Powell, and Stephen D. Johnson. 1989. Innovation Theory and Religious Nones. *Journal for the Scientific Study of Religion* 28: 216–29.

Tocqueville, Alexis de. 1954. *Democracy in America*. 2 vols. New York: Vintage.

Troeltsch, Ernst. 1931. *The Social Teaching of the Christian Churches*. 2 vols. London: George Allen and Unwin.

Trueheart, Charles. 1996. The Next Church. *Atlantic Monthly*, August, 37–58.

Turner, James C. 1999. Something to Be Reckoned with. *Commonweal* 126(1):11–3.

Turner, Ralph H. 1994. Ideology and Utopia After Socialism. In *New Social Movements*, edited by Enrique Larana, Hank Johnston, and Joseph R. Gusfield, 79–100. Philadelphia, PA: Temple University Press.

Turner, Victor, and Edith Turner. 1978. *Image and Pilgrimage in Christian Culture*. New York: Columbia University Press.

Viorst, Milton. 1998. *In the Shadow of the Prophet*. New York: Doubleday.

Voll, John O. 1991. Fundamentalism in the Sunni Arab World: Egypt and the Sudan. In *Fundamentalisms Observed*, edited by Martin E. Marty and R. Scott Appleby, 345–402. Chicago: University of Chicago Press.

Wacker, Grant. 1995. Searching for Eden with a Satellite Dish: Primitivism, Pragmatism, and the Pentecostal Character. In *The Primitive Church in the Modern World*, edited by Richard T. Hughes, 139–66. Urbana, IL, and Chicago: University of Illinois Press.

Warner, R. Stephen. 1990. *New Wine in Old Wineskins*. Berkeley, CA: University of California Press.

———. 1993. Work in Progress Toward a New Paradigm for the Sociological Study of Religion in the United States. *American Journal of Sociology* 98: 1044–93.

Weaver, Mary Anne. 1994. A Fugitive from Justice. *New Yorker*, 12 September, 48–60.

Weber, Max. 1958. *The Protestant Ethic and the Spirit of Capitalism*. New York: Charles Scribner's Sons.

———. 1963. *The Sociology of Religion*. Boston: Beacon Press.

———. 1978. *Economy and Society*. Berkeley, CA: University of California Press.

Webster, Richard. 1990. *A Brief History of Blasphemy*. Suffolk, UK: Orwell Press.

Weisman, Steven R. 1991. A Translator of Rushdie's Novel Is Slain at a Japanese University. *New York Times*, 13 July, Y1–5.

Whitehead, Alfred North. 1925. *Science and the Modern World*. New York: New American Library.

Wilcox, W. Bradford. 1998. Conservative Protestant Childbearing: Authoritarian or Authoritative? *American Sociological Review* 63:796–809.

Withrow, Oral, and Laura Withrow. No date. *Meet Us at the Cross: An Introduction to the Church of God*. Anderson, IN: Church of God.

Witten, Marsha G. 1993. *All Is Forgiven*. Princeton, NJ: Princeton University Press.

Woodhead, Linda, and Paul Heelas, eds. 2000. *Religion in Modern Times*. Oxford, UK: Blackwell.

Wuthnow, Robert. 1988. *The Restructuring of American Religion*. Princeton, NJ: Princeton University Press.

———. 1994. *Sharing the Journey*. New York: Free Press.

Yamane, David. 1998. Charismatic Movement. In *Encyclopedia of Religion and Society*, edited by William H. Swatos, Jr., 80–2. Walnut Creek, CA: Altamira Press.

Zoba, Wendy Murray. 1997. First Church of the Millennials. *Christianity Today*, 3 February, 20–1.

INDEX